THE BRITISH ORGAN

The British
ORGAN

Cecil Clutton and Austin Niland

B. T. BATSFORD LTD
LONDON

First published 1963
Second impression 1964

© Cecil Clutton, Austin Niland, 1963

Made and printed in Great Britain by William Clowes and Sons, Ltd
London and Beccles, for the publishers
B. T. BATSFORD LTD
4 Fitzhardinge Street, Portman Square, London W.1

FOREWORD

By Francis Jackson

The increased interest that has been accorded the Organ during the past few years—to which this book bears tangible witness—and its acceptance by musicians of all kinds as an instrument of music is a matter of great moment to its players and admirers.

There was a time when to be an organist was to be looked upon by other musicians with a certain amount of amusement mingled, perhaps, with a certain amount of pity. Here was someone, they thought, who, at the press of a switch, was able to unleash any quantity of thunderous noise, or to perform sentimental ditties on the Vox Humana; someone who, finding his repertoire severely circumscribed, was obliged to poach on the territory of any other branch of music he might choose, and who did it all most waywardly and unrhythmically as he pushed and pulled the stops on either side of him. In any case, how could a machine so huge, so diffuse, so loud, so dominating in volume of tone, be considered a musical instrument?

Probably there was some justification for this attitude. There were a few spirits, however, who found this kind of organ—the Romantic-Symphonic Organ—unsuitable for the playing of real organ music, as opposed to the transcription. They began to look elsewhere for their models and they found ancient examples on the Continent, in need only of restoration, which produced their original sounds. Thus began the revolution which split the organ world into two sharply divided camps. Whatever is to be said in favour of either side, it is the Classical ideal which has gained ground increasingly until it is, at the moment of writing, the rule rather than the exception. For even where there is a romantic specification, the voicing of the pipes has, willy nilly, come under the classical influence for the very simple and sound reason that a better blend is thus arrived at.

They also discovered England's own product, the excellent Victorian organ, where it had not been spoilt in the quest for Wagnerian power. It was most likely to be found in the remote country church or in the impecunious parish; and such gems are still to be found. Unfortunately they are still in danger of undergoing the modifications thought necessary

7

to make them louder or easier to control, but where there is a sympathetic understanding of these instruments, a thoughtful restoration can take place, and the instrument be allowed to retain its own character. For from such an instrument it can be seen what stage the Organ had reached when high wind pressures and enormous pipe scales came along to disrupt its development, the development which it should be allowed to continue, rather than follow an imported example. It is to be hoped that, when the few such organs that remain become due for restoration, they will be as carefully handled and preserved as the rest of our rich heritage of historic possessions.

The result of this revolution is that, once again, the organ can hold up its head as an instrument of music in its own right, with its own repertoire of music, much of which has been rediscovered and found to sound right at last on the kind of instrument for which it was written. No longer is it considered necessary to fill out the manual parts or add pedal parts to the music written for organs without pedals.

These are some of the points dealt with in the present volume. Two of the best-informed authorities on the organ have produced a work which gathers the history and aesthetic of the instrument concisely and readably between the covers of one book; and a story of absorbing interest has resulted.

The visual aspect, which often receives less than its due attention, here receives generous treatment, and the interesting review of organ cases is made readily intelligible by the collection of plates which, for variety and range of style, must be almost incomparable. This facet alone should stimulate interest among the increasing number of those who find pleasure and enlightenment in the sounds of the organ.

PREFACE

Anyone who writes a history of the British organ must be primarily indebted to the works of E. J. Hopkins and E. F. Rimbault, W. L. Sumner and Andrew Freeman. Without the researches of Freeman, in particular, it is doubtful whether any worth-while book on the British organ could ever be accomplished. The authors gratefully acknowledge their indebtedness to these authorities.

The authors also wish to thank the following for their generous help in the provision of illustrations: V. C. Bradley, Mus.B. (Dunelm), F.R.C.O., A.R.C.M.; Lord Dunleath; the Rev. B. B. Edmonds, M.A., F.R.G.S.; the Rev. W. A. Hepher, M.A.; Wm. Hill & Son and Norman & Beard Ltd.; J. R. Knott, F.R.S.A.; Cynthia Legh, O.B.E., J.P.; N. P. Mander Ltd.; H. Stubington, F.R.C.O., A.R.C.M.; J. W. Walker & Sons Ltd.; A. F. Wright; and Roger Yates.

Much valuable assistance has also been received from the Librarian and Staff of the British Museum Reading Room; Michael I. Wilson of the Victoria and Albert Museum; and Miss Mary E. P. Wilkinson, A.T.C.L., Honorary Librarian of the Organ Club.

The authors wish to express their sincere thanks to the following for kindly drawing attention to a number of corrections which have been incorporated in the second edition of this book: Kenneth Condon; Ralph Bootman; Dr. J. Dykes Bower, Mus.B. (Cantab), M.A., F.R.C.O.; Michael Gillingham, M.A., Ll.B.; Eric Hyslop; Noel Mander; Michael Sayer; H. Stubington; Colonel G. I. B. Winn, O.B.E.; and Dr. W. L. Sumner, A.K.C., B.Sc., F.L.S., F.I.M.I.T.

CONTENTS

FOREWORD *by Francis Jackson*   7

PREFACE   9

ACKNOWLEDGMENT   13

LIST OF ILLUSTRATIONS   15

chapter

I EARLY HISTORY and the European Background   19
    The Primitive Organ   20
    Germany   25
    France   36
    Italy   39
    Spain and Portugal   40
    After 1800   40

II TONAL HISTORY   45
    Middle Ages and until 1650   45
    The Restoration Organ before Father Smith   62
    Father Smith   68
    Renatus Harris   76
    The Eighteenth Century   81
    The Hill-Gauntlett Revolution, 1830–50   89
    1851–1900. Willis, Schulze, Hope Jones   97
    1900–40. Arthur Harrison   107
    The Post-war Revival   115

III MUSICAL USE   120

IV ARCHITECTURAL HISTORY   147
    1 Position   147
    2 Casework   156
    Purpose, Ingredients and Evolution   156
    Existing Pre-Restoration Cases   171
    Renaissance Cases of the Restoration and After   189
    Revivalism and the Caseless Organ   233
    Contemporary Styles   275

GAZETTEER   280

SELECTIVE BIBLIOGRAPHY   305

INDEX   307

ACKNOWLEDGMENT

Figure 1 is reproduced by gracious permission of Her Majesty The Queen.

The Authors and Publishers wish to thank the following for permission to include the illustrations appearing in this book:

British Travel and Holidays Association, for fig. 23.

Eric de Maré, for figs. 59, 83, 86 and 87.

J. Arthur Dixon Studios, for fig. 78.

Lord Dunleath, for figs. 19 and 53.

Rev. B. B. Edmonds, for figs. 5–7, 24, 30, 51, 52, 62, 67, 68, 71, 79–81, 94, 96, 97 and 103–5; and for fig. 98 (from a photograph by the late S. Harvey).

Rev. L. Edwards, for fig. 102.

William Hill & Son and Norman & Beard Ltd., and Frederick Watson, for fig. 108.

Imperial Chemical Industries Ltd., for fig. 76.

A. F. Kersting, for fig. 36.

J. R. Knott, for fig. 41.

D. J. McNeill, for fig. 53.

N. P. Mander Ltd., for figs. 39 and 84.

Sydney W. Newbery, for figs. 25, 34, 40, 43–5, 55, 56, 60 and 84.

The Provost of the Cathedral Church of St. Nicholas, Newcastle-upon-Tyne, for Fig. 20.

Nicholson and Co. (Worcester) Ltd., for fig. 27.

The Marquess of Northampton, for fig. 33.

The Organ, for figs. 37, 46–50, 54, 65, 66, 72, 90 and 92.

Photowork Ltd., for fig. 57.

Pitkin Pictorials Ltd., for figs. 21 and 35.

H. Stubington, for figs. 3, 8, 9, 70, 77 and 95.

Studio 'J', Dublin, for fig. 19.

J. W. Walker & Sons Ltd., for fig. 107.

A. F. Wright, for figs. 89 and 99; and for figs. 14, 69, 73, 74 and 100 (from photographs by the late E. Adcock).

Roger Yates, for figs. 2, 4, 13 and 101.

Figs. 28, 29, 32, 38, 42, 61, 88 and 106 are from the Publishers' collection.

THE ILLUSTRATIONS

The numerals in parentheses in the text
refer to the figure numbers of the illustrations

figure	page
1 Fifteenth-century positive organ: Hugo van der Goes triptych, National gallery of Scotland, Edinburgh	113
2 St. Stephen, Old Radnor	114
3 Gloucester Cathedral	123
4 St. Michael, Framlingham	124
5 St. Nicholas, Stanford-on-Avon	133
6, 7 King's College Chapel, Cambridge	134
8 St. Mark, Old Bilton: Robert Dallam case	143
9 Tewkesbury Abbey, 'Milton' organ	143
10 Lincoln Cathedral	144
11 St. George's Chapel, Windsor: chaire organ	144
12 St. George's Chapel, Windsor: great organ	144
13 Nettlecombe Court: Loosemore case	153
14 Exeter Cathedral: Loosemore double case	153
15 St. Mary-the-Virgin, Oxford	154
16 St. Lawrence Jewry, London: Harris double case	154
17 Basic organ pipe	158
18 German table organ, 1627	160
19 St. Mary, Dublin: Harris organ	163
20 Newcastle-upon-Tyne Cathedral	163
21 All Hallows-by-the-Tower, London	164
22 All Hallows, Twickenham: Renatus Harris case, formerly at All Hallows, Lombard Street, London	164
23 Adlington Hall	167
24 St. Margaret, King's Lynn: Snetzler case	168
25 St. Leonard, Shoreditch: Bridge case	168
26 Lip shapes	170
27 Birmingham Cathedral: Schwarbrick case	173

figure   *page*
28 St. Magnus-the-Martyr, London Bridge: Jordan case   173
29 Pembroke College Chapel, Cambridge: Father Smith double case   174
30 St. Katherine, Little Bardfield: Renatus Harris organ   174
31 Old Radnor organ case before restoration   176
32 St. Paul's Cathedral, London: north case   179
33 Compton Wynyates: Father Smith chamber organ   180
34 St. Peter's Organ Works, Bethnal Green: Father Smith chamber organ   180
35 Bristol Cathedral: Harris cases   185
36 St. James's, Piccadilly: Renatus Harris main case; chaire case   186
37 Canterbury Cathedral: case of Lancelot Pease's organ   190
38 St. Peter, Tiverton: Christian Smith case   193
39 St. Mary, Finedon   193
40 St. Vedast, Foster Lane, London   194
41 St. Mary, Rotherhithe   194
42 St. Mary Magdalen, Holloway Road, Islington   199
43 Our Lady of the Assumption, Warwick Street, Westminster:
    Byfield case   199
44, 45 Dingestow Court: Father Smith chamber organ   200
46 St. Mary-the-Great, Cambridge: Father Smith case   201
47 Durham Cathedral   202
48 Trinity College Chapel, Cambridge: Father Smith case   203
49 Emmanuel College Chapel, Cambridge: Father Smith case   205
50 Temple Church   207
51 Dulwich College Chapel: George England case   209
52 St. Mary, Stafford: Geib case   209
53 Down Cathedral: case of Green organ   210
54 St. Sepulchre, Holborn Viaduct: Harris case   212
55 Bryceson barrel organ   215
56 Bates chamber organ   215
57 York Minster: case of Elliot and Hill organ   216
58 Salisbury Cathedral: Renatus Harris case on choir screen   219
59 Royal Naval College Chapel, Greenwich   221
60 St. John, Waterloo Road, Lambeth   221

figure   *page*

61 Jesus College Chapel, Cambridge: case by A. W. N. Pugin   222

62 All Saints, Theddingworth: case by F. H. Sutton   222

63 St. Catherine Cree: Father Smith case   224

64 Sculthorpe Church: Snetzler case   227

65 St. Stephen, Walbrook: George England case   230

66 St. Mary Redcliffe, Bristol: Harris–Byfield case   232

67 Assumption of Our Lady, Harlton   235

68 St. Mary-the-Virgin, Great Bardfield   235

69 St. Bartholomew, Armley: Schulze organ   236

70 Sherborne Abbey: case by R. C. Carpenter   236

71 Ely Cathedral: case by Sir Gilbert Scott   239

72 St. Mary, Nottingham: case by Sir Gilbert Scott   239

73 Selby Abbey: case by J. O. Scott   240

74 St. Albans Cathedral: case by J. O. Scott   240

75 St. Martin-in-the-Fields: Allom case   242

76 St. George's Hall, Liverpool: case by C. R. Cockerell   243

77 St. James, Weybridge: case by J. L. Pearson   245

78 Westminster Abbey: north case   245

79 St. Mary-the-Virgin, Pulham: case by Bodley   246

80 St. Mary-the-Virgin, Cheshunt: case by Bodley   246

81 All Saints, Danehill: case by Bodley   246

82 St. Mary, West Tofts: case by Pugin   247

83 St. John-the-Evangelist, Oxford: case by Bodley   249

84 St. Michael-and-All Angels, Croydon: case by Bodley   250

85 St. John's, Stockcross: case probably by F. H. Sutton   251

86, 87 Brasenose College Chapel, Oxford: case by Jackson   253

88 St. Catherine's College Chapel, Cambridge: case by Garner   254

89 Sheldonian Theatre, Oxford: case by Jackson   254

90 Sketch of proposed interior of Ushaw College Chapel by
A. W. N. Pugin   255

91 St. John, Hampstead: case by Jackson   259

92 Chichester Cathedral: double case by A. G. Hill   259

93 Double organ case design for Hythe Parish Church   259

THE ILLUSTRATIONS

figure   *page*

94 Peterborough Cathedral: case by Hill   260

95 Beverley Minster: case by Hill   260

96 St. Andrew, Kirkandrews-on-Esk: case by Temple Moore   263

97 St. Peter, Yaxley: case by Temple Moore   263

98 Southwark Cathedral: case by Sir Arthur Blomfield   264

99 Winchester College Chapel: case by Caröe   264

100 All Saints, Hove: case by F. L. Pearson   267

101 St. Mary, Egmanton: case by Comper   268

102 All Saints, Carshalton   268

103, 104 Norwich Cathedral: case by S. E. Dykes Bower   273

105 St. Nicholas, Standish: case by S. E. Dykes Bower   273

106 Hyde Park Chapel, South Kensington   274

107 St. Columba, Glenrothes   274

108 Christ the King, Glasgow   274

109 Flentrop work-principle case at Doetinchem, Holland   277

110 'Denham' organ   278

CHAPTER I

EARLY HISTORY
and the European Background

The organ has a continuous history stretching back for over 2000 years, and it has been closely connected with Christian worship for well over half as long. By the fourteenth century it was recognised as the 'King of Instruments' and the peak of its musical pre-eminence was during the seventeenth and eighteenth centuries. For various rather curious reasons it retained its popularity throughout the nineteenth century, although it had but little aptitude for music of the 'romantic' era. For this reason, it failed any longer to attract the foremost composers and the whole of the nineteenth century produced only the handful of works by Mendelssohn, Liszt, Franck and Brahms. The first quarter of the twentieth century saw its continuously decreasing musical significance, accompanied by a spate of undistinguished compositions. Little but the French school, and the three sonatas of Hindemith, stand out from a mass of mediocrity.

However, during the second quarter of the century there has been a great revitalisation of the organ in Germany, Holland and Scandinavia, reaching France and America rather later. This movement cannot be said to have made any serious headway in Britain until within the last decade, but as often in our history, where we have been late starters we have made the most rapid progress, and British organs are now as advanced as any, and increasingly attract the attention of the musical public.

On the Continent of Europe the organ had a continuous history of development from about 1450 to 1800, some three and a half centuries. Then came a complete break with tradition, with interesting but generally unfortunate artistic results. In England we produced organ-music of the utmost importance from about 1540 onwards, but as a continuing development our history of organ-building does not start until 1660, since when there has been a steady development over three centuries up to the present day.

Our organ history is therefore quite different from that of any other country, but despite this it cannot be considered in isolation. It can only be appreciated clearly in perspective with the Continent, and the purpose of this chapter is to supply that necessary background.

As a matter of general interest, the history is very briefly described from its beginnings up to 1450, from which date the development of the modern organ may be traced without interruption to the present time. It is done so here in a necessarily sketchy way, but in sufficient detail to enable the study of the British organ to be undertaken in proper perspective.

THE PRIMITIVE ORGAN

The organ dates from the third century B.C., at latest, and by the beginning of the Christian era it had become an instrument of considerable sophistication. The earliest type of which any details or remains have survived was the 'hydraulus', so-called from the type of wind-reservoir used. The air was compressed by cylinder-type pumps and forced into a dome-shaped reservoir. A pipe from the top of the dome led to the wind-chest and pipes. It had no bottom but stood in another vessel, partly filled with water, which thus sealed the air in the reservoir. As the reservoir became filled by the pumps, the water was forced out of it into the containing vessel, until finally the air would escape as bubbles through the water. But when the organ was being played the air would be used up as fast as the pumps could supply it to the reservoir. Thus a fairly equal pressure of wind was ensured. The organ itself developed a balanced keyboard by an early date and a stop action similar to the slider system still used. Up to four stops seem to have been common, which must have been about the limit of what the pumps could supply.

The hydraulus was popular in the Roman Empire and apparently was loud enough to use even at open-air gladiatorial entertainments. With the collapse of Roman civilisation the hydraulus survived in Arabia and was made at any rate into the tenth century.

The pneumatic organ, supplied by bellows, may well go back as far as the hydraulus; but the earliest record of one is carved on the obelisk of Theodosius, at Constantinople, set up in 395.

Organs seem to have been introduced into Christian worship from about the eighth century, by which time they were also known in England.

By the tenth century the organ had attained to a considerable stature, as is evidenced by the following well-known description of the organ in Winchester Cathedral in the middle of the century, taken from a poem by Wulstan.

> Such organs as you have built are seen nowhere, fabricated on a double ground. Twice six bellows are ranged in a row, and fourteen lie below. These, by alternate blasts, supply an immense quantity of wind and are worked by seventy strong men, labouring with their arms, covered with perspiration, each inciting his companions to drive the wind up with all his strength, that the full-bosomed box may speak with its 400 pipes which the hand of the organist governs. Some when closed he opens, others when open he closes, as the individual nature of the varied sound requires. Two brethren of concordant spirit sit at the instrument and each manages his own alphabet. There are, moreover, hidden holes in the forty tongues and each has ten pipes in their due order. Some are conducted hither, others thither, each preserving the proper disposition of its own note. They strike the seven differences of joyous sound, adding the music of the lyric semitone. Like thunder the iron tones batter the ear, so that it may receive no sound but that alone. To such an amount does it reverberate, echoing in every direction, that everyone stops with his hands to his gaping ears, being in no wise able to draw near and bear the sound, which so many combinations produce. The music is heard throughout the town, and the flying fame thereof is gone out over the whole country.

While this description may not conjure up a particularly vivid picture of what this organ looked like or how it worked, it seems to have had a remarkably inefficient system of wind supply, requiring 70 men to supply only 400 pipes; but as to its powerful effect, Wulstan at any rate leaves us in no doubt at all.

However, we possess remarkably precise information about organ-building in the early twelfth century from the work *De Variis Artibus*, by an anonymous monk 'Theophilus', who probably lived in northern Germany. In this instrument, the pipes were made of copper. It is not stated how many pipes there were to a note. They stood on a common wind-chest and were sounded by a number of sliders, one to each note. These sliders were pulled out by the player, as required, and pushed in again to stop the sound. There was no automatic, spring-operated return, and thus the sounding of more than one note at a time was hardly practicable. The bellows were a number of whole sheep-skins fitted into a nozzle, connecting with the wind-chest, and each fitted with a clack-valve, for drawing in fresh supplies of air. Several such crude bellows and, probably, blowers were required, even for a small organ. The wind-chest might be made either of wood, as today, or, surprisingly, of copper.

There was no means of equalising the pressure, so that much depended upon the skill and judgment of the blowers, and even so the intonation of the pipes must have been very uncertain. However, by this time a system of bellows had probably been evolved elsewhere which continued to be used for some small instruments into the eighteenth century and, despite what has been written about it by those without practical experience, can provide a perfectly steady pressure of wind.

It is essential that there should be a minimum of two bellows, looking not unlike a modern domestic fire-bellows. One (the lower) side of each is fixed, and the upper, movable side has a lead weight attached to it. The blower raises one bellows, whereupon the weight starts to force it down again, supplying wind to the chest as it falls. When it is almost deflated the blower raises the other bellows, and lets it go just as the first becomes empty, and so on. The lead weights provide a steady pressure of wind. In larger organs the bellows were of very large size and were raised by the whole weight of the blower, worked like a treadmill. There might be as many as twelve blowers and twice as many bellows for a large organ. It is even possible that this type, known as diagonal bellows, may have survived continuously from the earliest times, since it is the one depicted in the fourth-century obelisk of Theodosius; but equally, like other aspects of the earliest organs, such as the balanced keyboard and stop mechanism, it may have been forgotten and subsequently re-invented.

The balanced keyboard seems to have reappeared by the end of the thirteenth century, but still the organ had no stops nor any other means of varying the power or quality of tone.

At about this time there began to be a marked cleavage between the large church organ and the smaller kind of instrument, known as a positive, such as that illustrated by Van Eyck in the Ghent altar-piece, or the one in a fifteenth-century picture in Holyroodhouse by Hugo van der Goes (smaller instruments, which could be carried in processions, were called 'portatives'; smaller ones still, which were slung round the neck, were played with one hand and blown with the other).

The large instruments, of crude mechanism and considerable power, could do no more than pound out a plainsong, but the positive was much more tractable, and certainly by the middle of the fourteenth century it could sustain feats of considerable dexterity. This is borne out by the Robertsbridge Manuscript of about 1325 with its organ estampie, and by the fame of Landini, the blind organist of St. Peter's, Rome, at the same time.

Organists therefore took to establishing a positive near the keys of the great organ so that they could play either, as occasion demanded. From this it was but a short step to combine the two in one instrument, with two sets of keys, or manuals. Similarly, as organs got larger, and incorporated longer and longer pipes, the effort of opening the pallets became too much, and the control of these largest pipes was delegated to a separate keyboard operated by the feet of the player. Certainly this state of affairs had been reached by the middle of the fourteenth century, and the 'console' of the organ built for Halberstadt Cathedral in 1365, with two manuals and pedals, was illustrated in the *Syntagma Musicum* of Praetorius in 1619. The keys followed the present arrangement of accidentals, though very much wider than the present octave, which reached its present dimensions towards the end of the fifteenth century (however, varying widths continued, and still do in certain modern clavichords).

By this time, therefore, the player could play loud or soft, but he could not produce any intermediate stage; it remained for a stop mechanism to be re-invented to produce all the essentials of a modern organ. There is no direct evidence as to when this happened, but almost certainly it was during the first half of the fifteenth century. The oldest surviving organ with stops is at S. Petronio, Bologna. The older of the two organs there (that on the south side) dates from 1470 and has a stop to each rank of pipes, operated on the ventil, or (in German) 'Springlade' system. In this system there are no sliders, but the stop simply shuts off the supply of wind to its rank of pipes. The slider chest may well have appeared first in Germany, but owing to the difficulty of making airtight joints in a slider chest, the Springlade chest seems to have become almost universal in the sixteenth century, and the slider chest only re-established its popularity in the seventeenth. Nevertheless, Springlade chests continued to be made in Italy until well into the nineteenth and even twentieth century.

The use of stops in Germany was different from that in Italy where, from the first, there was a separate stop to each rank of pipes. Germany and, no doubt, northern Europe generally, continued to keep the undivided great organ, known as the Blockwerk, and only gradually detached individual ranks from it. Thus, it might often happen that the great organ had independently available principals at only 8, 4 and 2 ft. pitches, backed by a huge Blockwerk mixture of as many as fifteen ranks, such as still exists in the Abbey Church at Klosterneuberg near Vienna (the organ dates substantially from 1555 and reached its present form in 1642).

Alternatively, the great might remain an entirely indivisible Blockwerk, with independent stops on the positive only. This arrangement survived at St. Bavo, Haarlem until 1630 and still exists in an organ taken out of the church at St. Nicolai, Utrecht, now awaiting reconstruction.

The ranks of the Blockwerk consisted of a number of unison and octave ranks from 16 ft. pitch upwards; and an almost equal number of ranks sounding at a fifth from the unison (such as the twelfth in a modern organ). Some of these ranks were of such high pitch that if they continued to the top of the compass the pipes would become unmanageably small. These ranks therefore broke back an octave at some point in the compass. Thus, although the pitch of the whole Blockwerk goes up as a scale is played from bottom to top of the keyboard, there is a shift in emphasis, the bottom note being *relatively* brighter than the top note. The modern mixture is in fact a direct descendant of the mediaeval Blockwerk, and behaves in exactly the same way. The breaks, which were certainly introduced at first only as a matter of practical convenience, have come to have great musical utility, since they give point to the lower voices, which tend to be ill-defined; and solidity to the upper voices which otherwise tend either to be too soft or too shrill. Also, there is a distinct limit to which the power of any instrument can be increased by adding more and more ranks at the same pitch. Ranks at many different pitches are much more effective in producing an effect of power. W. T. Best, the great Victorian organist, wrote in 1881:

> It is particularly necessary to stress the extreme importance of mixture-work, artistically tempered and of melodious sonority. No other legitimate means exist, nor can ever exist, of adding harmonious power to an organ.

Not all mixtures achieve these objectives.

Until the introduction of separate stops there was, of course, no incentive to develop different shapes of pipes and tone-colours; but this had certainly begun by the middle of the fifteenth century, and soon after the organ began to develop its own repertoire. One of the earliest forms of specifically organ-music consisted of a plainsong played on the pedals, and embroidered by more rapidly moving manual parts. This art was practised by the two early Netherland masters, Obrecht (1430–1505) and Isaac (1450–1517). By 1455 the Nieuwekerk at Delft had an organ with two manuals and pedals, the pedal department possessing an independent trumpet stop, for playing this type of music.

As soon as this stage had been reached it was inevitable that differing regional and national schools of composition should begin to appear, and

24

from 1500 onwards these can easily be traced. The most important schools are the German, French and Italian. Although there was a mature school of organ composition in England from the early sixteenth century, we did not have an identifiable school of organ-building before 1600, and even then the influences at work are exceedingly difficult to identify. The attempt to do so cannot even be ventured upon until the histories of the much older German, French and Italian (and to some extent Spanish) schools have been traced.

GERMANY

The German school was the first to reach a very early maturity, by the first half of the sixteenth century, and it also produced by far the largest bulk of important music culminating, of course, in J. S. Bach.

For practical purposes the Dutch school may be identified with the north German; south Germany and Austria developed along slightly different lines. Of these, the northern faction is the more important, because it was these northern composers who first exploited fully the use of the pedals.

The early St. Bavo organ has already been mentioned, the great organ remaining as a Blockwerk department, while the positive had separate stops of differing tonalities. It was only a short step to combine the two on one keyboard which then had at its command three distinct tonal families, namely:

(1) The principal chorus, including a Blockwerk section.
(2) Other flue stops, each controlling separate ranks of pipes, of varying shape and pitch.
(3) Reed stops.

Quite soon, each department, the pedal organ included, became complete in itself, with all three families of stops. This state of affairs was reached early in the sixteenth century and continued to be the basis of the German organ throughout the Renaissance, Baroque and Rococo eras. In terms of German organ-building it is really impossible to differentiate the Renaissance from the Baroque and indeed it may be said with some truth that Germany never espoused the artistic Renaissance at all, but went straight from Gothic to Baroque. Certainly north German fifteenth-century art (especially its sculpture) has far more in common with the Baroque than with the Renaissance.

At this time also emerged the names of the departments, which follow strictly their location in the organ.

The pipes of the Hauptwerk or great organ stood in the main case, above the head of the player. In the days when the great organ and positive were separate instruments, the positive was probably placed behind the player, wherever this was possible, so that he only had to turn round to play it. It remained there even after its keyboard became part of the main console; it was only necessary to take the mechanism, or 'action' under the floor. Its stop-knobs, however, frequently remained in the positive case, until well into the eighteenth century, and the organist had to turn round to change the stops. Many such consoles survive. The positive became the second most important department of the organ, frequently as large as the Hauptwerk itself, and it was known appropriately as the 'Rückpositiv' or back-positive. If there was a third manual department it might be placed high above the Hauptwerk, in which case it was known as the 'Oberwerk' or over-work. More often it was placed below the Hauptwerk, about level with the player's head, when it was called 'Brustwerk' or breast-work. This was convenient because early organs had a type of reed stop called 'regal' (to be discussed in detail later) which was extremely unstable as to pitch and so needed constant tuning. By putting the regals at the front of the Brustwerk they were thus readily accessible to the organist without his even having to leave the console.

The pipes of the pedal organ were either divided, at each side of the Hauptwerk, or sometimes occupied separate towers, standing each side of the Rückpositiv, in advance of the main case and on each side of the player. This arrangement is found in the famous instrument at Steinkirchen and survives in modern Dutch and north-German organ-building as, for example, at Doetinchem, in East Holland (*109*).

This placing of the departments, or 'works' at different levels, and naming them by their location, is known as the 'Werkprinzip', or workprinciple. It was not only sound musically, as will be discussed later, but also mechanically. To make tracker action work efficiently it is most important for the action to operate vertically from the keys; long horizontal travels, either backwards or sideways, never work well for long, and in fact, the pedal organs, with their necessarily sideways travel, always developed excessive mechanical clatter before the manuals. The workprinciple remained universal in north Germany until well into the eighteenth century and has now been almost universally revived there, and in Holland and Scandinavia. When an organ is efficiently laid out, tracker action can remain crisp, responsive and light, even in such huge organs as the present, eighteenth-century instrument at St. Bavo, Haarlem. That neither pneumatic nor electric action can ever be so responsive and prompt as good tracker action is now held almost universally in Germany, Holland and Scandinavia, and it is becoming increasingly recognised in France, America and Britain.

The music and the instruments of the north German school grew up hand in hand and the music demands a minimum of two manuals and pedals, each with the three tone-families (principal chorus, flutes and reeds) already mentioned. In fact, two manuals can meet all the musical requirements, and more than two were only called for by mechanical considerations when the number of speaking stops rose much above 30. Organs of larger size tend to manifest tonal reduplications, and an instrument of about 30 speaking stops is about the most convenient size to consider, in order to understand its tonal constitution and musical uses. Such an organ is at Capel, on the Jutland Peninsula, which has the advantage of being widely known because of the gramophone records made upon it by Helmut Walcha. The organ contains much sixteenth-century pipework by the famous Scherer family, and it was finally rebuilt by the even more famous Arp Schnitger (probably the world's finest and most important builder of organs) in 1695. It was moved to Capel from the Johanniskirche, Hamburg, in 1816 and contains the following 29 speaking stops.

Hauptwerk		Rückpositiv		Pedaal	
Quintade	16	Quintade	8	Untersatz	16
Principal	8	Gedact	8	Octava	8
Hohlfloit	8	Principal	4	Octava	4
Octava	4	Floit	4	Nachthorn	2
Spitzfloit	4	Octava	2	Rauschpfeife	II
Nasat	2⅔	Siffloit	1⅓	Mixtur	IV–VI
Gemshorn	2	Sesquialtera	II	Posaune	16
Rauschpfeife	II	Scharf	IV–VI	Trompet	8
Mixtur	V–VI	Dulcian	16	Cornet	2
Zimbel	III				
Trompet	8			Tremulant	
				Cymbelstern	

These may be divided into the three tone-families as follows:

On the Hauptwerk the principal, or diapason chorus consists of the Principal, Octava, Rauschpfeife and Mixtur.

The flute family consists of the Hohlfloit, Spitzfloit, Nasat and Gemshorn.

27

The Quintadena 16 ft. and Zimbel are common to each of the above.
The reeds are represented by the Trompet.

On the Rückpositiv the principal chorus has a 4 ft. foundation and comprises the Principal, Octava and Scharf.

The flutes are the Gedact, Floit, and Siffloit.

The Quintade and Sesquialtera are common to both.

The reed is a 16 ft. regal, labelled Dulzian.

The pedal organ, with a 16 ft. foundation, is mainly devoted to the principal chorus of

Untersatz	16
Octava	8
Octava	4
Rauschpfeife	II
Mixtur	IV–VI

Only the 2 ft. Nachthorn really comes into the flute series, but in fact was combined with the higher pitched principals for solo purposes.

There are no less than three reeds.

The music for which this instrument was designed falls into three main classes.

The first is polyphonic music in which the parts are of equal importance and do not call for any one to be emphasised. Such music is to be played on part or all of the principal chorus of Hauptwerk and pedal. If the work is of sufficient length to have a contrasting section in the middle, this will be played on the principal chorus of the Positiv which is more penetrating in tone than that of the Hauptwerk, but little if any softer. This is only a broad statement, which must be reconsidered in greater detail later.

The second class of music may be in the form of a trio or duo calling for each voice to be taken by an independent, and sometimes contrasted, tone quality. J. S. Bach's trio sonatas are the best-known example of this sort. The two manual parts may be represented by 8 ft. and 4 ft. flutes on each manual, or 8 ft., 4 ft., and 2 ft.; or 8 ft. and 2 ft., or any of these plus a mutation stop; or by a reed stop alone or combined with flutes and mutations. The pedal part might be represented by flue stops of 16 ft., 8 ft. and 4 ft., the 16 ft. pitch always being required by the continuo style bass. In each instance a satisfactory balance between voices would be obtained by selecting stops of similar pitches on each department, every stop being of more or less equal volume.

The third main class is music in perhaps four or more parts in which one of the voices takes the form of a melodic solo, either in coloratura style or a simple cantus firmus, accompanied by the other voices. Various chorale preludes of Bach and his contemporaries fall within this group, and it is here that solo reeds and mutations are of the greatest utility.

The 'mutation' stops are an all-important feature of the German, and all Baroque organs, and call for a fuller explanation. The best-known mutation stop today is the 'nazard' which is a stop at $2\frac{2}{3}$ ft. pitch, of flute tone. This pitch is, in fact, the second harmonic of 8 ft. pitch and is present to a greater or less extent in all 8 ft. stops. The nazard therefore merely emphasises a natural harmonic (it is, of course, tuned as a true fifth and is not a tempered interval). Similarly, the fifteenth 2 ft., seventeenth $1\frac{3}{5}$ ft., nineteenth $1\frac{1}{3}$ ft. and twenty-second 1 ft. are also components in the harmonic series and may appear as separate mutation stops. The harmonic series continues upwards indefinitely, at closer and closer intervals, but it cannot usefully be represented by separate stops above the 1 ft. (however, see later as to the Italian organ). These mutations, strictly solo stops, were introduced into the organ solely as colouring matter and their function is to produce composite tone colours of a purely solo character when used selectively with foundation stops. For this purpose they might be of quite dull flute tone, such as a nazard, in which case they would colour the foundation tone while sinking into it almost indistinguishably; or they might be of quite bright, diapason tone, in which case the colouring element would be much more vivid. Such stops were the Sesquialtera (combining the $2\frac{2}{3}$ and $1\frac{3}{5}$ ft. on one stop) and Terzian (combining $1\frac{3}{5}$ and $1\frac{1}{3}$ on one stop) in a typical north German organ.

Solo mutation stops must be distinguished quite clearly from the chorus mixture stops which they resemble only superficially. The 'solo' function of the one and the 'chorus' function of the other are quite distinct. However, such a stop as a narrow-scaled Sesquialtera can, for special purposes, be added to the principal chorus, to colour it when for some special reason it is desirable musically to give it a reedy intensity.

The Cymbel is a stop which may belong impartially to either the flute or the principal series. It consists of very small pipes throughout the compass, involving very frequent breaks. It may have only quint and unison ranks or it may also include the third (when it is known as a Terz-cymbel). When drawn with some flutes it adds a remarkable bell-like effect; when drawn with the principal chorus it merely adds brightness.

Summing up the flute and mutation series, its purpose was to produce a wide range of colourful effects by combining stops of generally similar tone-quality, at different pitches. For contrasting purposes, different combinations of flutes and mutations on two manuals achieve the desired result perfectly. And since all the stops on a Baroque organ (except the chorus mixtures) are of very similar power, an equal number of stops on two manuals are certain to balance each other. Solo mutations went out of fashion in the romantic organ which thus became deprived of one of the organ's most characteristic effects. In fact, much music written before 1750 absolutely demands their use and cannot be performed effectively without them. Fortunately, an adequate supply of solo mutations is included in nearly every modern organ.

There remain only the reeds. These may have inverted conical resonators, such as the trumpet in a modern organ; or they may have half-length cylindrical resonators, like a modern clarinet stop; or they may have very short resonators of peculiar and varied shape, in which case they belong to the 'regal' family.

The old trumpets differed from modern examples only to the extent that they were voiced on light pressure wind and had open shallots and unweighted tongues. They were of moderate power, prompt speech and fairly brilliant tone. Similar stops (some better, some worse) may be found in many old British organs today. They were used either as solo or as chorus stops. The extent to which they were used with the principal chorus is doubtful, and probably depended upon the quality of the trumpet (and whether it was in tune) and the taste of the organist. It may be reasonable to suppose that the manual trumpet would have been drawn in a Bach prelude but not in the fugue, where it would have confused the polyphony. On the whole, the north German reeds were not up to the level of the fluework, but this does not apply to the pedal reeds. At their best, these were of moderate power and fairly solid tone (that is, they lacked the rasping quality of some old, light-pressure pedal reeds) and this was invaluable in giving definition to the pedal part. The pedal line had plenty of definition in so far as this was produced by its independent mixtures, but the 16 ft. and 8 ft. flue stops were of somewhat slow and indefinite speech (at any rate before the eighteenth century) so that the reeds were invaluable in restoring a proper (but not excessive) emphasis.

The 'clarinet' class, called Krummhorn, has a thinner, sharper, less sugary and orchestral tone than a British organ clarinet, and it is being re-introduced into many modern British organs. It is a true organ tone, not imitative of an orchestral quality, and one of great beauty and utility.

The regals produced a variety of highly individual, snarling tone qualities (whence their generic German name of 'Schnarrwerk') of which the only (but highly refined) relic found in British organs is the vox humana. However, whereas the vox humana has quarter- or eighth-length resonators, the resonators of a regal had no mathematical relationship to the pitch of the reed and modified the tone only by their varying and often outlandish shapes. Because of this lack of resonator control they were extremely unstable in pitch, and needed constant tuning, as has already been stated. For this reason, and because of their bucolic tone quality, they were abandoned in the eighteenth century and it may be thought that their disappearance was not to be regretted. Indeed, a first encounter with a regal is apt to be distinctly putting-off, but the strangely haunting quality grows upon one, especially when it is realised that they were not often used alone, but more frequently with the flutes and mutations, in which way some startlingly beautiful tone-colours may be produced. Regals are being introduced into modern organs of the revived German school, where these new stops are proving more stable than might be expected.

To return to the principal chorus, this was based upon a unison stop of moderate scale and power, not greatly unlike such few seventeenth- or early eighteenth-century British open diapasons as remain in their original condition and on their original wind pressure. The difference between German and British choruses lies in the upperwork which, in the German organ, is considerably more plentiful and generally somewhat higher pitched. It consists entirely of unison and fifth-sounding ranks, unlike British choruses which contained third-sounding ranks, at least from 1660 onwards. The result is one of great homogeneity, considerable power, great brilliance and, generally, notable clarity. The brilliance succeeded well enough in the resonant German churches, coming from organs placed high up against the reflecting surface of a west wall; but when reproduced in normal British acoustic conditions it is not generally successful. Here, a fuller treatment is desirable, but this does not imply a reduction in the *amount* of upperwork; merely a different form of *treatment*, in the scaling of the pipes and arrangement of the breaks.

The omission of third-sounding ranks in German organs (and all other schools except the British) produces a much 'cleaner' sort of noise. The thirds have a thickening and reedy effect which has special uses but becomes wearisome after a short time. For these special purposes the Germans had their Sesquialtera and Terzian.

In the north German organs the principal choruses of the subsidiary manuals (especially that of the Rückpositiv) were more penetrating in

31

tone than that of the Hauptwerk, but little if any softer. In the south German school the huge Blockwerk mixtures survived longer on the great, so that the subsidiary choruses did tend to be considerably softer. The chorus of the pedal organ was proportionate in size and layout to the Hauptwerk, so that it was entirely independent of manual to pedal couplers (indeed, there seldom were any) but as has been said, they did rely to some extent upon the reeds.

Naturally, the most important use of the choruses, with or without reeds, was to accompany congregational singing, and to appreciate their effectiveness for this purpose it is necessary to attend a service in a large Dutch Reformed Church and hear how much better these brilliant choruses lead the powerful singing of an immense congregation than does any amount of powerful unison or reed tone.

In organ-music the choruses were used for music in which all the parts were regarded as being of equal importance. In all Baroque organ-music, as well as certain other instrumental forms such as the Italian concerto, composers thought in terms of terraced dynamics, or contrasted levels of volume and tone. This is a kind of musical expression to which the Baroque organ is admirably suited, the nineteenth-century romantic conception of expression as crescendo, diminuendo and sforzando being completely alien to it. In Baroque organ-music the climaxes are inherent in the musical structure, and call for no particular dynamic emphasis. Stylistically therefore, no changes of registration during the course of a movement are called for, and it is very unlikely that any were in fact made. The stop handles of a seventeenth- or eighteenth-century console of any size are so difficult for the player to reach while playing (some of them cannot be actually reached at all without getting up) that the addition or subtraction of stops during performance is practically impossible.

An historically correct way of registering one of the major fugues of J. S. Bach is to draw the full principal chorus on Hauptwerk, Positiv and pedal (without any couplers) and go straight through the work without any change of registration. During the episodes (when the pedals are silent) the hands are transferred from the Hauptwerk to the Positiv manual, if the structure of the part-writing permits, but 'unnatural breaks' are avoided. This method is adopted by some purists today. Other performers feel obliged to make some concessions to romanticism, and make use of assistants. With one or two of these, practical experience of an Arp Schnitger organ suggests the following procedure. For the opening, full to 2 ft. would be drawn on Hauptwerk, Positiv and pedal.

When the player moves on to the Positiv for the first episode, the assistants add a mixture to each of the Hauptwerk and pedal in preparation for the return to these departments. When this has taken place a mixture is added to the Positiv for the second episode, during which a further mixture is added to the Hauptwerk and one or two reeds to the pedal, for the final statement. The essential point is that stops are never added to a department when it is actually in use. The only exceptions to this are at some well defined break, for example, after the Neapolitan sixth on the last page of the *tema fugatum* of Bach's Passacaglia in C minor. Here it might be felt necessary to couple the manuals together or add a manual reed.

Whether assistants were employed in Bach's day is likely to be always a matter of conjecture. But it must be remembered that many of his performances would have been improvised (*vide* Forkel), in which case pre-arranged stop alterations by assistants seem rather improbable. Further, if assisted performances were at all frequent, it would be reasonable to suppose that a few scores marked with instructions for the assistants would have survived. So far as is known, there is nothing which enables any firm conclusions to be drawn.

The practice of old-fashioned players today, of starting a fugue on a soft stop and gradually working up to a tremendous climax (frequently with disastrous injury to the rhythm) is totally estranged from the musical approach of a seventeenth- or eighteenth-century player. Bach frequently writes at the commencement of a piece '*pro organo pleno*'. This does not mean 'full organ' in the modern sense, but a more or less full principal chorus, in the form just described. The French equivalent, to be discussed later, is '*pour le grand plein jeu*'.

One further aspect of the German organ needs to be mentioned before passing to the French school, and this is the method employed for voicing the flue stops, especially the principal chorus.

The whole organ was voiced on one pressure of wind which, in the sixteenth century, might vary from two to three inches, according to the size of the organ. This is a very low pressure in terms of all but the most recent British organs. The footholes of the pipes were then of such a size as to give a maximum supply of wind to the mouth; that is to say, the area of the foothole was at least as large as that of the flue (that is, the slit between the languid and lower lip)—frequently larger. Sometimes, as at Klosterneuberg (where the pressure is only 2 in.) the feet of the pipes of one foot speaking length and less are almost cylindrical in shape, with little or no taper at all, so that the diameter of the foothole is the same as the diameter of the pipe itself.

This ensured a very prompt 'attack' in the speech of the pipe and no attempt was made to delay this by 'nicking' the edge of the languid into a sort of saw-edge as was usual in the first half of the twentieth century and as, indeed, is necessary with heavy-pressure voicing, if a disagreeable 'spit' is to be avoided. Some modern, neo-Baroque builders have deliberately introduced such a 'spit' into their voicing, but it is not characteristic of an old chorus, although it *is* found in isolated stops, especially stopped flutes, where it is perfectly acceptable.

This form of voicing is known as 'open-foot' or 'flue-controlled' voicing, since no attempt is made to regulate the power of a pipe by what is the easiest means of doing so—by increasing or reducing the size of the foot-hole. Regulation is done only by widening or narrowing the flue (by manipulating the lower lip) and to some extent by increasing the height of the mouth (its 'cut-up') by cutting away the upper lip.

When carried out in conjunction with a sufficiently low pressure (preferably not more than $2\frac{1}{4}$ in., or $2\frac{1}{2}$ in. at most) this kind of voicing produces a characteristically open sort of "head tone", coupled with a very good attack, which is undoubtedly most effective. However, it is somewhat difficult to produce satisfactory reed tone on so low a pressure, and as pressures rose to about 3 in. towards 1700, the power of the flue-work had to be controlled by narrowing the flues to such an extent that a scratchy sort of tone tended to result. To overcome this disability, voicers began to vary the size of the foot-hole as a convenient and artistic method of voicing. In effect, making the foot-hole smaller than the languid has the effect of reducing the pressure of wind inside the foot and, therefore, the effective pressure upon which the pipe speaks. Only when foot-hole control is carried to extremes, as in the late nineteenth and early twentieth centuries, does the tonal result become objectionable. But on pressures between $2\frac{1}{2}$ in. and $3\frac{1}{2}$ in., the minimum necessary use of foot control and of nicking, in order to produce a musically acceptable result, is perfectly logical and was, in fact, used by nearly all eighteenth-century voicers.

Also up to about 1700, the principal chorus, and the flutes and mutations, were kept strictly apart for purposes of registration, but throughout the eighteenth century there is evidence to show that the families began increasingly to be mixed, and no doubt Bach himself was an innovator in this direction, whose unconventional registration was famous in his own day.

As the eighteenth century wore on, German organ-building began to

34

move in two different directions, one of which may be described as 'Rococo' and one 'Classical'. The 'Rococo' school tended towards more and more dramatic effects, including very powerful climax mixtures, 32 ft. reeds and even some attempt at string tone. Curiously enough, they made no use of the swell-box which was steadily establishing itself in England. The 'Classical' school tended to produce a more unified effect, and eschewed such bizarre effects as regals and, because it was mostly developed by the great artist, Gottfried Silbermann, it became somewhat the better known. By 1800 both schools had really come to an end, as musical interest moved increasingly towards the orchestra, opera, and the 'romantic movement', in none of which could any serious part be found for the organ.

The German organ up to 1750 is unquestionably the most important musically, since the greatest bulk of the most important music was written for it.

Of the mediaeval type of German organ, it is difficult to form any very accurate impression, but it is safe to assume that despite a conservative rebuild in 1712, the seven-stop organ at the old cathedral church of Notre Dame de Valère, Sion, in Switzerland, sounds substantially as it did in the fifteenth century. It is very loud and of a ringing, almost bell-like quality. The wind pressure is $1\frac{3}{4}$ in. No finer example of Renaissance German-school organ can be found than the great instrument in the Abbey Church at Klosterneuberg, near Vienna. Most of it dates from the middle of the sixteenth century and the final rebuild took place in 1642. Arp Schnitger was unquestionably the greatest builder of the high Baroque. The best surviving small organs by him are at Steinkirchen, near Hamburg, and Capel, in Jutland. Probably the finest large organ of the Schnitger school is in the great Dutch church of St. Laurance, Alkmaar. Of the Rococo builders, the Dutch Christian Muller was one of the most important, and the fully-restored instrument by him at St. Bavo, Haarlem, finished in 1735, was and is regarded as his *magnum opus*. Of quite a different type is the remarkably dramatic organ in the Fürstlichen Hofkirche at Amorbach, on the northern edge of Bavaria, built in 1782 by the brothers Stumm. Silbermann's work has suffered badly and no important untouched specimen survives, at any rate this side of the Iron Curtain; but so far as reeds and choruses go, the instrument in the abbey church at Ottobeuren, built in 1764, although by Karl Riepp, may be taken as representative and is an extremely fine instrument. The study of the above eight organs will give an excellent picture of the whole German school throughout its history up to 1800.

FRANCE

Next in importance to the German school is the French, and of the Continental schools, it is more like the English than any other. Not only have typical French and English stop-lists considerable affinities, including short-compass subsidiary manual departments, but the French organs, although they possessed pedals, had them in only a rudimentary form, as a small solo department (as will be shown later, the British organ had none at all until well into the eighteenth century). Tonally, too, the two were remarkably alike, especially in the late seventeenth century, when they lacked the forcefulness and excitement of the north German instruments.

Very few French lists of stops survive from before the last half of the sixteenth century but by 1575, at latest, the type had reached a full maturity from which it departed very little for the next two centuries.

The following specification of an organ built by N. Barbier for the church of Saint-Gervais and Saint-Protais at Gisors in 1580 is about the earliest mature example to have survived (the instrument itself no longer exists).

Grand Orgue

PLEIN JEU		MUTATIONS		ANCHES		PÉDALE	
Montre	16	Flûte	4	Trompette	8	Huitpied	
Montre	8	Nasard-quinte	2⅔	Clairon	4	ouverte	8
Bourdon	8	Sifflet	1	Voix		Saqueboute	12
Prestant	4	Quinteflûte	1⅓	Humaine	8		
Doublette	2	Cornet	V				
Fourniture	IV						
Cymbale	III						

Positif

Bourdon	8	Larigot	1⅓	Cromorne	8
Bourdon	4				
Doublette	2				
Cymbale	II				

When this is compared with the instrument of comparable size built for the Church of Notre Dame du Port, Clermont-Ferrand by Rabiny, in 1777, it will be seen how similar they are (p.37).

Like the German type, the foundation of the French organ was its two balanced manual departments, the grand orgue and positif. The latter was almost invariably in a separate case, like the German Rückpositiv, the console and player being placed between the main case and the positif.

Grand Orgue

PLEIN JEU		MUTATIONS		ANCHES	
Montre	8	Flûte	4	Trompette	8
Bourdon	8	Nasard	$2\frac{2}{3}$	Clairon	4
Prestant	4	Tierce	$1\frac{3}{5}$	Voix Humaine	8
Doublette	2	Cornet	V		
Fourniture	IV				
Cymbale	III				

Positif

Bourdon	8	Nasard	$2\frac{2}{3}$	Cromorne	
Montre	4	Tierce	$1\frac{3}{5}$		
Doublette	2				
Fourniture	III				
Cymbale	II				

Récit (short compass)

Cornet	V	Hautbois	8

Pédale

Flûte	8	Trompette	8
		Clairon	4

The two principal choruses were fairly well balanced in power, but that of the positif tended to be pitched an octave higher than the grand orgue. Thus, if the grand orgue had a montre of 16 ft., the positif had one of 8 ft; and if the grand orgue had one of only 8 ft., then the positif had nothing lower than a prestant of 4 ft. Apart from this distinction, the voicing was very similar. The mixtures contained quints and unisons only (never the tierce; wherein the British contemporary mixtures differed) of which (unlike the Germans) the quint ranks were slightly subordinated in power to the unisons.

In the seventeenth century these choruses had a fairly restrained, almost silvery quality, but during the eighteenth century a wider scaling was gradually adopted, together with higher wind pressures ($2\frac{1}{2}$ in. was usual in the seventeenth century, but by 1780 Clicquot, at any rate, sometimes used as much as 4 in.). A late eighteenth-century French chorus has a breadth of tone never to be found in British instruments, and a degree of power rarely if ever approached by us, although not reaching German levels of forcefulness and brilliance.

The grand orgue principal chorus was called 'le grand plein jeu', and that of the positif was 'le petit plein jeu'.

Quite distinct from the principal choruses were the flutes and solo mutations, and the two were never intermixed at any time during the history of the instrument.

The foundation of the mutation series was the bourdon of 16 or 8 ft. pitch. These stops were of wide scale and all but the extreme basses were metal pipes. The tone was of great beauty, and very sombre, quite unlike the 'perky' quality of the English, small scale, wooden-piped stopped diapason. The mutation ranks consisted of nasard $2\frac{2}{3}$, quarte de nasard 2, tierce $1\frac{3}{5}$ and larigot $1\frac{1}{3}$. The 1 ft. hardly ever appeared, and then only very early. Later, large organs also included the 16 ft. series in the form of grosse nasard $5\frac{1}{3}$. All of these were of wide scale, voiced as flutes, including the tierce. In this the French differed from the German organs, where the tierce rank never appeared by itself, being always attached to a quint (either as a Sequialtera, 12.17, or Terzian, 17.19), both of narrow, principal scaling. Owing to this foundational treatment, the French mutations tend to lose their identity in a synthetic resultant more completely than do the German equivalents.

The French cornets are also of wider scaling than the English, which more resemble the south German type. The French stops (also of short compass, from middle C) are extremely broad and sombre in tone. Their composition is like the British, consisting of a chimney flute 8 ft., and wide scale, lightly blown open ranks, at 4, $2\frac{2}{3}$, 2 and $1\frac{3}{5}$ ft. pitches.

These mutations were used in duos and trios and the cornets were much used in contrast with a 'basse de trompette' or 'basse de cromorne'.

The reeds formed the third tonal family and again, with two exceptions, were not supposed to be drawn with the fluework. However, it seems possible that this rule was more rigidly enforced during the eighteenth century than earlier, since the early reeds are not often strong, or regular enough to stand up by themselves. The exceptions to this segregation are the prestant 4 ft. and the cornet. The prestant was generally drawn with an 8 ft. trompette or cromorne, mainly to cover up its irregularities, when used as a solo stop. But when the reeds were used as a chorus, known as 'le grand jeu', the cornet was drawn with them, when it went far to bolster up the trebles, which were quite outclassed by the enormously powerful reed basses.

An eighteenth-century French reed chorus is without parallel in any other country, except perhaps Spain and Portugal. The stops are very powerful and free in tone, yet the basses have a remarkable roundness coupled with a very prompt attack. Unlike the Germans, the French did not use their 'plein jeux' much for polyphonic music, but reserved them more for homophonic treatment. The 'grand jeu', by contrast, was generally used fugally.

The other reeds were cromorne (equivalent to the British cremona),

38

voix humaine and, occasionally, hautbois (the latter always in a short compass department). Regals were not used in France after 1600.

The grand orgue and positif were always of full compass, but the next two manual departments, the récit and echo, were always short. Each consisted of seldom more than three or four stops and sometimes only a solitary cornet. The récit was not enclosed, being quite different from the récit expressif of the nineteenth century.

The pedal department was entirely a solo department, used in trios, or as a reed cantus firmus against the Plein Jeu. Only quite late in the eighteenth century did it become at all common to introduce 16 ft. stops; first a bombarde and subsequently a flûte, and then only in the largest instruments.

French organ music of the seventeenth and eighteenth centuries is highly stylised and sophisticated. The registration to be used is invariably stated precisely. The instrument and its repertoire were very closely related. Although gayer and more superficial than the German school, the French music is of great beauty; but to make sense of it, it is essential that something resembling the correct tonalities should be available, and used.

Not many old French organs survive unaltered. Perhaps the most representative, accessible, and in fair condition is the late eighteenth-century instrument by Clicquot, in the Cathedral at Poitiers.

ITALY

Entirely different from the French or German schools is the Italian, which had an even longer existence than either, since it survived with little or no alteration from the fifteenth century until well into the nineteenth century; at least 450 years altogether.

As will appear later, very little is known of British organs in the sixteenth century, but it seems safe to assume that from the time of Henry VIII onwards the Italian influence was considerable.

The Italian organ never had more than one manual and consisted of a diapason chorus of which all the ranks (quints and unisons) drew separately. Small organs were complete to the 1 ft., larger instruments went up to the thirty-sixth (3 in. longest pipe). In addition, there was a 4 ft. flute and a 'voce humana' consisting of a principal-scaled, short-compass, céleste. The latter stop can be of great beauty, and was used melodically.

The mutation ranks were not used melodically, being simply a split-up mixture and each rank breaks back an octave as it reaches $1\frac{1}{2}$ in. C.

39

The largest instruments go down to 16 ft. C, but almost none have independent pedals, though an octave of rudimentary pull-downs was quite usual, and Frescobaldi often requires long-held pedal points. Reeds only appeared right at the end, in the nineteenth century, and then rarely.

The biggest concentration of early Italian organs is to be found in Bologna and Brescia (which was the home of Antegnati, the foremost Italian builder), but perhaps the most beautiful of all is the late sixteenth-century instrument in the Silbernenkapelle at Innsbruck, in Austria. Its specification is as follows:

Principale	8
Ottava	4
Decimaquinta	2
Decimanona	$1\frac{1}{3}$
Vigesimaseconda	1
Flauto in ottava	4
Voce Umana (mid. C)	8

The organ is voiced on $1\frac{3}{4}$ in. wind.

SPAIN AND PORTUGAL

The Spanish and Portuguese organs call only for passing notice since they produced no important school of composition and, indeed, there is very little ordinary organ music that can be played upon them. Their flue choruses follow mostly the Italian pattern, but two manuals are quite usual, although pedals are rare, and generally only pull-downs. Unlike the Italians, however, the Spanish organs from early times have been rich in reeds of immense stridency, which can sound very exciting in a large building when reasonably in tune, which they mostly are not. Indeed, the number of old Spanish or Portuguese organs now in playing order is remarkably small. Their use is also complicated by the fact that all the stops are divided, and frequently a treble has no corresponding bass, and vice versa.

Cavaillé-Coll is said to have been much influenced by the Spanish reeds, whose impact was enhanced by many of them projecting horizontally from the case, called by Cavaillé-Coll 'en chamade'.

AFTER 1800

Classical organ-building in the Continent of Europe came to an abrupt end between 1790 and 1800; only in England can a steady history of development be traced into and throughout the nineteenth century. In

Holland, certainly, the old traditions lived on into the middle of the nineteenth century, but generally, elsewhere, the first 40 years of the century saw very little organ-building activity. This was logical enough, at a time when the romantic movement was coming into its own, and large orchestras were being heard for the first time. The organ had nothing to contribute to this artistic new world, at any rate for the time being.

The parent of the romantic organ was Aristide Cavaillé-Coll (1811–99), without any question. He envisaged the organ as something quite different from anything that had gone before, entirely romantic in concept. He produced his first, fully developed organ as early as 1841, at Saint-Denis, Paris. The different manual departments no longer had any separate identity and often enough the grand orgue was the only one to possess chorus upperwork. The fluework was all of moderate power, made up of diapasons, flutes and strings. Although the mixtures can be drawn with a flue foundation only, Cavaillé-Coll thought of them only as adjuncts to his immense reed choruses. Although these were voiced on light pressures, Cavaillé-Coll kept up the power of the trebles in a way his predecessors had been unable to do, by putting the trebles on a higher pressure (usually about 5 in.) than the basses (usually about 3½ in.). He also used double-length, or harmonic trebles, for many of his trompettes and, as already mentioned, disposed the most powerful ones horizontally, or 'en chamade'.

At first, separate mutations found no place in the Cavaillé-Coll organ, although he quite often retained a cornet. Only later, under the influence of Saint-Saëns and Guilmant, did he make some concessions to classical design.

The different manual departments were therefore used more for ease of registration than anything else. They had no separate identity and merely contributed to the massive 'grand chœur' of all coupled together.

Curiously enough, Cavaillé-Coll was no great devotee of the swell box, and was content to enclose only one department of even a five-manual organ and that, as likely as not, a handful of solo stops without any chorus ensemble.

To match this essentially symphonic concept of the organ Cavaillé-Coll devised a system of stop-control which was also the first of its kind. Each department had two wind chests. On one stood the 'fonds' consisting of the flue stops up to 2 ft. On the other stood the 'jeux de combinaisons', comprising the reeds and mixtures (there are unimportant exceptions to this broad classification). Each of these chests was controlled by a ventil, which cut off its wind-supply. Each ventil was controlled by a pedal (similar to a composition pedal). The interdepartmental couplers were also controlled by pedals. To play a large composition, requiring a succession of diminuendi and crescendi, it was therefore necessary only to draw most of the stops in the organ, put most of them out of action by the ventils, and play throughout on the grand orgue, registering only by use of the pedal-operated ventils and couplers.

This concept of the 'expressive' organ, using crescendo and diminuendo, was of course an entirely new one. Not only was it entirely foreign to Baroque music, which relied on terraced dynamics, but it would have been physically impossible to achieve on any eighteenth-century console. Nor could it have been achieved in an organ of any size with tracker action, since the coupled manuals would have been uncomfortably heavy. In this, Cavaillé-Coll was helped by the 'Barker lever' action, invented by the English Charles Spackman Barker. Barker interposed pneumatic motors between the keys and the trackers of the principal manual which thus not only reduced the weight of the action of that department, but also of the others when coupled to it.

The outstanding merit of the Cavaillé-Coll organ, as seen through the eyes of his contemporaries, was demonstrated by the great school of organ composition which grew up, literally around it, of which César Franck and Widor are among the earliest and most illustrious. It was, however, an entirely symphonic concept, closely connected with the romantic movement; and when musical taste began once more to look back, or perhaps onwards, to more classical forms, the Cavaillé-Coll organ quickly lost its lustre. It is, in fact, absolutely impossible to make sense of most eighteenth-century or earlier music on a Cavaillé-Coll organ (or, at any rate, only on one or two exceptional instruments). His influence was therefore immense, but limited in its duration to about 70 years. During this time he obliterated all but a handful of the great school of classical French organ-building and left France with a vast collection of instruments of superb, almost indestructible craftsmanship and extremely limited artistic utility.

No one Cavaillé-Coll organ can be quoted as entirely typical, but that at Sainte-Clotilde, Paris, is characteristic, and famous because César Franck was its first organist from 1859 to 1890. The instrument has not been greatly altered from its original state.

Germany followed very much after Cavaillé-Coll, but preserved a considerable background of classical design, so that the grotesquely large and ponderous German organs of the nineteenth century are of greater general utility than are the more thorough-going romantic French instru-

SAINT-CLOTILDE SPECIFICATION

Grand Orgue		Récit Expressif	
Montre	16	Bourdon	8
Bourdon	16	Flûte Harmonique	8
Montre	8	Viole de Gambe	8
Gambe	8	Voix Céleste	8
Flûte Harmonique	8	Flûte Octaviante	4
Bourdon	8	Octavin	2
Prestant	4	Basson-Hautbois	8
Octave	4	Voix Humaine	8
Quinte	$2\frac{2}{3}$	Trompette	8
Doublette	2	Clairon	4
Plein Jeu	V		
Bombarde	16	Tremblant	
Trompette	8		
Clairon	4	**Pédale**	
		Quintaton	32
Positif		Contrebasse	16
Bourdon	16	Flûte	8
Montre	8	Octave	4
Gambe	8	Bombarde	16
Flûte Harmonique	8	Basson	16
Bourdon	8	Trompette	8
Salicional	8	Clairon	4
Prestant	4		
Flûte Octaviante	4	14 Pédales de	
Quinte	$2\frac{2}{3}$	Combinaison	
Doublette	2		
Plein Jeu	IV		
Clarinette	8		
Trompette	8		
Clairon	4		

ments. For aids to registration they relied largely on the 'Rollschweller', being a general stop-crescendo pedal.

In addition to the great French symphonic school of organ composition, the organ became popular during the latter half of the nineteenth century as a medium for playing arrangements of orchestral works. This is now regarded rightly as being in very poor taste, but a century ago this would not have been a valid criticism. At that time, orchestras were few and far between and there is no doubt that organ arrangements of orchestral works served to bring great music to a vast number of people who otherwise could never have heard it at all. The great virtuosi of the day, among whom the Englishman, W. T. Best, was undoubtedly pre-eminent, developed a measure of skill and ingenuity in this direction which few modern players, fortunately, would care to emulate; especially with the limited aids to registration available a century ago.

With improving musical taste, organ-building split into two different schools of thought, and the point of cleavage, throughout Europe, was in the early 1920s.

The French, with their great romantic composers, naturally did not want an organ which would not do justice to them. At the same time, they wanted to be able to play Bach, and their own early composers, intelligibly. This they did in a variety of ways, but the most usual, in a fairly small organ, was to place the diapasons up to 2 ft. on the grand orgue, and trumpets and mixtures on the récit expressif. The récit also contained strings and flute stops, and thus served most 'romantic' requirements. Alternatively, the grand orgue and récit together comprised a classical French grand orgue, consisting of a complete principal chorus, and reeds. The positif then closely followed eighteenth-century lines, with solo flute mutations and a chorus mixture.

Germany, the Netherlands and Scandinavia, however, had produced no equivalent school of romantic organ composition, apart from the six Mendelssohn sonatas and the few towering works, of immense difficulty, by Liszt and Max Reger. The tendency there, therefore, has been to write off the romantic organ and its music entirely, and revert to a completely eighteenth-century idiom of organ building. Unless this kind of organ soon attracts a virile and significant school of modern composition it seems doubtful if it can long survive, but in the meantime, its finest manifestations, particularly by Dutch and Scandinavian builders, are very good, within their self-imposed limits.

Early American organs closely followed the British pattern, but in the first third of the present century they evolved a dreadful kind of instrument, conceived as a sort of one-man band. The renaissance was led by an Englishman, Donald Harrison, who obtained control of the Aeolian Skinner Company in the early 1930s and developed a very fine type of general purpose instrument, which attained a rapid and complete success. This, in its turn, has supplied a model for much in modern British organ-building, as will be seen later. The latest trends in America are towards a more severe classicism.

With this background of Continental history we are in a position to follow the curious history of the British organ.

CHAPTER II

TONAL HISTORY

Middle Ages and until 1650

The history of the British organ is one of intransigent insularity; not until 1950 did it begin to take on any sort of international character.

It must be confessed that this sturdy independence has not generally been to its artistic advantage and we only held the lead on other countries for a short time in the middle of the nineteenth century. On the other hand, there is a natural tendency to judge every school of organ building by the standards of the north German school, not perhaps so much because of its manifestly superior logic in design, as because it produced such composers as Buxtehude and Bach, much of whose music cannot be played effectively on any other kind of instrument. As has been shown in the preceding chapter, the other national schools—French, Italian and Spanish—were as limited in scope as our own.

Ironically it is of the pre-Commonwealth organ, when Byrd, Gibbons and Bull were producing some of the world's finest keyboard music, much of it for organ, that we know and understand least. There is enough surviving evidence to form a valid conception of what a typical German, French or Italian organ sounded like in 1600, but we can only guess what a British organ sounded like at this time. Hardly any pipes and very few specifications survive, and the latter are so peculiar that it is extremely difficult to probe the ideas underlying them.

Nor are we any better off in the middle ages.

The famous description of the tenth-century organ at Winchester was quoted in the last chapter. This was evidently a large and powerful instrument of a kind that continued to be built on the Continent, especially in Germany, and finally developed into the mature organs of Scherer in the sixteenth, Schnitger in the seventeenth and Silbermann in the eighteenth centuries.

In England there is no evidence that such massive machines long survived. There are plenty of references in churchwardens' accounts to organs throughout the middle ages, mostly for repairing or moving them. But the money amounts are always so small (even after allowing for currency depreciation) as to indicate pretty clearly that the organs were small, as also does the frequency with which they were moved, not only about the church, but from one parish to another, often on hire. This may be partly accounted for by the layout of our Gothic churches with their great west windows. These left no room for a west-end gallery inside the church with a large organ upon it. The Continental tradition of a western screen façade, with no window, left a west wall inside the church which had to be covered up somehow, and a large organ case was an obvious functional way of doing so.

By contrast, the typical British Gothic church provides all too few places in which an organ, however small, can be stowed away. Most parish churches now house Victorian or later organs which are unnecessarily large for their requirements, and have had to be tucked away in nooks and crannies which enable them neither to be seen nor heard to any advantage nor even, often enough, maintained.

In the middle ages it is therefore clear that our organs were small, and mostly so small as to be readily portable. Frequently there was more than one in a large church, of which one generally stood on the rood screen, as in St. Dunstan in the West, London, where in 1522 repairs were done to the 'organs in the quyer' and 'the organs in the Rode loffe'.

Among the earliest references to organs, after the Winchester affair, is one in York Minster in 1147; and in 1304 Westminster Abbey possessed two pairs of organs. The reference to 'pairs' of organs has no special significance. It is not to be inferred that the Abbey had in fact four organs, nor yet that its organs had two manuals. It just happens that organs, like clavichords and virginals later on, were always referred to as a pair, like scissors and trousers today.

It is fitting that York Minster, which has so often played a leading part in the history of British organ-building, should provide us with the oldest surviving contract for building a British organ. This is dated January 24th, 1338 (the English is modernised):

'Master Adam of Darlington undertakes to make a new organ. He is to start on Thursday next. He is to receive from the Chapter for his work 11 marks. Lead, materials and other needful things are to be supplied by the Chapter. He shall associate with him as many other workmen as are necessary, at his own expense. He shall enter upon no other undertaking until this one has been completed. He shall do the work as quickly as he possibly can.'

Unfortunately this document tells us nothing about the organ, except its price, which in current values might be put at about £2,000. This would be rather larger than to be portable, but small enough for a building so large as the Minster. The most interesting fact is that the organ builder was even at this early date a free-lance lay craftsman. The same was true of St. Paul's Cathedral at about the same time where 'Walter L'Orgoner' built a clock in 1344. The clock is described in considerable detail, though unfortunately not sufficiently to be sure whether it was a weight-driven clock with a mechanical escapement, or merely an unusually complicated water clock. Mechanical clocks were known in Italy by 1300 and the world's oldest surviving complete clock is that in Salisbury Cathedral, dating from 1386. Before this, it seems reasonably certain that mechanical clocks had reached England by the middle of the century and Walter is therefore, with Adam of Darlington, the earliest recorded native maker. It is interesting, but logical enough, that these two ecclesiastical crafts, both demanding considerable mechanical skill, should have been practised by one man. A century and more later, as clock-making became more precise, it was more usually combined with the craft of the locksmith, while the increasing complication of organs called for entirely specialist skill.

As early as the fifteenth century the records of the Brewers' Company mention a guild of 'Orgelmakers' as one of three 'crafts exercised from old and still continuing in this ninth year of King Henry V'. This went on until 1531, in which year, on August 29th, the City authorities recorded: 'Fforasmoche as this court is credeblye enformed that the olde name and companye of organ makers ys nowe consumed and dyssolved, wherefore now at the speciall request of John Howe ye yonger, organ maker, he ys transposed to the mistery and company of skynners' (they, of course, being concerned to supply leather for bellows).

In 1447 Nicholas Rawnce made a pair of organs for Canterbury Cathedral for £3 6s. 5½d., which suggests a substantially smaller instrument than Master Adam's at York, and roughly comparable is one made by John Chamberleyne for Magdalen College, Oxford, for £8, in 1508.

Apart from these, contemporary references are scant but 'springs for the basses' are frequently replaced, suggesting that the larger pallet-springs were chronically unreliable.

Even the sixteenth century brings us very little closer to established facts. Only in the last year of the century do we get an actual list of stops, and that only for the large musical clock sent by Queen Elizabeth as a present to the Sultan of Turkey. The clockwork was supplied by the famous maker Randolph Bull and Thomas Dallam made the organ which had the following stops:

Open principal
Unison recorder
Octavo principal
Flute
Drum
Nightingale
Shaking stop

This may be read as two 4 ft. and two 2 ft. stops, such as organ clocks might have at any time up to the nineteenth century; it does not lead very far towards an understanding of church organs in the sixteenth century.

The few organ cases that survive from the sixteenth century indicate that ordinary organs were at any rate sometimes of a quite impressive size. The oldest case is that at Old Radnor, on the Welsh border. Even allowing for the living having been in the royal gift from 1502–34, and for the then flourishing school of woodcarving at Llanano, it is difficult enough to account for the presence of this sumptuous case, standing 18 ft. high, in this small and remote Welsh village. But as it cannot anyway be put later than 1550 it does at least show that sizeable organs existed in British churches, other than cathedrals, during the sixteenth century.

Apart from Dallam's Turkish organ the only other surviving sixteenth-century specification is ambiguous in the extreme and has vexed the ingenuity of musicologists ever since. It relates to the organ made by Antony Duddyngton for the important church of All Hallows, Barking, in 1519:

> This endenture made the yere of our Lorde God MVXIX an the moneth of July xxv day witness that Antony Duddyngton, Citizen of London, Organ Maker, hath made a full bargayn ... to make an instrument, that ys to say, a payer of organs for the foresed churche of dowble c-fa-ut, that is to say xxvii playne keys and the pryncipale to conteyn ths length of v foote so following wt Bassys called Diapason to the same conteyning length of x foot or more: and to be dowble pryncipalls throweout the said instrument, so that the pyppes wt inforth shall be fyne metall and stuff as the utter parts that is to say of pure Tyn, wt as fewe stops as may be convenient.

The price was £54 which, like the York organ of nearly 200 years earlier, suggests the modern equivalent of about £2,000 which would buy a

48

single-manual organ of adequate size for such a church today. 'xxvii playne keys' (i.e. naturals as opposed to sharps) suggests a compass of four octaves, C–C, with the customary short bottom octave giving E[1] as apparently the lowest note: or the shorter compass C–A, including a full bottom octave with all accidentals. Neither solution is entirely satisfactory, as no keyboard music before late in the century goes above A; nor does it demand the lower accidentals. However, it was evidently a not unusual compass, as the organ built by John Howe for Holy Trinity, Coventry, also had 'xxvii pleyn keyes'. The pitch also is curious, since the C pipe today is either 4 or 8 ft. long, and 5 or 10 ft. suggest a very low pitch. However, it may be that these pipes were to stand in the case, so that their overall length was important, and the length is to be read as including the feet. This would agree with the apparently casual 'x foot or more'. Many deep interpretations have been put on 'Bassys called Diapason to the same'; but from the fact that the principals were to be 'dowble throweout' it is not necessary to assume anything more complicated than that the principal from 4 ft. had two pipes to a note, but the bottom octave had only one pipe to a note. As was already usual on the Continent, the show pipes were to be of pure tin, presumably burnished; but it was distinctly unusual at that time for the pipes inside the case also to be of tin, always an expensive metal. The closing words 'wt as fewe stops as may be convenient' may be taken at face value. British builders had certainly broken down the blockwork into separate stops by 1500. Thus, in 1513, at St. Lawrence, Reading, the accounts record payment for 'two lokks . . . one for the stopps and the other for the keys', which can only be interpreted literally. And in 1521 Danyell Lokyar was paid 1s. 'for the making of iiii stoppys of iron for the same organes' at St. Andrews, Canterbury. The Leckingfield Proverbs, dating from the beginning of the sixteenth century, also refer to organs with stops:

The swete orgayne pipis comfortith a stedfast mynde
Wrong handlynge of the stoppis may cause them sypher fro their kynde
But he that playeth of pipes wher so grete nowmber is
Must handill the keyes all lyke that by misgovernaunce they sounde amyss.

And again, in 1526, John Howe built for Holy Trinity, Coventry, a 'Peir of organs with vii stops' (and xxvii pleyn keyes, as mentioned earlier) for £20.

There is evidence of five stops (perhaps even seven) at Old Radnor.

---

[1] E key played C. F♯ played D. G♯ played E. Then from F upwards each key played its proper note, B♭ being the lowest accidental.

If £20 could buy seven stops at Coventry, the £54 of All Hallows, Barking, would clearly buy a much larger number, yet it is stipulated that the organ is to be 'wt as fewe stops as may be convenient'. The inference is that as much as possible of the money was to go into the blockwork, with only a minimum of separate stops.

The John Howe mentioned at Coventry was the middle and most famous of three generations of organ-builders whose names occur constantly between 1485 (when John's father was working at York Minster) and about 1570. In 1557–8 we find him at Eton dealing with the usual chronic defect of the times 'for xii springes for the great basses iii s'; but in 1565–6 is the enigmatical entry 'for his charge commyinge hither and other reparacions done upon the organiste ut patet per billam vii s'. The Elder John died in 1519 and the second John in 1571. In the last 12 years or so of his life he was affectionately referred to as 'Father Howe'—an epithet of endearment and respect earned subsequently only by Father Smith and Father Willis. He is the John Howe previously referred to as being 'transposed' to the Skinners' Company. The third generation was Thomas Howe, but it is not clear if he was an organ-builder.

After about 1563 the growing puritan movement was almost as inimical to organs as the time of the Commonwealth, and certainly very little new organ-building was done; to revive only for a short period under Archbishop Laud in the reign of Charles I. In many churches organs were disused, while at the visitation of Bishop Bancroft to St. Paul's Cathedral in 1598 it is complained:

> Item the Orgayns are so misused in the Blowing and other ways wt jogging the bellowes that the Bellowes be broken and the winde is not sufficiente to geve sownde to the insterment.

and further:

> The Organ lofte is greatly abused by yᵉ bell ringers letting up of many people for monye to yᵉ decaye of ye instrument, yᵉ pipes beinge manye of them under feete, and (to) yᵉ hazardinge of ye people underneath.

Some idea of what this organ looked like may be formed from the 'Rites of Durham', written in 1593, containing the following mention of three organs there at that time: 'the fairest paire of the three did stand over the quire dore only opened and played upon at principall Feasts, the pipes beinge all of most fine wood and workmanshipp, very faire, partly gilded upon the inside & outside of the leaves & covers up to the topp with branches and flowers finely gilted with the Name of Jesus painted with gold. There was but two paire more of them in all England of the same makinge, one paire in Yorke and an other in Paules'.

The reference to wooden pipes is of special interest. Wooden pipes have at no time been used at all commonly on the Continent, but from this reference, up to the time of Bernard Smith a century later, they were apparently very popular in England and this might supply a clue to the influences at work in Britain in the sixteenth century, although no one has yet succeeded in identifying it.

Of slightly later date (*c.* 1610) is the famous Compenius organ in the castle of Frederiksborg in Denmark, where the pipes are all of wood, but this organ is so much of a freak that it is difficult to suppose it exercised any influence elsewhere.

It is much more likely that Italian influences were at work in England. Henry VIII introduced Italian craftsmen of all kinds and surviving stringed keyboard instruments in England are almost all Italian. Elizabeth's own Virginal (a superlative instrument, now in the Victoria and Albert Museum) is of Italian make. It therefore seems most likely that Italian influence would have been strong in organ-building. Unfortunately for this theory, early Italian organs have nearly all metal pipes; certainly the great instruments of the Antegnati school surviving in Bologna and Brescia. Only in the late sixteenth- or early seventeenth-century Italian organ in the Silbernenkapelle at Innsbruck do we find an instrument with mostly wooden pipes (only the trebles being of lead). This may be the survivor of a type which was influential in Britain. The pipes are of small scale, with thin walls and an amazingly bold tone, highly comparable to those of Bernard Smith. But the possibility cannot be overlooked that the tradition was a native one and in an inventory of an organ-builder's stock as early as about 1515 there is mention of a number of wooden pipes, as well as material for making metal ones:

Imprimus ii grete organ cacez with carven worke
Itm ii cobbordes for to ley in the belowes in the same casez
Itm ii smaller casez with carved worke and the song-bordes redy wrought
    to set in pypes
Itm xviii of fyne tynne in plate redy wrought
Itm in ley metall xiii lb weight
Itm in lede iiii lb. weight
Itm a pytt of erthe to melte tyn inn
Itm iiixx pypes of tymber, the most part redy-made
Itm a stoke and a grete hammer for the same
Itm a long planke for to plane metall uppon
Itm an organ case peynted grene with keyes and a song-borde redy made
    to set in pypes, with a case of white tymber therefor, redy made
Itm ii planes for to plane metall with and the irons to the same

Itm iiii planes with irons to the same
Itm iii hollow planes
Itm v gowges and formes and metal coffyns
Itm ii irons for to shave metall bright in square
Itm iii mawndrells
Itm a grete knyff for to cutt lede with
Itm iiii rowndes for to tune pypes with
Itm iiii peces for to caste with metall
Itm ii swages with branches and byrdes.

Before leaving the sixteenth century reference must be made to a quite different sort of organ which was fashionable throughout most of the century and continued with decreasing popularity into the eighteenth. This was the regal.

The nature of a regal has already been explained in Chapter I. In England it very rarely—before 1660 probably never—appeared as a stop in a pipe organ, but as an instrument on its own it seems to have enjoyed considerable popularity. In the inventory of Henry VIII's possessions there are no less than 13 pair of single and five pair of double regals. The distinction between 'single' and 'double' relates only to the pitch of the instruments, single being in 4 ft. and double in 8 ft. pitch. Not until about 1625 did 'double' signify an instrument with two manuals. Usually, a regal had only the single set of reeds, but several in Henry's inventory had two or even three stops—'one stoppe pipe of tinne, one regale of tinne and a cimball'. This was unusual and the set of stopped pipes would make it quite a bulky instrument. But several had a cymbel. This consisted of a very small mixture, or may even only have had one pipe to a note like the cymbel in the Compenius organ at Frederiksborg, which has wooden pipes, the longest of only 2 in. speaking length, and breaking back repeatedly throughout the compass. Such a stop would go far to cover up the roughness and inevitable irregularities of the regal stop and make the instrument sound far more like an organ, while taking up a negligible amount of room. Regals were used to accompany singing and also in concerted music, where they can be most effective. Sometimes they were used in churches together with the main organ, as at St. Martin-in-the-Fields where between 1561–3 was 'payed the xxii of June to the organ maker for brase to tonge the small regalls to the pryncipall xii[d]'.

A very small organ having four flue stops, all with wooden pipes, and a regal, survives at Blair Atholl castle. It was made by John Loosemore in 1650. A 'bible' regal is in the Galpin collection, kept at Fenton House, Hampstead. Bible regals can be folded up for ready transport and are so made that when folded they look like a large book. It must be emphasised that regals had beating and not free reeds, which accounts at once for their characteristic tone, and for their pitch instability. A modern English reproduction has free reeds and bears no resemblance tonally to a true regal; it is simply a small harmonium.

With the seventeenth century we come at last to complete lists of stops although it is still extremely difficult to judge how the instruments sounded.

Eton College acquired a new, single-manual organ in 1613. The Howe family had looked after the organs there from 1553 to 1570, after which the accounts have no further references to organs for over 40 years, until 1613-14, when a new organ was supplied by Thomas Dallam. The expenses in and about making the organ included the following items:

Item the Soundeborde bellowes and other necessaries excepting the case £xxvii

It to Mr. Dallam the organmaker for provision of wanscott for the organs ut per billam 5.l.

It to Joyce the waterman for carrying of the wanscott from London at ii severall times and for carrying the same from the bridge xiiid. in toto xvi.s. vid

It to Mr. Dallam for blewe painted paper v.s.

It to Willm Person painter for gelting paynting and vernishinge the organe xxiiii l.

It to Robt Kettle joyner for the making of the organ case (the Colledge finding all stufe) 10 l.

It to him for glewe and nailes ut per billam ii s. xi d.

It to the Smith for work about the penthouse over the organ, nailes holdfast xxxvii s. iiii d; to the Smith for hewing the wall to lett in the organ case vi d.

The organ contained the following stops:

1 a diapason of Tynn fyve foote longe stopped
2 a principall of Tynn a open stopp fyve foot longe
3 a fflute unison to the principall fyve foote longe of Tynn
4 an octavo to the principall of Tynne
5 a ffyftenth of Tynne.

It apparently also had a tremulant, as in the next year Dallam mended 'the bellowes and the shaking stopp'.

It is known that the following pre-Commonwealth organs had two manuals:

King's College, Cambridge	1606
Trinity College, Cambridge	1610

Worcester Cathedral   1613
St. John's College, Oxford   *c.* 1620
Chirk Castle   1631–2
York Minster   1632
Salisbury Cathedral. Choir organ added 1635
Magdalen College, Oxford   1637 or earlier.

The organ at King's College, Cambridge, was made by Thomas Dallam and its case is the splendid one that survives to this day. The organ was taken down for safety in the Rebellion, and the choir organ case, on the east front, was probably added when it was re-erected after 1660. The specification is not known.

Trinity College had a single-manual organ to which John York added a 'chaire' organ in 1610.

At Worcester Cathedral a new two-manual organ was built by Thomas Dallam in 1613, which is the earliest two-manual specification we possess:

The particulars of the Great Organ
Two open diapasons of metall. CC fa ut a pipe of 10 foot long
Two principals of metal
Two small principals or 15ths of metal
One twelfth of mettall
One recorder of mettal, a stopt pipe

In the Chaire Organ
One principal of mettal
One diapason of wood
One flute of wood
One small principal or fifteenth of mettal
One two & Twentieth of mettal.

Worcester already possessed an organ bought in 1556 which stood on the north side of the choir. It may therefore have survived the arrival of Dallam's organ, which stood on the screen. It remained there until 1646, when the city was surrendered to the Parliamentarians. On July 23rd 'many gentlemen went to six o'clock prayers to the college [i.e. cathedral] to take their last farewell of the Church of England service, the organs having been taken down the 20th'. The Dallam organ was safely preserved and re-erected with some alterations after 1660.

The organ at St. John's College, Oxford, had an identical specification and was also by Dallam.

Chirk Castle, in Denbighshire, belonged to Sir Thomas Myddleton, who contracted for a new organ to be built by John Burward of London. The contract is dated February 28th, 1631.

On the upper sett of keys
Stopt diapason (of metal)
Open diapason from gamut upwards
Principal (large)
Principal (small)
Recorder
Fifteenth
Twenty-second
On the Lower sett of keys
Diapason
Principal (large)
Principal (small)

The Magdalen College instrument has had a remarkable history. For some reason it was allowed to remain *in situ* until as late as 1654 when John Evelyn saw it in July. His diary says: 'Next, we walked to Magdalen College, where we saw the library and chapel, which was likewise in pontifical order, the altar only, I think, turned tablewise; and there was still the double organ, which abominations (as now esteemed) were almost universally demolished; Mr. Gibbon [i.e. Christopher Gibbons] that famous musician giving us a taste of his skill and talents on that instrument'.

This, incidentally, is an early instance of the use of 'double' as applied to a two-manual instrument and not merely to one of full compass (i.e. extending below gamut g).

Shortly after Evelyn's visit the College 'presented' their organ to Cromwell who removed it to Hampton Court where it was set up in the great hall, and it is said that it was played upon by John Milton the poet.

In the inventory made after Cromwell's death in 1659 the organ appears as 'Value about £300—one large Organ and a Chaire Organ which was brought from Maudlin College in Oxford'. Whether or not the removal from Oxford to Hampton Court was strictly a present, a warrant was shortly issued to the Housekeeper at Hampton Court to deliver up the organ for it to be returned to Oxford, and this was probably effected by Robert Dallam who had the care of it from 1661 to 1685, after which it passed to Renatus Harris. In 1686 the college agreed 'with Mr. Harris for the repairing of the organ, who being at Oxford offered his services the rather because his grandfather made it at first, and he was sufficiently known to be as skilful an artist as any in England'. From this it was long supposed that the organ was built by Harris's paternal grandfather, since one Harris was paid £40 in 1637 'pro ecclesia'. That, however, might mean almost anything, not necessarily connected with the organ, and the Rev. Andrew Freeman pointed out that Harris was more likely referring to his mother's father, Thomas Dallam, who is known to have been employed on the organ between 1615 and 1624. If the 1637 Harris was an organ-builder he would have been Thomas Harris, the father of Renatus. The date of the organ may thus be anywhere between 1615 and 1637, but the case (which survives in Tewkesbury Abbey, who acquired it in 1737 when Magdalen had it replaced by a new organ by Thomas Schwarbrick) may well be earlier (the organ was built, or perhaps rebuilt, by John Chappington in 1597).

When Renatus Harris was called upon to rebuild the organ in 1686 he recorded its specification as then existing, which was clearly also its original form.

Great Organ	Chaire Organ
Open Diapason	Stopped diapason
Stopped diapason	Two principals
Two principals	Recorder
Two fifteenths	Fifteenth
Two two-&-twentieths	

He made the following interesting remark about the old doubled ranks:

Whereas the great organ consists of eight stops, namely, two diapasons, two principals, two fifteenths and two two-and-twentieths, one of which stops, and several pipes in the other, have been spoiled by Preston; finding by experience that when two unisons are together in an organ as two principals, two fifteenths, etc., that they never agree well together in tune, and one stop of each sort is in a manner as loud as two of the same name; for which reason neither in my organ at the Temple, nor in those which I make for the King, after the open and stopped diapasons, none of the rest are of the same denomination; so that I propose to make your eight stops to consist of these following, one open diapason, one stopped diapason, one principal, one great twelfth, one fifteenth, one tiers, one furniture of two or three ranks, according as there is room for it, in place of the two two-and-twentieths. In the choir organ there are one stopped diapason, two principals, one recorder and one fifteenth, so that in these five stops there are no less than three unisons; which five stops ought to be reduced to these four, namely, one stopped diapason, one principal, one stopped twelfth and one fifteenth; the recorder being left out will give more air to the rest of the work. With these amendments, alterations, additions and varieties of stops, it will be an extraordinary good instrument, and the best old organ in England, and exceed the best organ in your university, with only the cost of one hundred and fifty pounds.

Before leaving this famous organ, its further history may briefly be traced. In 1797 Holland added a swell and in 1848 Henry Willis rebuilt it comprehensively, this being one of his first commissions. It has finally been rebuilt by Messrs. Walker since 1950, still containing many seventeenth-century pipes, although so much revoiced by Willis and others as to be unrecognisable tonally.

The Salisbury Cathedral organ was taken down and stored during the Commonwealth. Its choir organ of five stops was added by John Burward in 1635 and its specification, as recorded by Renatus Harris in 1688, differed very little from that of the 1613 Worcester organ.

The Magdalen College organ was not the only one to be preserved during the Commonwealth by moving into secular quarters. A visiting Frenchman wrote in 1659 (as translated by Evelyn): 'That nothing be wanting to the height of luxury and impiety of this abomination, they have translated the organs out of their Churches to set them up in taverns, chaunting their dithyrambics and bestial bacchanalias to the tune of those instruments which were wont to assist them in the celebration of God's praises.'

The largest pre-Commonwealth organ of which details survive is that made by Robert Dallam for York Minster in 1632. It stood on the north side of the choir but, having survived the Commonwealth, was moved in 1688 on to the screen. It contained the following stops:

Great Organ (51 notes)
Imprimis two open diapasons of tynn to stand in sight, many of them 8′
    to be chased
Item one diapason stopp of wood [Query, a 'stopped diapason'?]   8′
Item two principals of tynn   4′
Itm   one twelft to the diapason   2⅔′
Itm   one small principall of tynn   2′
Itm   one recorder unison to the said principall   2′
Itm   one two and twentieth   1′

Chaire Organ (51 notes)
Imprimis one diapason of wood
Itm   one principal of tynn to stand in sight, many of them to be chased
Itm   one flute of wood
Itm   one small principall of tynn
Itm   one recorder of tynn unison to the voice

The 'small principalls' in this organ are clearly fifteenths which otherwise are lacking (in the same way, after 1660, a nineteenth was invariably a 'small twelfth'), but this interpretation can hardly be applied to the Chirk Castle specification quoted on p. 55. There, there is a fifteenth on the Great as well as a large and a small principal. This would be more difficult to understand were it not for the one remarkable survival of any consequence from this period, which is a house organ bearing the name and date 'Christianus Smith 1643'.

This belonged in 1825 to Edward Taylor, Gresham Professor of Music, to whom it had descended from his great-grandfather, which would thus carry its recorded history back a further century at least. It was in perfect condition up to 1939, when it fell prey to London evacuees to the country house where it then stood, who removed or broke several of its pipes and generally did a good deal of damage, so that it cannot now be played. Fortunately, it has now been acquired by Noel Mander, the organ builder, who has shown such outstanding skill and taste in the restoration of early organs. Its early restoration is planned, when it will be the most valuable evidence of pre-Commonwealth British organ-building. Its specification is apparently as follows [the stop-names are modern, as no old labels survive]:

Stopped diapason, bass $\Big\}$	8
Stopped diapason, treble	
Large open diapason from middle C up	8
Small open diapason from middle C up	8
Principal	4
Fifteenth bass $\Big\}$	2
Fifteenth treble	
Twenty-second breaking to twelfth at middle C	1

Several significant facts emerge from a study of this organ. In the first place all the pipes are of wood. On one of the pipes is the signature 'Christianus Smith, 1643'. The date is also carved into the case, but the name does not appear anywhere else. The tradition in the Taylor family was that it was made by Christianus Schmidt and brought here in 1660 by Bernard Schmidt as a specimen of their skill in voicing wooden pipes. In view of the signature of plain 'Smith' this story cannot be taken very seriously, and it will appear to be of considerable importance later in this chapter when Smith's origins come to be considered.

In the second place, the presence of two open unison stops of differing scale and power, especially in such a small organ, is entirely without precedent in any other country at this period. It suggests that a need was felt for varied power in unison pitch, and this would certainly be useful in solo anthems with organ accompaniment. Subtly graduated power would also be consistent with the great organ pieces of Byrd, Gibbons and Bull, whose well-defined sections seem to call for slight additions in registration, but never for a chorus of destructive power. If this line of reasoning is acceptable, so that all the pairs of duplicated ranks in pre-Commonwealth organs were graduated in power, it certainly makes them appear to be more logical than has hitherto seemed to be the case.

Thirdly, the break in the twenty-second, at middle C, to a twelfth, is extremely interesting. It has hitherto seemed most difficult to account for the provision of 1 ft. stops, but never of a nineteenth, although the twelfth is quite common. But if, as here, the twenty-seconds broke back into a twelfth, they do become more sensible and logical. In support of this probability, it may be noted that at Worcester the twenty-second is on the chaire organ and not on the great, where there is an independent twelfth.

In every way therefore, this instrument is of the utmost historical importance and its survival has made it much easier to understand the pre-Commonwealth British organ than could otherwise have been the case.

Before leaving the pre-Commonwealth scene, we have some evidence of how these instruments sounded to their contemporaries, noted down in the diary of a tour of England made in 1634 by three members of the Military Company of Norwich.

At York they saw and heard 'a faire, large, high organ, newly built, richly gilt, carv'd & painted; and deep & sweet snowy row of quiristers'. There was only one other organ in the whole of York, beside that at the Minster. At Lincoln the organs and voices were 'deep & sweet' and the organ at Exeter 'most sweet'. At Bristol the organ was 'neat, rich & melodious'. It will be noticed that 'sweetness' is the quality most admired; not power, or brilliance, as would have been the appropriate description of a large German organ of the period. Nor are the three soldiers to be regarded as undiscriminating critics, for at Carlisle 'the organs & voices did well agree, the one being like a shrill bagpipe, the other like the Scottish tone'.

A different viewpoint is made by Thomas Mace in *Musick's Monument*, published in 1676, when he describes his memories of a service in York Minster during the siege of 1644. 'Now here you must take notice that they had then a Custom in that Church (which I hear not of in any other Cathedral, which was) that always before the Sermon, the whole Congregation sang a Psalm, together with the Quire & the Organ; And you must also know, that there was then a most Excellent-large-plump-lusty-full-speaking-Organ which cost (as I am credibly informed) a Thousand

Pounds. This Organ I say (when the Psalm was set before the Sermon) being let out, into all its Fullness of Stops, together with the Quire, began the Psalm. But when That vast-concording-unity of the whole Congregational Chorus, came (as I may say) Thundering in, even so, as it made the very Ground shake under us: (oh, the unutterable ravishing Soul's delight!) in which I was so transported, & wrapt up into High contemplations that there was no room left in my whole man, viz., Body, Soul & Spirit, for any thing below Divine & Heavenly Raptures.'

One cannot help suspecting that the passage of 30 years had somewhat enhanced Mace's memories—at any rate so far as the organ is concerned —and that the contemporary description by the three soldiers is more to be trusted. Perhaps it would not be far out to describe the pre-Commonwealth British organ as based on an Italian model, but without its mutation ranks; adapted primarily to accompanying choral singing, and playing the serious and undramatic English organ music of that time.

It has been argued by one or two historians that British organs before the Commonwealth possessed pedals. The evidence adduced is as follows:

Some of the early organ music, about the time of the Reformation, has very wide stretches for the left hand, or at least is difficult to play without pedals.

In the Duddyngton contract of 1519 quoted on p. 48, the reference to 'the pryncipale . . . wt Bassys called Diapason to the same . . .' is held to mean pedals, as are many references for repairs to 'springes for the great basses' as at Eton on p. 50.

In a poem of 1598 the following remarkable passage occurs:

> *Where, as by Art one selfly blast breath'd out*
> *From panting bellowes, passeth all about*
> *Winde-Instruments; suters by th'under clavers*
> *Which with the keyes the organ-maister quavers.*

In Thomas Dallam's account for work at King's College, Cambridge, in 1605 is the following:

> Item for ebony for the kayes
> Item for studds to make claves,

and in 1635 Robert Dallam was paid the large sum of £13 for adding pedals of a type and purpose unspecified, to the organ at Jesus College, Cambridge.

In Dandle Cotsgrave's *Dictionairie of the French and English Tongues*, published in 1611, appears 'Basses Marches—Pedalls; the low keys of some organs to be touched with the feet'.

As will be seen, while all are suggestive, only the last is unequivocal, but it can hardly be accepted as conclusive, since it is merely making a statement of fact as regards *French* organs and does not necessarily imply that *British* organs already possessed pedals.

From the known early seventeenth-century specifications, all of which have already been quoted, it is clear that at this time, at any rate, British organs did not have pedal pipes, though this does not rule out the possibility of their having had pull-downs. The double-organ music of John Lugge and others, on the other hand, clearly has no use for pedals. The bass passages for the 'double' are clearly to be played with the left hand and would be very difficult to execute on pedals, even with a modern technique and pedal board. They are obviously the British substitute for an obbligato pedal part. Nor does the organ music of such advanced organists as Orlando Gibbons and John Bull offer any advantages to an organ with pedals; even after Bull had settled in Holland he still wrote no organ music for pedals—even long pedal-points, as much used by Frescobaldi. It therefore seems conclusive that pedals were not used in England in the late sixteenth or early seventeenth century, although the possibility cannot be ruled out that isolated examples may have been made for musicians who had learnt the use of pedals abroad. Jesus College, Cambridge, may have been such a case, though £12 seems a very large sum for a set of pull-downs.

As to the pre-Reformation period, the evidence can only be regarded as very tenuous. The organ music of Preston, Redford and others is mostly in the form of elaboration of a plainsong theme. Nearly all of it lies easily under two hands and all of it *can* be played without pedals. But where this is difficult, as in Redford's 'O Lux on the faburden', it is at least equally likely that he intended the plainsong to be played by another instrument such as a sackbut.

Taking a general view, it seems most unlikely that if pedals were at any time commonly used in England, they would ever have been given up; and neither the late sixteenth century, nor the Commonwealth disuse of organs was long or complete enough for their advantages to have been so far forgotten that they would not have been revived in 1660.

The case can therefore only be regarded as non-proven, though the possibility of pull-down pedals having existed in isolated cases cannot be ruled out.[1]

[1] A lengthy correspondence on this subject took place in the *Musical Times* from September 1960 onwards.

The Restoration Organ before
Father Smith

The immediate post-Restoration era started with two entirely different schools of organ-building. One was the new style brought in by Bernard Smith, inevitably having a considerable measure of Continental influence; the other was a revival of the native, pre-Commonwealth school. For a short time the two existed side by side, but the old soon gave way to the new. While it lasted, it really belonged more to the pre-Commonwealth and may properly be considered with it. Altogether, apart from a handful of instruments that had been allowed to remain *in situ* throughout the Commonwealth, about eight important organs were either built or planned after 1660, on traditional lines.

The first and most remarkable of these is a scheme proposed by Robert Dallam in 1661 or 1662 for a new organ at New College, Oxford. Dallam was introduced to the College by Philip Timber, the 'Chaunter' of Westminster, in a letter dated May 15th, 1661:

> These for the right wor[ll] Dr. Woodman, Warden of New College in Oxford—Rev[r]nd S[r].
> Your former love & respects to me whilst I was a poore member of your Colledge haue imboldened me to write to you in the behalfe of my friend, Mr. Dallum, that if you haue a desire to erect an organ in your chappell for the Quire service, you would be pleased to enterteine him for the worke thereof, who is generally conceiued to be the best organmaker in England, as his father was before him: he is at this time imployed in the making of Windsor organ, but he hath two sonnes very excellent in the same faculty whom he can leaue to finish that worke that he may waite upon you when-soeuer you shall be pleased to send for him: I can send to him at any time & for that respect sake which I owe to the Colledge it is my hearty desire that the worke may be well donne. If you will honour me with a letter you may be pleased to direct it to me Chaunter of Westminster (by which title I am best knowne) at my house in Deanes Yard there, and you shall much ingage
> Your most humble servant—Philip Timber.

Dallam had been in France during the interregnum and was keen to bring some grand foreign ideas into play. The spelling suggests that his stay abroad had left him somewhat out of practice in writing his native tongue:

Great Organe

1. The fore frante of the organe the bigeste pipe—24 fote long fittinge for the place & for the decorment of the church
2. The nixte stope—in the organe 16 fote longe a 8 a bove him
3. The nixte stope—12 fute longe a 8 aboue the 16 fote
4. The bordane 8 fute long a 8 from the other above him
5. The recorder—4 fote longe a 8 to the burdane a bove him
6. The Simbale in 2 stopse [i.e. 2 ranks] rininge throu in 5's
7. The furnitor 3 stopes goin throu in 8's
8. The prinsepale 6 fote longe
9. The small prencepal [i.e. 15th]
10. The 2 & 20
11. The sifflet 1 fut longe
12. The 5 to the recorder [i.e. 12th]
13. The nasone stope
14. The flut de alman
15. The sagbot
16. The Cleron

I oblise My self to performe and mack all thes stopes conformabel to the Churce and agmentacion of good musick and give contentment to them that hiris it

1. The Chere organe the for fronte of it 8 fote longe
2. The bordone 6 fote longe stoped
3. The recorder stop
4. The antheme stop in vids
5. The prinsepal
6. The small prinsepal
7. The 2 & 20
8. The flute

These stopes the number of the pipes 12 hudreth—16 in the grit organe and 8 in the chaire organ wher vpon I vld bind and ablisz to put in 24 stops in the 2 organes and byde the triele of all the arganists in England and organ makers.

The nature of the 'antheme stop' is a mystery. In some later notes to the scheme Dallam writes: 'Item timber for the Sound-bord, bellowes, the antheme stopp and diurse other parts of the Organ within it'—which is the only stop mentioned separately, and suggests it may have been something like a tremulant rather than a set of pipes. 'In vids' also does not get us much further but probably means 'in wood'.

This scheme is a curious mixture of the traditional with the new, in the form of mixtures, reeds and very deep compass; although still without any suggestion of pedals. In the event, Dallam did build an organ for New College, but to a more modest specification that has not survived.

The next instrument, and perhaps the first to be completed after 1660, was built by Lancelot Pease, of Cambridge, for Canterbury Cathedral. The contract is dated July 17th, 1662. It contains an early use of 'double' as meaning two manuals—'A Double Organ, vizt a great Organ and a Chaire Organ'. The Chaire organ was to be finished by the Christmas following and the Great by Christmas 1663. The specification was as follows:

> *Great organ*—13 stops
> One diapason of mettall
> One diapason stopt of wood
> Two principalls of mettall
> Two fifteenthes of mettall
> A small and great twelft of mettall
> Two two and twentieths of mettall
> A flute of mettall
> A recorder of wood
> A tierce of mettal
>
> *Chaire organ*—6 stops
> Two stopt diapasons of wood
> One principall of mettall in the front
> One fifteenth of mettall
> One fifteenth of wood
> One flute of wood.

It will be seen that this follows strictly early seventeenth-century lines, such as the Worcester Cathedral organ of 1613, with its duplicated ranks. The only additions are a seventeenth and nineteenth; but no reeds or mixtures.

There is an analogy to this in the very remarkable surviving organ at Adlington Hall, near Macclesfield, for long, and still, the seat of the Legh family. Owing to its strange history this organ stands as a wonderfully complete example of early Restoration organ-building in England, and is specially interesting in that in style it stands midway between the old tradition and the new. The only unlucky thing is that no contract survives, so that neither its date nor its maker can be fixed with certainty. Both the specification and the style of the case suggest a fairly early date after 1660, probably incorporating some parts of the case and pipework of an earlier instrument.

The specification of the organ is as follows, the spelling being taken from the contemporary labels on the stop jambs, with the exception of the vox humana and trumpet, where they are missing:

Great Organ (upper keyboard)		Choir Organ (lower keyboard)	
Opn diapason	8	St diopason ch	8
St diopason	8	St flute ch	4
Principall	4	Bassoon ch	8
Gt twelfth	$2\frac{2}{3}$		
Fifteenth	2		
Bl flute bas ⎱ Bl flute trib ⎰	2		
Ters	$1\frac{3}{5}$		
Sm twelfth	$1\frac{1}{3}$		
2 & twenty	1		
Vox Humana	8		
Trumpet	8		

The compass is ostensibly four octaves and a third, from B to d, but bottom B and C♯ sound G and A in the 16 ft. octave respectively.

Both departments stand on a common chest, and the stopped diapason has two sets of pallets so that it is playable independently on either keyboard. This was an arrangement much used by Renatus Harris, as will be seen later. He termed it the borrowing of stops 'by communication'.

The wind pressure is $2\frac{5}{8}$ in.

During the eighteenth century, Handel was a friend of the Leghs and stayed at Adlington Hall in 1741 and again in 1751. There still exists at the Hall an autograph copy of his 'Hunting Song' endorsed 'Presented by him in his own hand to Charles Legh Esqr in the year 1751'. Handel must therefore have played the organ, and there was a tradition that it was made to his specification by the local firm of Glynn & Parker, which would date it at about the middle of the eighteenth century. In view of the style of the case and the specification, this tradition could never have stood up to critical examination; but perhaps because the organ had been unplayable for longer than any living memory, no one had ever questioned it until 1956, when its restoration became a matter of serious discussion. It then became apparent that far from having been designed by Handel, the organ must certainly have existed in its present form before even he was born. Internal evidence also suggested that it had been unplayable since before 1800.

The condition of the organ was indeed horrifying, a very large proportion of the pipes being squashed flat out of all recognition; but the restoration was entrusted to Noel Mander who contrived to salvage all but 30 of the original pipes. Owing to its long silence of 150 years the organ was never 'improved' during the nineteenth or twentieth century and thus now stands in perfect order and in its entirely original condition. As such, it is unique as a large seventeenth-century organ, surpassed only by the 50-years-earlier Compenius instrument in the Frederiksborg Castle in Denmark; but even more important than the latter, which was a freak, even in its day, suited best to the performance of light dance music, and thus not at all representative of its period.

As a medium for the performance of seventeenth-century organ music the Adlington Hall organ affords quite exceptional facilities, although it is not perfectly adapted to the English 'Double Organ Voluntary', which calls for a choir organ not much less in power than the great; and for this purpose the Adlington choir is not quite strong enough. A fifteenth in place of the choir bassoon would have been better in every way, and more usual for the period, but the bassoon is obviously an original stop. The mutation stops on the great organ show that these were regarded as part of the diapason chorus in seventeenth-century English organs. The open diapason is among the most beautiful of any age and the trumpet and vox humana show that British artists at that time were producing reeds as fine as any.

Mr. Mander considers that Bernard Smith was the rebuilder of the organ and there is a good deal of stylistic evidence to support him. On the other hand, the semi-archaic specification somewhat suggests one of the older English builders. The problem is unlikely to be solved, but in any event, the organ stands today as a unique and precious example of seventeenth-century British organ-building. It bears upon it an ivory plaque with the inscription:

> This organ was built by Bernard Schmidt about 1670 incorporating parts of a previous instrument. After being silent for about 150 years it was restored by Noel Mander in collaboration with Cecil Clutton.
> Cynthia Legh   1959

The restoration was carried out with a grant from the Historic Buildings Council.

Possibly even earlier than the Canterbury organ was one built by Robert Taunton for Wells Cathedral under a contract entered into in 1662, which is completely archaic, being almost a replica of Thomas Dallam's organ at Worcester, 50 years earlier. It has no mixtures nor reeds and, as at Worcester, the only mutation rank is a solitary twelfth. The organ stood on the screen, as the present one does, having two fronts, one facing east and one west. This, apart from any other considerations, provides one practical reason for having two open diapasons.

Robert Dallam having failed to bring off his ambitious New College scheme, the largest of the immediately post-Restoration organs was John Loosemore's 1665 instrument in Exeter Cathedral. This was notable for its large basses, the longest pipe having a speaking length of 20 ft. 6 in. and a diameter of 1 ft. 3 in. The Hon. Roger North writing at the time, remarked: 'I could not be so happy to perceive that, in the musick, they signified any thing at all, but thought them made more for ostentation than use; for there are terms in sound which will not be exceeded; for, when the vibratory pulses are so slow as may be distinguished, sound vanisheth; which is nearly the case with this great pipe'. A critic of the present century similarly, but more succinctly, described a 32 ft. stop as 'nothing but an expensive draught'.

Loosemore inclined to the old order, and used wooden pipes, especially in his smaller organs, such as one made for the Song School at Exeter, which had the following stops, all the pipes being of wood:

Open diapason	8
Stopped diapason	8
Principal	4
Flute	4
Twelfth	$2\frac{2}{3}$
Fifteenth	2

The compass was four octaves, C–C, with a short bottom octave.

Loosemore made another single-manual organ for Sir George Trevelyan at Nettlecombe Court, which still exists, having been rebuilt in the eighteenth century.

Another instrument to be built in the old style was at Winchester Cathedral, by Thomas Thamar, in 1665. It was, in fact, completely traditional and apart from one mixture stop could well have been devised 50 years before. Thamar contracted to provide 'a faire substantial, good and perfect double organ, . . . Item the said double organ shall consist of a faire great organ and a choir organ'.

The term 'double' by this time means only two manuals. This is, however, probably the first time that the second manual was called a 'choir' instead of a 'chaire' organ.

The great organ contained the following stops:

In the front one open diapason of tynn the biggest pipe containing thirteene foote in length with his bigness according to the monicords.
One Principall of Tynn, the biggest pipe thereof to fill up the front
One stopp diapason of wood
One recorder of wood, unison with the great Principall

Two small Principalls, also (i.e. 'known as') Fifteenths of tynn
One Twelfth of Tynn
One Fourniture of tynn
One Two and Twentieth of Tynn
And the Choir organ shall conteyne five stopps of pipes, every stopp
conteyning one and fifty pipes, viz—
  One great Principall of Tynn to stand in the front
  One diapason of wood
  One flute of wood
  One small principall of tynn
  One two and twentieth of tynn

This organ stood on the north side of the choir, where the present instrument also stands. It was next rebuilt by Renatus Harris in 1693, with more mixtures and mutations, but still without reeds.

Most of Thamar's work was done in Cambridge, including Pembroke College, from whence his organ was moved in 1708 to Framlingham Church in Suffolk, where much of his pipework still survives.

The last recorded new organ in the old style was built by Thomas Harris (father of Renatus) for Worcester Cathedral, as late as 1666; but as the specification is practically identical with the 1613 Dallam organ, which seems to have been taken down and preserved through the Commonwealth, it is possible that Harris merely restored and re-erected Dallam's instrument. See p. 223, however, for mention of the new case.

After this, we hear no more of the old English style, and by soon after 1670 Bernard Smith had entrenched his new type of organ in an unassailable position.

Father Smith

According to an old tradition related by Dr. Burney, the demand for organs immediately after the restoration of the monarchy in 1660 was so great, and the number of surviving organ-builders so small, that premiums were offered to foreign organ-builders to settle in this country. Of Smith he says: 'Bernard Schmidt, as the Germans write the name, brought over with him from Germany, of which country he was a native, two nephews, Gerard and Bernard, his assistants; and to distinguish him from these, as well as to express the reverence due to his abilities, which placed him at the head of his profession, he was called *Father Schmidt*. The first Organ he engaged to build for this country was for the Royal Chapel at Whitehall, which being hastily put together, did not quite

68

fulfil the expectations of those who were able to judge of its excellence. It was probably from some such early failure, that this admirable workman determined never to engage to build an Organ upon short notice, nor for such a price as would oblige him to deliver it in a state of less perfection than he wished. And I have been assured by Snetzler, and by the immediate descendants of those who have conversed with Father Smith, and seen him work, that he was so particularly careful in the choice of his wood, as never to use any that had the least knot or flaw in it; and so tender of his reputation, as never to waste his time in trying to mend a bad pipe, either wood or metal, if it had any radical defect; he instantly threw it away & made another. This, in great measure, accounts for the equality & sweetness of his stops, as well as the soundness of his pipes to this day.'

What Burney wrote about Smith has been accepted ever since as an accredited fact, but in this book it is represented for the first time that the whole story is without foundation upon fact.

In the first place, the story of the premiums to foreign builders is highly suspect. Who, especially at that time, was likely to offer such a premium? Hardly an impoverished government, and even more improbably anyone else. Nor would it have been likely to pass without opposition from the native craftsmen, however overloaded with orders they may have been.

Next, it is believed that Burney and Hawkins were among the first people to refer to Smith as 'Schmidt'. Certainly none of his contemporaries did so; nor did Smith ever so subscribe himself. That Smith came over from Germany, or at any rate, some part of the Continent, is easy enough to believe, but the submission here is that he was a son or nephew of Christian Smith, maker of the 1643 organ, and that he went abroad during the Commonwealth perforce, for want of employment at home. He would naturally return home as quickly as possible after the restoration of a civilised régime. He would not have been the only English builder to emigrate during the Commonwealth; Robert Dallam went abroad in 1641 and made several organs in Brittany during the interregnum, returning in 1661. Smith's age was perfectly consistent with such an adventure, as we can fix the date of his birth with fair accuracy at 1628 or 1629, so that at the Restoration he was about 31.

Smith's predilection for wooden pipes is inconsistent with a Teutonic upbringing. As has already been argued, in nowhere but England is it possible to find a continuous tradition of wooden pipe-making for the previous century and a half.

Not only did Smith never refer to himself as Schmidt, but experts in the British Museum agree that there is nothing German about his handwriting, and the peculiarities of his English and its spelling more suggest a north-country than a German background. This may perhaps be borne out by the fact that the contract for Durham, made in 1683, was one of his first important contracts. The following extract from a letter of November 12th, 1686, to the Dean's Registrar at Durham is fairly typical of his style: 'I cam save hom last Saturday, out of the Contree, wher I found your kind letter & the bill in closet, wher for I give you humble thanck for your kesn and grat kindness, which I all wayes knolleg. I have receeved the hondert & fifty pound yesterday. I shall be all wayes ready to serve you & yours when so ever it may be your pleasur. As for the organ I have made for your Catedrall Church, I know it is so good and sound mad as anny as in the holl worrelt. I must confes I have out gon the pris, for this I declare that it cost mee a bove a thousent pound, lett anny body think or say what the plees.' (Smith was always 'outgoing his price', despite Burney's remarks to the contrary.) While 'hondert' is German, it is not inconsistent with north-country pronunciation, rather badly spelt; while such words as 'worrelt' are pure north-country.

The 1643 instrument now being found to be by Smith and not Schmidt is yet another indication of Bernard's true nationality. Its pipework and scaling bear too close a resemblance to his work to be at all accidental.

If further argument is needed, Smith's will provided 'Imprimis I give & bequeath unto all my Brothers & sisters & unto all & every of their children the sume of one shilling apeece in full of all their Rights & pretentions to my estate'. Now if Smith was German, it is hardly likely that all his brothers and sisters would have come with him to England in 1660; while if they had stayed in Germany he would hardly have bothered to cut them off with a shilling nearly 40 years later (the Will is dated November 4th, 1699, and Smith died in February 1708 and was buried at St. Margaret's, Westminster, where he was also organist).

It is therefore suggested that there is considerable evidence for saying that Bernard Smith was completely English and that the fable of his being German goes back no further than Burney, who was a notoriously inaccurate historian.

Apart from the Chapel Royal instrument of 1662, which seems to have been built by Smith under a sub-contract from John Hingeston (Organist to Charles I, Cromwell and Charles II; a pupil of Orlando Gibbons and the tutor of John Blow), there is no record of Smith having built a new organ until 1671 when he supplied a small single-manual organ for the

Sheldonian Theatre, Oxford. This is the only time when there is any contemporary suggestion of Smith being anything but English, Anthony Wood, the Oxford antiquary, relating on May 18th, 1671, that 'we had vocall & instrumentall musick in our Theater to the new organ set up there . . . by Smith, a Dutchman'; but this does not seem very substantial evidence against what has just been adduced, except possibly for the fact that Bernard is a not uncommon Dutch name. But it could well mean that Smith's stay abroad was in Holland and not in Germany, and this would be consistent with his having made no apparent attempt to introduce pedals into this country, upon his return. For while pedals were not unknown in Holland in the mid-seventeenth century, they were by no means common, and there still survive quite large three-manual Dutch organs of this period with no pedal organs (for example, Loppersum and Medemblik). By this time, too, he is being referred to as 'the celebrated Smith' and even as 'the King's Organ Maker', although he was not confirmed in this office until ten years later. But it was not until 1680 that Smith was really flooded with orders and from that year comes the earliest contemporary record of a two-manual specification by him. This was for Christ Church Cathedral, Oxford, as follows:

Great Organ		Choir Organ	
Open diapason	8	Stopped diapason	8
Stopped diapason	8	Principal	4
Principal	4	Flute	4
Twelfth	$2\frac{2}{3}$	Fifteenth	2
Fifteenth	2		
Tierce	$1\frac{3}{5}$	Compass GG (short	
Sesquialtera	III	octave) to C, 50	
Cornet (to middle C sharp)	IV	notes	
Trumpet	8		

It seems certain that Smith introduced the cornet into England. It is a solo stop consisting of a stopped 8 ft. unison (usually a chimney flute) principal, twelfth, fifteenth and seventeenth. Its compass was from middle C, or C sharp upwards. It was a powerful stop, usually of large scale, although the English examples have never been so large in scale as the French. To save soundboard space it was usually mounted on its own chest, above the great, from which it was conveyanced, and for this reason it was often referred to as a 'mounted cornet'. Cornets were fairly common in Holland, but never in north Germany; another pointer to Smith's training having been in Holland, not Germany.

It will readily be seen how much more versatile and less wasteful in its

71

resources this organ was than anything that had gone before, with its complete diapason chorus, solo cornet, and trumpet and all within the space of 13 stops. No English organ-music of this (or, for practical purposes, any subsequent) period demands a complete chorus on the secondary manual. What Smith did remained standard practice for the next hundred years and more. 1683 brought a contract with Durham Cathedral for a slightly more ambitious organ with a second open diapason on the great, a 'voice humane' on the choir and two extra flutes. This was contained in a magnificent double case on the choir screen where it remained until 1847.

Smith went on working up to the time of his death, producing upwards of 70 organs, but his two most famous were those made for the Temple Church and St. Paul's Cathedral. The former was the subject of the famous 'battle of the organs'. In 1683 Smith thought that he had actually obtained the contract, but Renatus Harris, who by that time was beginning to make a name for himself, somehow persuaded the Benchers to allow him to install a rival instrument in another part of the church, the final order to go to the one judged to be the better organ. They were erected in 1684 and then Harris (who was undoubtedly a better reed voicer than Smith) challenged Smith to produce some additional reed stops, including a vox humana, cremorne and double courtel. Smith complied, but during the night before the final trial some friends of Harris (never over-scrupulous in his behaviour) cut the bellows of Smith's organ so that it could not be used—a stupid prank which can hardly have disposed the Benchers in Harris's favour. But in the end, it was not until 1688 that they finally decided in favour of Smith (according to Burney, on a casting vote by Judge Jeffreys). Harris removed his organ with his reputation enhanced rather than otherwise, but its specification has not been preserved. The final specification of Smith's organ was as follows:

Great Organ

Prestand	61	pipes	12	foote Tone
Holflute of mettle	61	,,	12	,, ,,
Principall of wood & mettle	61	,,	06	,, ,,
Quinta of mettle	61	,,	04	,, ,,
Super Octavo	61	,,	03	,, ,,
Cornett of mettle	112	,,	02	,, ,,
Sesquialtera of mettle	183	,,	03	,, ,,
Gedackt of wainescott	61	,,	06	,, ,,
Mixture of mettle	226	,,	03	,, ,,
Trumpett of mettle	61	,,	12	,, ,,

Chair Organ

Gedackt of Wainescott	61 pipes	12 foote Tone	
Hohlflute of mettle	61 ,,	06 ,,	,,
A sadt of mettle	61 ,,	06 ,,	,,
Spitts flute of mettle	61 ,,	03 ,,	,,
A Violl & Violin of mettle	61 ,,	12 ,,	,,
Voice Humane of mettle	61 ,,	12 ,,	,,

Ecchos

Gedackt of wood	61 ,,	06 ,,	,,
Super Octavo of mettle	61 ,,	03 ,,	,,
Gedackt of Wood	29 ,,		
Flute of mettle	29 ,,		
Cornett of mettle	87 ,,		
Sesquialtera	105 ,,		
Trumpett	29 ,,		

This is the first appearance in England of an echo organ, of which the pipes were placed in a completely and permanently closed box. It was generally of short compass, and the two stops here of complete compass were unique. Another version of the specification, written by Christopher Shrider in 1708, differs only in detail, but shows that the violin stop was in fact a cremona, or krummhorn. Such names as hohlflute and sadt betray the Dutch or German influence of Smith's sojourn abroad.

The compass was from FFF (no low F sharp or G sharp) to C, 54 notes; but above gamut G on great and chair G sharp and D sharp keys were divided, the back part being raised above the front. These were tuned to A flat and E flat respectively, so as to overcome the evils of unequal temperament tuning (as will be seen shortly, this spurred Harris on to some remarkable *tours de force* in the way of subdivided notes).

A substantial number of Smith's pipes survived in the organ until it was destroyed by enemy action in 1940.

Smith's other *magnum opus* was at St. Paul's Cathedral, built between 1695 and 1697; but despite the much greater size of the building, it contained only four stops more than the Temple. However, this was because the Dean insisted (contrary to the wishes of Sir Christopher Wren) that the organ should stand upon the screen. Smith provided a compass to CCC, but Wren would not allow the lowest five pipes of the diapasons to go in, nor a bassoon, a clarion, and perhaps one other, declaring that he would not have the beauty of his building spoilt by 'the damned box of whistles'. Smith kept the pipes in readiness, but Wren outlived him, so that he was never able to install them. Thus, the effective compass was FFF to C (no low F or G sharp) with the echo to tenor C only.

Great	Chayre	Echo
Open diapason	Quinta Dena Diapason	Diapason
Open diapason	Stop. diapason	Principal
Stop. diapason	Principall	Nason
Principall	Hol fleut	ffifteenth
Hol fleut	Great Twelfth	Cornet
Great Twelfth	Fifteenth	
ffifteenth	Cimball	Trumpet
Small Twelfth	Voice Humaine	
Cornet	Crum horne	
Mixture		
Sesquialtera		
Trumpet		

It is difficult to form an accurate impression of what Smith's organs sounded like since no important organ remains in original condition. Only two or three do so, and they are chamber organs. One belongs to the Marquis of Northampton and is at Compton Wynyates (*33*). It has two manuals and six stops but is not at present in good repair. The second is an even smaller organ belonging to Noel Mander (*34*) containing a stopped diapason and principal of wood, and a fifteenth and divided two-rank mixture of metal. A slightly larger organ is at Dingestow Court, Monmouthshire, the seat of the Bosanquet family for whom it was built. It was subsequently rebuilt with new case and action by Gray, who put on it the following inscription: 'This organ was originally built by that celebrated artist commonly called Father Smith and erected in its present position by Robert Gray of London 1773'. In this way the best of both worlds was achieved, since Smith's action was notoriously unpleasant and soggy to the touch. The pipes were entirely untouched and are almost all of wood, of very small scale, despite which the tone is so powerful and ringing as to suggest metal (*44, 45*).

Smith's diapasons are recognisable as the ancestors of all subsequent British work and so far as one can judge what is left of his chorus-work, it was strong and ringing. His wooden stopped diapasons have a marked quintadena quality and are of exceptional beauty. It is difficult to say why he generally included a tierce rank in his mixtures, thus setting a fashion which has been followed in England almost to this day, although it was hardly ever done abroad. Probably it was so that in a small organ, with only one compound stop, it could be divided and the upper part available as a cornet solo. This he certainly accomplished, but as a result his mixtures when used as chorus stops have a somewhat thick and reedy quality which palls after a fairly short time. According to Hopkins and

74

Rimbault, Smith made the principal, twelfth and fifteenth one pipe narrower than his open diapason, and the mixtures two pipes narrower, so that the twelfth was the same scale as the fifteenth.

Smith enjoyed a considerable social position, and his great reputation was perhaps founded almost as much upon his straight dealing and amiable character as upon the undoubted excellence of his instruments. He was a member of a very select club founded by Richard Bentley, the Master of Trinity College, Cambridge, a Fellow of the Royal Society and holder of other distinctions. The Club included John Evelyn, John Locke, Isaac Newton, Christopher Wren—in fact, the most eminent minds of the day. It was probably Bentley who first referred to Bernard as 'Father Smith'. Smith also enjoyed the friendship of Blow and Purcell. He died in 1708 and was succeeded in business by his son-in-law, Christopher Shrider, his own nephews Gerard and Christian Smith having set up separately, each on his own, in 1689 and 1690 or thereabouts, neither attaining any great eminence.

Smith's portrait hangs in the Examinations Schools, Oxford.

Before passing to his only serious rival, Renatus Harris, it is interesting to quote the opinion of Sir John Sutton on both of them, from an excellent little book (now very rare) entitled *A Short Account of Organs built in England from the Reign of King Charles the Second to the present Time*. Although this was published anonymously, the identity of the author seems never to have been much of a secret, and at the time of writing it, in 1847, many instruments by both artists survived in practically their original state. Sutton, incidentally, owned both the Smith instruments described above and now belonging to Lord Northampton and Mr. Mander. Of Smith, Sutton says: 'The Chorus is also very fine & very brilliant in effect, though not quite so much so as the Chorus afterwards introduced by Snetzler in his Organs which, though extremely brilliant, is almost too shrill, and when heard in a small building rings unpleasantly in the ears'.[1] Of Renatus Harris he writes: 'His Diapasons are both sweet & rich and his chorus is vivacious & ringing, even more so than Schmidt's, and his reed stops, though far inferior to those made at present, are also superior to his'.[2] Nevertheless, it is clear from the book as a whole that Sutton's preference was for Smith, whom he followed Burney in calling 'Schmidt'. He considered that 'the great beauty of Schmidt's organs consists in the sweetness & brilliancy of the wooden pipes'.[3]

[1] *A Short Account of Organs* p. 28.   [2] Ibid., p. 58.   [3] Ibid., p. 28.

Renatus Harris

Renatus Harris is generally considered as having been a continuous rival of Smith, but in fact he is not heard of until about 1674 and it was not until about 1683 that he took over the management of the business from Thomas, by then referred to as his 'poore aged father'. He did not become a serious rival of Smith until the 'battle of the organs' in 1684. In any case, he was no less than 23 years younger than Smith, having been born in 1651 or 1652.

He had an already ancient organ-building lineage going back to the Dallams, and with the Byfields who followed him this covered well over two centuries of organ-building. The complete tree is as follows:

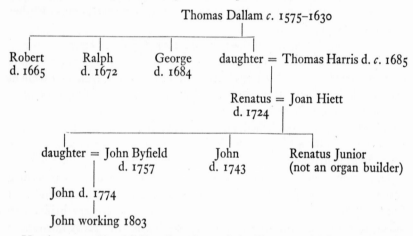

Thomas Dallam *c*. 1575–1630

Robert d. 1665

Ralph d. 1672

George d. 1684

daughter = Thomas Harris d. *c*. 1685

Renatus = Joan Hiett
d. 1724

daughter = John Byfield
d. 1757

John
d. 1743

Renatus Junior
(not an organ builder)

John d. 1774

John working 1803

Harris spent his childhood and youth in France, which accounts for the fuller tone of his diapasons and mixtures when compared with Smith's, and the reported superiority of his reeds, although of this we today can no longer form a judgment at first hand.

Harris was by no means content with the British organ as he found it, and made various attempts at improvement, as will be shown, including the introduction of pedals; but by the time he came on the scene the more conservative type had already been established so firmly by Smith that he was no more able to alter public taste than his uncle, Robert Dallam, had been at New College in 1662.

In all, Renatus built about six cathedral organs and a good deal of pipework from the first, at Chichester, made in 1677, still survives. His organs were generally larger than Smith's and he was more liberal in his provision of solo stops. A typical Renatus Harris specification is that of the organ he made for St. Bride's, Fleet Street, in 1696.

Choir Organ (lowest set) 50 notes

Stop^{e}d diapason all mettall except the first octave	8
Principal of mettall	4
fflute of mettall	4
Stop'd twelfth of mettall	$2\frac{2}{3}$
ffifteenth of mettall	2
Tierce of mettall	$1\frac{3}{5}$
Vox Humane stopp	8

Great Organ (middle set)

open Diapason of fine mettall in front	8
Stop'd Diapason all mettall except ye first octave	8
principall of mettall	4
Cornett of 5 ranks all mettall	V
Great Twelfth of mettall	$2\frac{2}{3}$
Cart of mettall	2
ffifteenth of mettall	2
Tierce of mettall	$1\frac{3}{5}$
Sesquialter stop of 5 ranks mettall	V
furniture of 3 ranks mettall	III
Trumpett stopp mettall	8

Echo Organ (top set) 25 notes

Tribles to the open diapason	8	
,, ,,	Stop'd diapason	8
,, ,,	Principall or fflute	4
,, ,,	Great Twelfth	$2\frac{2}{3}$
,, ,,	Cart or ffifteenth	2
,, ,,	Tierce	$1\frac{3}{5}$
,, ,,	Trumpet	8

The stop on the great organ called 'cart' had no equine proclivities, but was an Englished version of the French 'quarte de nazard' (i.e., a large-scale stop in the mutation series, a fourth above the nazard). Smith's equivalent was his block flute.

One of Harris's mechanical ingenuities was the borrowing of a stop from one department to another, as he called it, 'by communication'. This he achieved by putting his great and choir pipes all on one chest, with double pallets, one set controlled by each set of keys. The stops he wished to duplicate also had two stops and sliders, one registering with one set of pallets and one with the other. In this way the stop could be played on either keyboard. The disadvantage of the scheme was that the pipes had to stand over a set of clack-valves, to prevent wind sent up from one pallet disappearing down the other; but even so, this type of chest was considerably prone to runnings. However, at a time when there were no aids to registration the system possessed undoubted advantages. Harris's largest organ, which he built in 1710 for Salisbury Cathedral,

77

made extensive use of 'communication', and was the first four-manual organ to be made in England. Even without borrowed stops, it was a very large organ for the time and its specification comprised 50 stops in all.

The stops of the great organ all appeared twice with the exception of the second open diapason and the cornet, the second keyboard thus being almost a complete reduplication of it. The compass was GG (short octave) to C, 50 notes, for the great and choir; that of the echo was two octaves from middle C. The specification was as follows:

Great nearly all used twice		Choir		Echo	
Open diapason	8	Open diapason		Open diapason	8
Open diapason	8	(from gamut g)	8	Stopped diapason	8
Stopped diapason	8	Stopped diapason	8	Principal	4
Principal	4	Principal	4	Flute	4
Flute	4	Flute	4	Twelfth	$2\frac{2}{3}$
Twelfth	$2\frac{2}{3}$	Twelfth	$2\frac{2}{3}$	Fifteenth	2
Fifteenth	2	Fifteenth	2	Tierce	$1\frac{3}{5}$
Tierce	$1\frac{3}{5}$	Bassoon	8	Larigot	$1\frac{1}{3}$
Larigot	$1\frac{1}{3}$			Trumpet	8
Sesquialtera	IV			Vox humana	8
Cornet (middle C)	V			Cromhorn	8
Trumpet	8				
Clarion	4	Drum pedal tuned to CC			
Cromhorn	8				
Vox humana	8				

Harris's specifications in general are somewhat better than Smith's, who seldom used a separate seventeenth or nineteenth, but invariably included the tierce rank in his compound stops. Harris, by contrast, relatively seldom did so. His organ at St. Peter Mancroft, Norwich, had three mixtures on the great, called sesquialtera, mixture and furniture, none of which contained a tierce rank. The sesquialtera and furniture both included a unison rank (i.e. of 8 ft. pitch) in the treble, which is a very early example of this. In his Newcastle-upon-Tyne organ the sesquialtera, despite its name, did not contain a tierce, whereas the mixture did.

Fortunately, it is still possible to form a useful idea of how Harris's organs sounded. The single-manual organ at Little Bardfield, Essex (which is attributed to Harris and is said to have come from Jesus College, Cambridge) is almost intact (*30*), as are large parts (including the great chorus) of St. John's, Wolverhampton. It was previously thought that the pipework at St. Mary's, Dublin, is by Harris, but in fact this is not so.

At All Hallows, Twickenham, which came from All Hallows, Lombard Street, the great chorus survives up to twelfth and fifteenth. Harris's diapasons are more foundational in tone than is typical of British diapasons generally, but they are very fine all the same. The chorus has a broad, ringing quality of great nobility. Although he made wooden stopped diapasons, these do not compare with Smith's, but his metal chimney flutes are of great beauty. It seems to have been generally acknowledged that his action work and his reeds stops were better than Smith's and, over all, it can be said that his organs were at least as good as those of his rival. Smith had the advantage of having established his priority before Harris was effectively on the scene, and maintained it by the undoubted excellence of his instruments, by the honesty of his dealings, and by his agreeable behaviour. The last two, it seems, could not be said of Harris, who had a quarrelsome and jealous nature which sometimes led him into stupidly petty actions, such as the cutting of Smith's bellows at the Temple Church. At Christ's Hospital 'he by some means or other made the said chaire organ useless upon account of some money remaining due to him' and at St. Clement's, Christopher Smith was called in to remove 'the cheat Mr. Harris putt into the Organ in order to put the Organ out of order'.

Almost more important than what Harris actually achieved are the things he wanted to do, but was never able to accomplish, at any rate beyond the experimental stage. These were his scheme for a grand west-end organ at St. Paul's Cathedral, including pedals, and some means of expression, though precisely what those means were, it is not possible to determine.

Smith's quarter notes were regarded by Harris as a sort of challenge, to which he replied by dividing a note into 50 parts—a singularly useless *tour de force*, which he later excelled by dividing it into 100 parts. However the experiment seems to have put him in mind of endowing the organ with powers of expression—'this performance gave the Proposer a Notion of the swelling of the Notes upon the Organ which he finds to answer upon Tryal, though looked upon equally impracticable with the other'. It must therefore be assumed that his swelling 'notion' was not connected with a swell box (curiously enough, invented by Abraham Jordan in the very same year, 1712), but in some way with his multiple subdivision of a note. It would appear likely that having 10 pipes all within a few beats of each other, he tried bringing them on successively, and found that the resultant 'voix céleste' was in itself not disagreeable, and produced an effect of a real crescendo. Either he stopped short there, or else then tried the same operation with a number of pipes to a note, all in tune. This, however, would not produce so effective a crescendo, because of the effects of sympathy and it may be that he had in mind a modification of the multiple céleste. What is curious, and less easy to explain, is another passage saying that the device had to stand against a reflecting surface, though indeed it is obvious enough that by being so situated its effectiveness would be considerably enhanced. That, however, is true of any organ.

Here are several excerpts from the St. Paul's project which, it will be noticed, was not published until after Smith's death:

> The Inclos'd Proposal takes its rise from the organ I set up in Salisbury Cathedral in 1710 which was begun some Years since for a church in London, as a Masterpiece of Great Value to have been paid for by Subscription and was made capable of emitting Sounds to express Passion by Swelling any Note as if inspired by Human Breath. But the Place where it is now fix'd, not being proper for that Performance, which requires the Situation to be against a Wall, for the Sound to strike but one way, it loses that Advantage; & yet being prepar'd for that Intent, there may be more Varieties express'd thereon than by all the Organs in England, were thir several Excellencies united. You are desir'd to observe that the propos'd Organ for St. Paul's is intended to be plac'd at a great Distance from the Choir & not to interfere with the present Organ in the Performance of the Service, being chiefly consider'd in its Situation for the benefit of Swelling the Notes. . . . The use of it will be for the Reception of the Queen on all public Occasions of Thanksgiving for the good Effects of Peace or War, upon all State Occasions, St. Cecilia's Day, the Entertainment of Foreigners of Quality & Artists & on all Times of greatest Concourse. . . . Sir Christopher Wren approves it.

He finished by naïvely suggesting that it could be paid for out of the taxes. Turning to describe the instrument:

> This organ shall contain a double double Diapason of Profundity which shall comprehend the utmost notes of Sound. In this stop shall be pipes forty foot long, & above two foot diameter; which will render this Organ vastly superior in worth & value to any other Diapason organs; & that the rest of the work may bear a due Proportion, it shall consist of Six entire sets of keys for the hands, besides Pedals for the feet.
>
> The first Set to be wholly appropriated for a grand Chorus, intended to be the most firm & strong that ever has yet been made.
>
> The second & third Sets to answer all Sorts & Varieties of Stops & to represent all Musical Instruments.
>
> The fourth to express the Ecchos.
>
> The fifth to be a Choir or Small Organ, yet to contain more pipes & a greater Number of Stops than the biggest Organ in England has at present.

The sixth to be adapted for the emitting of Sounds to express Passion by swelling any Note as if inspir'd by Human Breath; which is the greatest improvement an organ is capable of except it had Articulation. On this set of keys the notes will be loud or soft, by swelling on a long Note or Shake, at the organist's pleasure. Sounds will come surprising & harmoniously, as from the Clouds, or distant Parts, pass, & return again, as quick or slow as Fancy can suggest; & be in tune in all Degrees of Loudness & Softness.

By means of the Pedals, the Organist may carry on three Fugues at once, & be able to do as much as if he had four hands, for the Feet would act upon the Pedal-Keys, when the hands were employ'd above, & the Sound would be proportionately strong; which in the grand Chorus in so vast a Church, ought to be as strong & bold as possible; & therefore Pedals are us'd in all the Great Organs beyond the seas.

The fact that there was an echo as well as a swelling keyboard is additional evidence that Harris's device was no mere swell box.

The Eighteenth Century

Renatus Harris died 12 years later, in 1724, his grand scheme unaccomplished, and for the rest of the century British organ-building continued along singularly placid and unadventurous lines that can be discussed in a much shorter space than the first exciting quarter century after the Restoration of the Monarchy. The kind of organ established by Smith by about 1680 continued to be made for well over a century by the younger Harris, the Byfields, Shrider, Snetzler, Green, the Englands and others, with no more than insignificant variants, except for the invention of the swell organ.

The Smith tradition was most ably carried on by his German foreman and son-in-law Christopher Shrider who inherited the business on Smith's death (his two nephews having set up each on his own in 1689-90, but neither to any great effect.) Perhaps the most representative surviving example of his work is at Finedon Church, Northampton, which also has its exceedingly fine original case, standing on the west gallery. The great is almost entirely his work and is very bold in effect, with a strong reedy flavour attributable to the powerful tierce rank of the mixture. Shrider died in about 1754.

The direct Harris tradition was longer lived, through Renatus's son John who lived until 1743 and worked in partnership with his brother-in-law John Byfield, the first of three John Byfields of whom the last was working as an organ builder until after 1800. One of the first and most important of their works was the large organ they built for St. Mary Redcliffe, Bristol, in 1726, only two years after the death of Renatus. This instrument was remarkable for its very long compass; the size of the swell organ; the number of its reed stops; and for having possessed the first absolutely authentic pedals in England (even though they consisted only of one octave of pull-downs, possibly with an octave coupler). Its specification was as follows:

Great		Chair		Swell	
CCC–d, 63 notes		GG–d, 56 notes		fiddle G–d, 32 notes	
Open diapason	8	Stopped diapason	8	Open diapason	8
Open diapason	8	Principal	4	Stopped diapason	8
Stopped diapason	8	Flute almain	4	Principal	4
Principal	4	Flute	2?	Flute	4
Twelfth	to 2⅔	Sesquialtera	III	Cornet	III
Fifteenth	GGG 2	Bassoon	8	Trumpet	8
Tierce	1⅗			Hautboy	8
Sesquialtera	V			Vox humana	8
Cornet (middle C)	V	**Pedals**		Cromorn	8
Trumpet	8	CCC–C, 13 notes			
Clarion	4	Octave coupler [to pedals?]			

The exact priority of the first pedal board is not quite clear as in 1720 Shrider was paid for the following work at St. Paul's:

> For adding 6 large Trumpet Pipes down to 16 ft Tone to be used
> with a pedal or without £36
> For the Pedal & Its Movements £20
> For adding the Loudning & Softning (that is) the Swelling Note
> & its Movements & other things thereto belonging £12

The bass trumpet pipes may only have been some of those prepared for by Smith but not allowed by Wren to be put in; and the pedal may have been only a shifting movement. But it is at least likely that a pedal board is implied and this is borne out by Burney, although he was certainly not the most reliable of historians. Burney wrote of the supposed pedals at St. Paul's: 'On Handel's first arrival in England, from Greene's great admiration of this master's style of playing, he had literally condescended to become his bellows blower, when he went to St. Paul's to play on that organ, for the exercise it afforded him in the use of the pedals. Handel, after three o'clock prayers, used frequently to get himself & young Greene locked up in the Church together; & in summer often stript unto his shirt & played until eight or nine o'clock at night.'

This was in 1722; but in default of indisputable evidence, the exact priority must lie between St. Paul's and St. Mary Redcliffe.

The second John Byfield was also a most capable builder. Fortunately, one of his finest organs, made in 1764 for St. Mary's, Rotherhithe, survives in a remarkably original state. The 1764 specification was as follows, being quite a late example of a sizeable organ without a swell organ. The compass was GG (short octave) to d.

Great		Choir	
Open diapason	8	Stop'd diapason	8
Stop'd diapason	8	Principal	4
Principal	4	Flute	4
Nason	4	Fifteenth	2
Fifteenth	2	Vox humana	8
Sesquialtera	III		
Cornet (middle C)	V		
Trumpet	8		
Clarion	4		

A swell organ and one pedal stop were added during the nineteenth century and other minor alterations effected. The organ was thoroughly restored by Noel Mander in 1959 and is now an important example of mid-eighteenth century tone. The diapason may be described as midway tonally between Renatus Harris and Bernard Smith, and a little louder. The sesquialtera contains no tierce and the diapason chorus is wonderfully full, clear and ringing and one of the finest to be heard in London. The trumpet is also extremely fine and quite as good as any Continental reeds of the period, although completely British in treatment. The organ has its original case and stands on the west gallery (*41*). It establishes Byfield as a builder of the top rank and is an instrument of great historic importance and beauty.

Another pupil of Renatus Harris was Thomas Schwarbrick, who was active until soon after 1750 and executed several important commissions, but very little of his pipework remains. In 1733 at St. Michael's, Coventry, he included a stop or stops named 'harp', 'lute' and 'dulcimer', but they were so difficult to keep in tune that they were removed in 1763.

Richard Bridge was also probably trained by John Harris, and a completely original specimen of his work survives at Great Packington Church, near Rugby, whither it was removed from Gopsall Hall, belonging to the Marquis of Ely. Its additional interest is that among the innumerable organs said to have been designed by Handel, it is well authenticated. The great has seven stops up to twelfth, fifteenth and seventeenth, and the choir three stops up to fifteenth.

Samuel Green was another important representative of the Harris school, though in his work he departed from it almost entirely. He was born in 1740 and probably after training with the family became a partner of the middle John Byfield in about 1770. In 1772 Green set up on his own, and after Snetzler's retirement he was so fortunate as to find favour with George III, and as a result built many important organs up to the time of his death in 1796. His organs were soft and sweet, but lacking in nobility, and he used excessively large scales for his diapason basses. He did, however, improve the status of the swell organ, both by giving it a longer compass than was usual (at Greenwich Naval Hospital down to FF) and by using the venetian shutters first made by Schudi on harpsichords. Although Snetzler is the reputed inventor of the dulciana stop, Green probably first made it in the form it is known today, and he also made dulciana cornets. Sir John Sutton described his organs in derisive terms as 'Emulating the tone of a musical snuff box rather than that of an organ'.[1] His specifications followed perfectly conventional lines.

Somewhat following the style of Green's work came John Avery, of whom Sir John Sutton wrote, 'Avery was a shocking drunken character and a person not in any way to be depended upon, being generally drunk and often in prison for debt, but was nevertheless an excellent workman when he was once set to work'.[2]

The Englands were the last indirect descendants of the Harris school, carrying it on into the nineteenth century. George England was trained by Richard Bridge, whose daughter he married, and set up on his own around 1750. He was active until about 1780 when he was succeeded by his son George Pike England whose work really represents the transition from the eighteenth century to the beginnings of the modern organ. Fortunately, a largely original specimen of his work survives at St. Mary Magdalene, Holloway Road (formerly known as Islington Chapel of Ease). This was one of his last organs, being finished in 1814 only two years before his death. It has an effective case of Spanish mahogany and the organ was conservatively rebuilt in 1867 by Henry Willis, who was for many years organist at St. Mary Magdalene's. The diapason is substantially louder than the upperwork (comprising twelfth, fifteenth and two mixtures) despite which it does not preponderate, and the chorus is remarkably brilliant. It has a noticeably more modern flavour than, for example, St. Mary's, Rotherhithe, attributable to the brighter quality of the individual ranks at all pitches.

In addition to the elder and younger Englands George had a brother John who worked in partnership with Hugh Russell from about 1780 to 1795.

[1] Ibid., p. 82.   [2] Ibid., p. 86.

Hopkins and Rimbault gives the following particulars of George England's scaling:

George England made his Principal one pipe smaller than his Open Diapason, his Fifteenth two pipes narrower, & every rank of his Mixtures to a varied scale. In a compound stop of 4 ranks comprising 17th, 19th, 22nd & 26th, he would make the 17th a small scale, the 19th rather larger, the 22nd large scale & powerfully voiced, & the 26th small again, & voiced almost as a Dulciana. This last rank, nevertheless, made itself heard & gave to the mixture a sound as of bells. England's Mixtures were of a very silvery & sparkling quality; though not so bold as Smith's nor so full as Harris's, on account of their different composition & smaller scaling.

England's great organs almost always contained a cornet but frequently no reed (the same also applies to Green). A typical, fairly large example of his organs was that built in 1765 for St. Stephen's, Walbrook. The compass of the great and choir was GG (no GG♯) to e, 57 notes, and the Swell fiddle G to e, 34 notes.

Great		Choir		Swell	
Open diapason	8	Dulciana (gamut g)	8	Open diapason	8
Stopped diapason	8	Stopped diapason	8	Stopped diapason	8
Principal	4	Flute	4	German flute	4
Nason	4	Fifteenth	2	Cornet	III
Twelfth	2⅔	French horn	8	Trumpet	8
Fifteenth	2	Vox humana	8	Hautboy	8
Sesquialtera	IV			Clarion	4
Mixture	II				
Cornet (middle C)	V				
Trumpet	8				
Clarion	4				

A very interesting specimen of George England's work was at St. Mildred's, Poultry. This had a conventional great, but the second manual was a compromise between swell and choir. The compass was GG to e, 54 notes. For the lowest 20 notes there were only two stops, stopped diapason and principal, both unenclosed. The top 34 notes, from fiddle G up, were then a normal enclosed swell containing:

Open diapason	8
Stopped diapason	8
Principal	4
Flute	4
Cornet	III
Trumpet	8
Hautboy	8

Thus, this second manual could be used either as a full compass choir organ or as a short compass swell.

Sir John Sutton wrote of England that his 'Diapasons are rich and sonorous, and the Chorus is very brilliant'[1] and this may be regarded as a fair and accurate assessment.

Finally, Joseph Walker was trained by George Pike England, later to found the great firm of J. W. Walker & Sons who continue to flourish. Thus, it may be said that there is an unbroken tradition of 400 years from Thomas Dallam up to the present time.

Only two important names from the eighteenth century remain to be mentioned; the Abraham Jordans and Johann Snetzler.

The Jordans, father and son, are notable principally for their invention of the swell organ; or at any rate for its introduction into England, since it is said that there were earlier swells in Spain and Portugal of which the Jordans were aware.

Their first swell box was installed at St. Magnus the Martyr, London, a large four-manual organ, in 1712. *The Spectator* of February 8th in that year contained the following notice: 'Whereas Messrs. Abraham Jordan have, with their own hands, joynery excepted, made & erected a very large organ in St. Magnus Church at the foot of London Bridge, consisting of four sets of keys, one of which is adapted to the art of emitting sounds by swelling the notes, which never was in any organ before; this instrument will be publicly opened on Sunday next, the performance by Mr. John Robinson. The above said Abraham Jordan gives notice to all masters & performers that he will attend every day next week at the said Church to accommodate all those gentlemen who have a curiosity to hear it'—if Jordan did know of the Portuguese swells he was at any rate not admitting to it.

Jordan's swell box consisted simply in the old echo box with its front side arranged to slide upwards, raised by a cord which ran over a pulley and connected with a pedal controlled by the player. Its powers of expression were very limited and if the pedal was let go accidentally the slider came down with a crash. One or two such 'nag's-head' swells still exist and one is in the Snetzler organ at Hillington Church, Norfolk.

Johann Snetzler is of great importance as he had almost a monopoly from about 1760 to 1780, seriously challenged only by Byfield. He was a Swiss, born in about 1710. Very little is known about his early history, but he was apprenticed in Germany and is known to have been employed in Holland. Snetzler came to England in about 1746, and he

[1] Ibid. p. 87.

seems to have taken to the British organ like a duck to water (the authenticity of an instrument dated 1742, attributed to Snetzler, now in America, is dubious). His voicing is entirely British in style and he made no attempt to alter the existing order of things. Sir John Sutton wrote of his work that 'his instruments are remarkable for the purity of their tone, and the extreme brilliancy of their Chorus-Stops, which in this respect surpassed any thing that had been heard before in this country, & which have never since been equalled. His reed stops were also much better than those built before his time. His Organs though they are more brilliant than their predecessors, fall short of that fulness of tone which characterized those of Schmidt, Harris, Schreider, etc., but they are nevertheless most charming instruments.'[1]

This is true enough of Snetzler's smaller instruments, especially chamber organs, of which he made a very great number. In these, the diapasons are smooth and sophisticated in tone and up to the fifteenth the effect is remarkably mild; but the mixture, containing a powerful tierce rank, comes on with a crash which puts all else quite in the shade. But in his larger church instruments the diapasons are made relatively more bold and the mixtures take on an agreeably silvery quality. They certainly bear no resemblance to the powerful contemporary German mixtures. The largest amount of Snetzler's pipework to survive in any organ is at Beverley Minster. The organ was rebuilt on several occasions by Hill, but always respecting Snetzler's work. The organ, which must be accounted one of the finest church organs in the country, stands on the choir screen and has one of Dr. A. G. Hill's cases. The great contains the complete Snetzler chorus up to two mixtures and there is a lot more in the

Great		Choir		Swell	
Open diapason	8	Open diapason	8	Open diapason	8
Open diapason	8	Stop'd diapason	8	Stop't diapason	8
Stopt diapason	8	Principal	4	Principal	4
Principal	4	Flute	4	Cornet	III
Twelfth	$2\frac{2}{3}$	Fifteenth	2	Hautbois	8
Fifteenth	2	Sesquialtera	III	Trumpet	8
Tierce	$1\frac{3}{5}$	Bassoon	8		
Sesquialtera	III	Vox humana	8		
Fourniture	IV				
Trumpet	8				
Clarion	4				
Cornet (middle C)	V				

[1] Ibid. p. 73.

swell and choir, including a delicate little trumpet. The original Snetzler specification, built in 1769, is given on p. 87. The compass was GGG to e and the swell organ fiddle g to e. There were one and a half octaves of pedals.

Snetzler built another large organ for Halifax parish church and on its completion there was a competition for the post of organist. The chances of Mr. Wainwright of Manchester were much fancied. Wainwright played with great execution, but not at all to the liking of Snetzler who ran about the church exclaiming (he never completely mastered the English language): 'Te tevil, te tevil, he run over te key like one cat; he vil not give my piphes room for to shpeak'. Afterwards came Mr. Herschel (later to achieve outstanding fame as an astronomer) who played with great solemnity so that Snetzler cried: 'Aye, Aye, 'tish is very goot, very goot indeet. I vil luf tish man for he gives my piphes room for to shpeak'.

Snetzler afterwards asked Herschel how he obtained such a sonorous effect (for the organ had no pedals), at which Herschel drew two lead weights out of his pocket and explained: 'One of these I placed upon the lowest key of the organ, and the other upon the octave above; thus by accommodating the harmony, I produced the effect of four hands instead of two'.

Herschel got the job.

Many examples of Snetzler's chamber organs survive.

In 1756 he made a two-manual organ for the Duke of Devonshire which is now in Hillington Church in Norfolk. It is noticeably bolder in effect than his later, more 'refined' and sophisticated work such as the instrument he built in 1769 for Teddesley Hall. This organ survived into the 1950s having, apparently, hardly ever been used and certainly never tuned; when it was heard by chance that the house was to be demolished. Mr. Mander, on being informed, managed to secure the instrument and arrived to remove it as the roof was being taken off by the demolition contractors. The organ has found a suitable and permanent home in the City of London church of St. Andrew-by-the-Wardrobe.

Another of Snetzler's chamber organs is at Eton College, and he also made an even smaller type of instrument, designed for easy transportation. These are in the form of a bureau, or writing desk, in which the pipes are most ingeniously coiled to the available space. They contain four stops; a stopped diapason 8, stopped flute 4, fifteenth and a divided two-rank cornet-mixture.

He is the reputed inventor of the dulciana, but he did not always make the stop in the form now known. At any rate his earlier specimens were of inverted conical shape and bearded (a very early use of this device). The narrow-scale cylindrical dulciana in its modern form was probably first made by Green. Snetzler also used a harmonic chimney flute (over-blown to its first harmonic and therefore, being stopped, of three times normal length.) This he called 'German flute'.

For his keyboards Snetzler generally used a most handsome form of sharp, consisting of a sandwich of ivory between two outer layers of ebony.

In 1773 he entered into partnership with one Jones, and one or two instruments, such as St. Mary Huntingdon, are signed 'Jones & Snetzler'. Jones was also an executor of Snetzler's Will. It is also said that Snetzler had an arrangement with Burkhardt Schudi for making claviorganums (combined harpsichord and organ) but there is no surviving specimen by them (although, paradoxically, a Snetzler-Kirkman claviorganum does survive). However, Snetzler was an executor to Schudi's Will.

Snetzler's last dated organ is 1781 after which it is said that he retired and returned to Germany; but finding that he could not do without English porter he returned towards this country, but died on the way, at sea. His Will was proved on October 20th, 1785, but the place of his burial is not known.

He was succeeded in business by his Swedish foreman Jonathan Ohrman of whom, however, not much more is heard.

Thus ends the school of British organ-building at its most typical and insular, starting with Bernard Smith and ending with George Pike England, who brought it to the brink of its next and perhaps finest phase of all.

Ohrman took into partnership one John Nutt and there is a tradition that they were later joined by Thomas Elliot, who subsequently worked on his own.

The Hill-Gauntlett Revolution
1830-50

William Hill, who was born in 1789, went to work for Elliot in 1815, married his daughter Mary, and became his partner in 1825. Elliot died in 1832 but was predeceased by Mary, and Hill subsequently remarried, setting up as an organ builder on his own.

Thus started the famous firm of Hill, much later to take its present style of 'William Hill & Son and Norman & Beard'. The Snetzler-Elliot tradition has not so far received historical proof, but if it is true, the firm thus has an origin second only to the Walkers in antiquity. Be that as it may, William Hill, the founder of the firm, was certainly the most power-ful influence in bringing the British organ to perhaps its highest peak of perfection and one which we may not be flattering ourselves in believing was ahead of all its Continental contemporaries.

This he did in an astonishingly short space of time, greatly assisted by Dr. Henry John Gauntlett.

Gauntlett showed such early musical promise that he became organist of Olney Church (in Buckinghamshire; also the home of Cowper the poet) at the age of nine. He later came to London to be articled to a solicitor, when he also became the organist at St. Olave's, Tooley Street. He was given a Canterbury doctorate of music in 1842 and from that time decided to devote his entire career to music. He was a keen advocate of the C compass for all manuals and pedals, and of properly developed pedal organs, and he found a willing ally in William Hill.

They had to some extent been anticipated by Dr. John Camidge, for whom Elliot had built a grotesque instrument at York Minster, dating from 1829. This had a CCC manual compass, but Camidge made the fatal mistake of including no manual doubles. The pedal organ, however, possessed four 32 ft. stops including one reed, a 'sackbut'. The instru-ment was an almost total failure, and the many additions which Camidge made to it were designed to enhance its faults rather than overcome them. But the York organ had at any rate accustomed the British to the idea of large organs and so to an extent prepared the way for Gauntlett & Hill.

The organ made by Booth of Wakefield in 1828 for the Brunswick Chapel, Leeds, also had a two-octave pedal-board and four pedal stops including a trombone. The remainder of its specification was un-distinguished, so it also may well have been designed by Camidge.

Even earlier pioneer work had been done by the remarkable Abbé Vogler, who put forward many schemes for reducing the size of the organ by extensions and borrowings, and the suppression of almost all chorus work, in favour of a number of solo stops. Born in 1749, he had a great effect on the Continent where the public taste in organs had reached a very low ebb towards the end of the century. In 1790 he toured several countries with an instrument which he called an 'Orchestrion'. In Holland he received the following eulogistic notice: 'The Abbé Vogler, director of the Royal Academy of Music to his Swedish Majesty, has constructed, after his own invention & design (& at his own expence) an organ with four rows of keys, sixty-three stops, thirty-nine pedals, &

three swells, with proper resources to modify the sound: of which the first opens & shuts the general case of the pipes; the second, which is a pneumatic measure, stops the wind; the third divides & reunites the resources proportionably to the harmonic progression. The breadth, height, & depth of this organ is nine feet; the temperament of it is beyond conception exact. With respect to the body of tone, when in full chorus, it is equal to a church organ of sixteen feet. In depth of sound, it surpasses those of thirty-two feet; in sweetness, the *armonica*. Its *crescendo* governs all it plays; its *diminuendo* is qualified by the most minute gradations; & with respect to variety, the connoisseurs have declared, that a concert given by the Abbé on his *orchestrion*, being a combination of all the instruments in Europe, & the result of thirty years travelling, is the utmost extent of perfection in the art of constructing organs.'

Arrived in London the same year we read, in Rees' *Cyclopaedia or Universal Dictionary of Arts, Sciences & Literature*, published in 1819:

> He had pedals put to the organ in the Pantheon, & a general swell contrived for the whole instrument, & in a series of morning performances on that organ, showed his dexterity in the use of the pedals, not only in the *crescendo* & *diminuendo*, but in innumerable imitations, many of which were thought imaginary, & but for the ample promises & descriptions on his bills of fare, would perhaps not have been discovered.
>
> The science of this extraordinary musician was thought by some to degenerate into pedantry, and the splendid promises in his advertisements to border on *charletanerie*; so that his success was not equal in our country to his real merit. Had he promised & attempted less, the public would have been more just, & even generous in the estimation of his talents; but having injudiciously promised seeming impossibilities, what was possible, & what he really did perform, was sullenly heard with an unwillingness to be pleased. What he really did achieve was often uncommon & well deserving of applause, though perhaps not so much as he expected.

In short, while Vogler was received here with a good deal of native scepticism, he must at any rate have opened the eyes and ears of many to the potentialities of the pedal board and the swell box.

Undoubtedly the greatest missionary works of a practical kind were the visits of Mendelssohn to England, of which the first was in 1829. By playing his own works, and those of Bach, on such few instruments as possessed pedal organs at all adequate to his needs (notably St. Peter's, Cornhill, and Christ Church, Newgate Street, which were rebuilt under Gauntlett's direction) he introduced an entirely new conception of organ music and organ playing to the British public.

To return at last to William Hill: he had first to overcome an early reverse in the form of a serious illness immediately after setting up on his own account. This put his work into serious arrears and some of his clients complained vociferously, particularly one Dr. Worthington, who said that his congregation were laughing at the imperfections of the uncompleted organ. Mrs. Hill fended him off as best she could until her husband was able to take up the cudgels himself which he did as follows: 'Sir—It must be distressing to you as a minister of the gospel to see your congregation laugh at the organ. I hope you will succeed in solemnising their minds to better things. At present, by your account, they must be in a very dark state, both as regards music & eternal life.'

In 1834 Hill built the important concert organ for Birmingham Town Hall, and in 1837 added to it the world's first heavy pressure reed, a 'grand ophicleide', on 12 in. wind, which still survives there as the present tuba mirabilis. But for the rest of the organ Hill was a keen advocate of light pressures, between 3 and $3\frac{1}{2}$ in. for all fluework. Later, he was willing to voice chorus reeds on up to 5 in. pressure which he considered (quite correctly) to produce the advantages of heavy pressure (properly maintained trebles and an ability to stand in tune) without losing the advantages of light pressures (a prompt attack in the bass and a quality which does not annihilate the fluework). He was always insistent that the diapason chorus, including a proper supply of mixtures, must be able to stand by itself, without reed support. He was also entirely opposed to extreme sonorities of all kinds, with the isolated exception of his heavy pressure tuba. On this sound and solid foundation rests his great work in bringing the British organ to full maturity, from its long-standing condition of delayed adolescence, in a space of barely ten years.

Gauntlett's and Hill's earliest attempts to produce an adequate pedal organ consisted of a pedal compass of $2\frac{1}{2}$ octaves, only the lowest octave of which had any pipes. These were a complete downward continuation of the stops of the great organ. Thus the second C of the pedal board was coupled to bottom C of the great and by this inconvenient arrangement the pedal department could at least balance whatever might be drawn on the great.

However, in 1841 came the organ in the George Street Chapel, Liverpool, to the altogether remarkable arrangement of 52 speaking stops (p. 93).

The manual compass was CC–f and the pedals CCC–D (27 notes).

The advances made in this organ are immense. From an archaic, chaotic state the British organ suddenly emerged at full stature, capable of dealing with all sorts of organ music instead of only the highly restricted

Great 16 stops		Swell 20 stops		Choir 8 stops	
Tenoroon to t.c.	}16	Tenoroon to t.c.	}16	Open diapason	8
Bourdon from t.c.		Bourdon from t.c.		Dulciana	8
Open diapason	8	Open diapason	8	Stopped diapason	8
Open diapason	8	Dulciana	8	Clarabella	8
Stopped diapason	8	Corno flute	8	Principal	4
Quint	5⅓	Stopped diapason	8	Stopped flute	4
Principal	4	Quint	5⅓	Wald flute	4
Flute	4	Principal	4	Oboe flute	4
Tenth	3⅕	Suabe flute	4	Cremona	8
Twelfth	2⅔	Twelfth	2⅔		
Fifteenth	2	Fifteenth	2	**Solo 1 stop**	
Sesquialtera	III	Flageolet	2	Tuba mirabilis	8
Mixture	III	Sesquialtera	III		
Doublette	II	Mixture	II	**Pedal 6 stops**	
Posaune	8	Echo cornet	V	Open diapason	16
Clarion	4	Contra fagotto	16	Bourdon	16
		Cornopean	8	Principal	8
		Trumpet	8	Fifteenth	4
		Oboe	8	Sesquialtera	V
		Clarion	4	Trombone	16

native school. The pedal organ, of normal Bach compass, became Hill's standard for many years to come and was independent for most purposes. Within six stops it would be impossible to find any better disposition. In view of this it is difficult to see why he retained his divided manual doubles, which were a relic of the days of the pull-down pedals. Pedal pipes had begun to appear in England during the second half of the eighteenth century (probably Westminster Abbey had the first, in 1778), but they were invariably a set of large-scale, lightly blown wooden pipes, designed solely to provide a deep-toned bass to the manuals and probably seldom used except for a final dominant and tonic. Such stops in fact continued as the basis of the normal British pedal organ until 1939 and a set of such pipes was often the only pedal stop in quite large organs up to well after 1850. In fact, these early stops were more useful than they appeared, because they spoke promptly and were soft enough to be used with soft combinations. But they seemed to gain strength as more manual stops were added and made themselves felt even in full organ. The later 'open wood' was a much more heavily-winded, ponderous and booming affair and was one of the worst banes of the British organ from the early twentieth century. Hill's pedal organ was therefore an immense improvement over practically anything that had gone before, in being able

93

to support an independent pedal part without a coupled manual. Though others followed Hill for a time, such independent pedal organs had almost completely disappeared by 1860, not to be revived until the late 1950s.

Indeed, there was continued opposition to pedals until an amazingly late date. When Holdich built a fine 10 stop pedal organ at Lichfield Cathedral in 1860, including an open 32 ft., two mixtures and two reeds, Samuel Spofforth the cathedral organist told him 'you may put them there but I shall never use them'. And W. T. Best said of Thomas Adams (1785–1858), a London organist, 'of much celebrity in his day & a very remarkable extempore player . . . he regaled himself by serving up one or two of Bach's 48, adding a droning pedal when his bunions were propitious'.

No less important than Hill's pedal organ was the new relationship between swell and choir. Previously, the choir had been of complete compass but only possessed a mixture in the very largest organs, and not always then. The swell was a short-compass echo-cum-solo department. Under Hill, the swell took over the duties of the old English choir as the second manual ensemble, leaving the choir as a sort of mixed accompani-mental-cum-solo department, although still unenclosed. The new swell flue chorus was not appreciably softer than the great organ chorus, so that with the box open it could do effective duty for the German Positiv in playing Bach's and similar French and German music. Because the swell box tended to make the department sound more distant than the great it was given a greater reed emphasis, and even at this early date we find a 16 ft. reed included in the swell before the great. For this reason, this Liverpool organ can be accounted as having possessed the first fully developed British 'full swell', and the organ as a whole was equally well equipped to deal with music of all periods; a state of affairs which had never existed before and has seldom done so since, for several reasons to be discussed later.

Not much of William Hill's work has survived in anything like its original condition, but the organ in the Ulster Hall, Belfast, is an important exception. As originally built in 1861 it had four manuals and 53 speaking stops. The specification was very good and the organ was not much altered during a minor rebuild in 1903. It is an instrument of great beauty and brilliance and the reeds are fine examples of medium pressure voicing as executed by Hill. The Ulster Hall organ must therefore be accounted of great historical importance and artistic merit.

Other builders followed the example of Gauntlett & Hill: notably Walker, and Gray & Davison. Frederick Davison was for a short time

Hill's partner, in 1837, but in 1838 he married a daughter of John Gray, already in practice on his own as an organ-builder, and in the same year they set up as Gray & Davison and made a number of extremely fine instruments of which very few survive in original condition. The parish churches at Chippenham, in Wiltshire, and Usk, in Monmouthshire, are among the few survivors. Henry Willis was apprenticed to this firm.

Joseph William Walker was apprenticed to George Pike England from about 1818 and was in business on his own after England's death. Many fine small organs by him survive in country churches and one of the finest surviving examples of this classical period of British organ building is the Walker instrument in Romsey Abbey, completed in 1848.

J. C. Bishop was in many ways a pioneer. As early as 1829, at St. James's, Bermondsey, he provided a two-octave pedal organ with three complete stops, including a reed. As an alternative to the use of pedals the stops could also be played by a second performer from a manual keyboard on the left of the main console. Bishop also invented composition pedals and introduced a large-scale open wood flute, called clarabella, which he substituted for an old cornet whenever he could. The largest surviving organ of the pre-1850 era is the Bishop at St. Giles, Camberwell, in South London. This church was one of Gilbert Scott's first important commissions and the organ was completed in 1844. It was designed by S. S. Wesley which may account for some of its rather archaic features, though Bishop was evidently strong enough to insist upon C compass, as against Wesley's devotion to the G compass. As a result, while one may regret that this unique survival should not have been a Hill, it is nevertheless a most important instrument historically. Having had practically nothing done to it throughout its long life, except that a string stop had been substituted for one of the swell mixtures, it was rebuilt by the original builders in 1960, the tracker action to the manual keys being, very properly, retained. Despite the presence of three mixtures on the great the effect in the treble is not so exciting or colourful as might be expected, owing to Bishop's practice of having more and more unison and less and less mutation ranks, going up the compass; until the top octave and a half is composed almost entirely of unison ranks (8, 4 and 2 ft.).

Many other builders were doing good work in this halcyon second quarter of the nineteenth century, but the finest specification of all came from the never very large firm of Nicholson of Worcester who, however, then, as now, turned out a limited amount of very good work. The organ they built for the Shire Hall, Worcester, in 1844 would be considered an exceptionally fine one if designed today. The designer is unknown, though some French influence is apparent in the specification and console layout. Unfortunately, the organ now existing in the Shire Hall is either much later, or greatly modified. The organ contained 53 speaking stops and one or two unusual accessories besides the usual couplers, which are therefore mentioned.

Great 15 stops

Great diapason, metal	16
Open diapason	8
Open diapason, small	8
Gamba	8
Bourdon	8
Quint	$5\frac{1}{3}$
Octave	4
Gemshorn	4
Wald flute	4
Twelfth	$2\frac{2}{3}$
Fifteenth	2
Tierce	$1\frac{3}{5}$
Mixture	V
Posaune	8
Clarion	4

Swell 15 stops

Great diapason, metal	16
Open diapason	8
Gamba	8
Stopped diapason	8
Keraulophon	8
Octave	4
Gambette	4
Wald flute	4
Superoctave	2
Mixture	V
Trombone	16
Cornopean	8
Hautboy	8
Clarionette	8
Clarion	4
Octave coupler	
Tremulant	
Sforzando pedal (coupling Great to Swell)	

Choir 11 stops

Open diapason	8
Viol di gamba	8
Dulciana	8
Clarabella	8
Stopped diapason	8
Harmonic flute	4
Dulcet	4
Suabe flute	4
Octave flute	2
Echo cornet	V
Trumpet	8

Pedal 11 stops

Great diapason, wood	32
Open diapason,	16
Open diapason, small, wood	16
Dulciana, metal	16
Violon	16
Bourdon	16
Quint	$10\frac{2}{3}$
Principal	8
Bass flute	8
Fifteenth	4
Mixture	III
Posaune	16
Octave coupler	
Pedal organ 'off' and 'on'	

This sudden development of large organs and their exploitation by the organists was not without its critics, especially for church use. Sir John Sutton wrote in 1847: 'The reason why these beautiful instruments [i.e. Smith's and Harris's] are so often destroyed is, that the Clergy and those in authority are persuaded by their organists that the instruments in question are not fit to play upon; by which they mean that it is impossible to show off upon them in the most approved fashion, for they have neither pedals, swell, or any of those complicated contrivances with which these modern *Music Mills* are crowded. Every lover of true Cathedral Music must have experienced how much these modern alterations and additions to the Organ, mar the effect of that most devotional manner of performing the Church Service. In the chanting of the Psalms, the attention is continually drawn from the voices by the perpetual changing of stops and clattering of composition pedals, for the modern Cathedral Organist scarcely ever accompanies six verses on the same stops, or even on the same row of keys, and keeps up a perpetual thundering with the pedals throughout the Psalms, when perhaps the choir he is accompanying, consists of ten little boys, and six or at most eight men, three or four of whom are either disabled by old age, or a long continued habit of drunkenness. The effect of Pedals in Fugue playing is truly magnificent; but in English Organs the pedals are very inferior to those in Germany, as they consist in this country of only one set of pipes, either a very large open or stop diapason and seem to require some connecting link between the Organ and the Pedals. In Germany, there is a chorus upon the pedals as well as upon the manual, which seems to have the desired effect. But as Fugue Playing is not the Chief object in an English Cathedral and the consequence of pedals, and *Pedal pipes most especially*, having been so mischievous, it is much to be desired that they should be removed from Cathedral Organs, certainly from the one that accompanies the Choir, for why should there not be two, as is commonly the case in France and Germany; and then the *Music Mill* even might have a fine effect, coming from a distant part of the Church, and used only upon extraordinary occasions.'—Sir John might almost have been quoting in places from Renatus Harris's St. Paul's project. But his words, sound in so many ways and applicable even today, went unheeded.

1851–1900. Willis, Schulze,
Hope Jones

The next important event in the development of the British organ was the Great Exhibition of 1851. Organs were exhibited by most of the leading makers, though Hill evidently felt his own position so secure as to call only for a somewhat perfunctory instrument. The important results were in introducing the work of the German builder Edmund Schulze and of Aristide Cavaillé-Coll to the British musical public and,

97

most important of all, in establishing firmly the reputation of Henry Willis.

The impact of Cavaillé-Coll was not great. He obtained several commissions, mostly for town halls in the north of England, of which Manchester was the most important. But his extremely brassy reeds call for resonant buildings and do not sound well in the dead acoustics of most town halls; and any way, they are not generally acceptable to British ears. The lasting effect of Schulze's work was much greater and it is significant that most of his English work has survived practically without alteration, namely St. Bartholomew's, Armley, St. Peter's, Hindley, and St. Mary's, Tyne Dock. Even his largest instrument at Doncaster Parish Church has not been greatly altered. Curiously enough, his 1851 Exhibition organ, which went to Northampton Town Hall, has since disappeared, mysteriously, but completely. Schulze's work was remarkable for several things. Despite the unkind things that have been said about his reed stops by several authorities, they are extremely fine examples of light-pressure voicing. His flutes are beautiful and his pedal string-toned stops, using wooden pipes, are of a beauty, attack and definition that has never been surpassed nor even, perhaps, equalled. But most outstanding were his diapasons which English taste enabled him to develop in a way which probably would not have found acceptance in his own country. His art lay in producing the maximum effect from light wind-pressures, which he achieved by wind-chests of generous proportions and exceptionally large foot-holes to the pipes. In the latter he was, of course, only reverting to sixteenth- and early seventeenth-century German practice and as exemplified in his Exhibition organ, which was voiced on only $2\frac{1}{2}$ in. of wind, the effect was probably excellent. It certainly made a great impression upon most of those who heard it. This pressure is, in fact, the greatest upon which 'open-foot voicing' can be used with artistic effect. On higher pressures a loss of quality is almost unavoidable, and Schulze used progressively higher pressures for his great organs culminating in $3\frac{3}{4}$ in. at Tyne Dock. Despite adjustments in scaling the result was an increasing coarseness in tone quality and a sluggishness in attack, while the great power of the basses could no longer be matched by the trebles. When carried up to mixtures in ranks of equal power, as in the celebrated five-rank mixture at Armley, the effect can only be described as devastating. This stop, whose composition is as follows,

CC.   15. 19. 22. 26. 29.
T.C.   8. 12. 15. 19. 22.
c.   1. 5. 8. 12. 15.

provides a climax to the full organ as crashing in effect as any tuba. It is quite useless as part of a diapason chorus.

Schulze showed how to produce diapason tone of ample harmonic development, which would make itself felt in even the largest building, and chorus work which would match it. In such conditions it may even be musically acceptable, although nothing can compensate for the sluggish attack. Unfortunately, it gave the British a taste for powerful diapasons which was to bedevil practically all British work for the next hundred years. Schulze himself was well aware of the artistic hazards, and when discussing the Armley organ he wrote: 'As to the great of your organ, to make the tone more delicate and more silvery I suggest instead of $3\frac{3}{4}$ inch wind only $3\frac{1}{4}$ inch. In tone, this will mean little loss of power and a gain in beauty'. However, although the Armley church is much larger than the Kennedys' music-room in which it was originally installed, 'silvery' is about the last epithet that could truthfully be applied to the instrument.

Schulze died in 1879 but several British builders followed upon the lines he had established, notably T. C. Lewis, who built a number of important instruments, culminating in Southwark Cathedral in 1896. Like Schulze, he was entirely opposed to the voicing of chorus reeds upon a pressure higher than the fluework, and the whole of the Southwark instrument was on $3\frac{1}{2}$ in. wind, except for two reeds in the solo organ, upon 12 in. The pressure of the pedal reeds has subsequently been greatly enhanced; in the opinion of some judges, not at all to their advantage.

Henry Willis must have staked a great deal on the 1851 Exhibition, for he showed there an instrument of three manuals and no less than 70 speaking stops. For a young man of only 30, whose only important commission had been the rebuilding of the Gloucester Cathedral organ in 1847, this must have stretched his financial resources to the limit. The specification was a curious one, archaic in many ways, very advanced in others. It was wasteful and contained many stops which could have been dispensed with; yet there was no 16 ft. reed in the 22 stop swell. But it had Barker pneumatic lever action to great and swell, and, for the first time in organ history, thumb pistons between the manuals. Willis remarked that: 'Altogether it is presumed by the builder to be the first successful large organ constructed in England.'

Of the excellence of the instrument there can be no doubt. As a direct result of it, Willis was commissioned to build a new organ of 100 speaking stops for St. George's Hall, Liverpool, while the Exhibition organ went in reduced, but improved, form to Winchester Cathedral.

The modern British concave and radiating pedal board also arose from the Exhibition. S. S. Wesley remarked to Willis that Schulze's organ had a concave pedal board, adding that it was a pity he had not also made them radiating—as had in fact been done by Hill at York Minster in 1831. Willis responded by producing the 'Wesley-Willis' concave and radiating board which is the standard used today with only minor deviations. This arrangement is now used in Italy, but seldom or never in France, Holland, Germany or Scandinavia, where the flat and parallel board is still preferred, as it was by W. T. Best, who described the Wesley-Willis board as 'a clumsy apparatus which makes a pedal-board resemble the bottom of a sailing boat'.

The instrument which Willis built for St. George's Hall, Liverpool, can be described without question as the first modern organ. Each of the great, swell, choir and pedal departments had its complete diapason chorus from 16 ft. to mixtures (five of them on the great) and very complete reed choruses. The solo organ, by contrast, had only five flue stops against ten reeds. The console, too, was completely modern with its inclined stop-jambs, thumb pistons, including general pistons, concave and radiating pedal board, pneumatic lever action to each department, and the couplers, and also to the operation of the swell pedal. The heavy-pressure wind was supplied by a steam engine. The only archaic features were included at the instigation of Wesley who insisted upon G compass for the manuals, and unequal temperament tuning, which was retained until 1867.

At the end of the long description of the organ in the first (1855) edition of Hopkins & Rimbault's classic work *The Organ, its History & Construction*, Hopkins could write with justice: 'To the combined exertions of Dr. Wesley and Mr. Willis, the Town Council and the inhabitants are indebted for an unrivalled instrument; and while the opulence of the Corporation has justified such a large expenditure (£10,000), the result is both satisfactory and creditable to the gentlemen who have conducted its erection.'

In 1867 the pressure of the four big solo organ reeds (two 8 ft. and two 4 ft.) was raised to $17\frac{1}{2}$ in. in the bass and $22\frac{1}{2}$ in. in the treble; and their effect was entirely unique in their scorching brilliance. The character of the whole organ suffered from the decision to alter them during the last 30 years.

Willis subsequently built several more town hall organs, including the splendid instruments in the Alexandra Palace and the Albert Hall, of which the former is not now playable and the latter was entirely transformed in an unfortunate manner in the early 1920s. But none of these ever equalled the unmatched beauty of the Liverpool instrument. One of the most remarkable was the quite small three-manual organ built in 1877 for the Sheldonian Theatre, Oxford, to the design of Sir Frederick Gore Ouseley. There, the choir organ was entirely abandoned in favour of a solo organ, including a tuba. Willis did this again in his organ for the Inventions Exhibition of 1885.

Willis's work gradually altered during his long life, partly, no doubt, in accordance with changing public taste, but there is little reason to believe that he was opposed to this change. On the one hand, he provided less mixture-work; and what remained was more restrained in treatment; and on the other he abandoned his differentiated wind-pressures between bass and treble, and seldom used any pressures but $3\frac{1}{2}$, 7 and 15 in. The first was for soft and solo reeds; the 7 in. pressure was for all chorus reeds; and the heavy pressure was for the tuba. Willis was able to use 7 in. pressure throughout by virtue of the loading of the reed tongues developed by his brother George (this is generally regarded as their invention, but in fact loading of the tongues is described by Mersenne in his *Harmonie Universelle*, published in 1635, where he says that 'the sound of the reeds is thereby softer and more agreeable'). Undoubtedly, however, Willis lost something by this uniform pressure, since the basses are noticeably deficient in attack, especially when compared with his tubas. But what Willis would never do was to force the power of his diapasons, or to employ exaggerated sonorities, and it is this quality which makes his organs so eminently versatile and musical, even though the later instruments may be less exciting than his earlier work. A defect of Willis's organs for playing eighteenth-century music is that the swell diapason chorus is invariably very much softer than that on the great, so that it is impossible to obtain the kind of balance that is essential for playing the music of Bach and his predecessors; but apart from this the flexibility of Father Willis's organs is always their outstanding quality.

In addition to his large cathedral organs he built some excellent small ones of which the 1881 'organ on wheels' at St. Paul's Cathedral must be accounted one of the most outstanding small organs of all time, for its effect is such that it is often mistaken for the large Willis. Its specification is as follows:

Great		Swell		Pedal	
Open diapason	8	Open diapason	8	Bourdon	16
Lieblich gedackt	8	Gemshorn	4		
Principal	4	Cornopean	8		
Fifteenth	2				

Willis's workmanship was without rival, and even when he installed one of the first large-scale electric actions, at Canterbury Cathedral, in 1886, it worked satisfactorily for 53 years until the organ was next rebuilt.

Although some of what he did led to the deterioration of British organ design when others tried to follow his lead and, worse still, improve upon it, in his own hands his technique was always perfectly safe and it can be said that he never produced an organ which was not a master-piece.

It was at the suggestion of F. G. Edwards, editor of the *Musical Times*, that he was called 'Father' Willis in his own lifetime, as Father Howe and Father Smith had been before him. He died on February 11th, 1901, at just short of 80, and was working until within a few hours of his death.

The work of Father Willis is in a class by itself, and it was exactly suited to the taste of his time, so that his advancement was largely at the expense of Hill's (William Hill died in 1870 at the age of 81 and was succeeded by his son Thomas, who died in 1893, he being succeeded in turn by his son Arthur George, who died in 1923). Nevertheless, with the present return to classical trends in organ building, William Hill would be more in sympathy with modern thought than would Henry Willis, and it is likely that in time his work will be thought of greater importance. Nevertheless, any organ by Willis is a work of art which should be jealously preserved and not altered.

Before turning to consider the work of Walkers, Michell & Thynne, Casson and, finally, Hope-Jones towards the end of the century, it is appropriate to examine the opinions of W. T. Best, who was the out-standing British organist of the century and the prototype of all sub-sequent concert virtuosi. He made and played many arrangements of orchestral works, which in 1892 Walter Parratt described as 'examples of misapplied skill'; but it must be remembered that he did this at a time when there were few provincial orchestras, and he thus brought good music to a public who could not hope to hear it in any other form. His packed weekly recital at St. George's Hall, Liverpool, showed that he supplied a need and there can be little doubt that he did much to improve musical taste in Liverpool. His views on tonal design are both sound and interesting and they show how clearly he discriminated between the needs of a church and a concert organ, while recognising the basic requirements of any organ, which must be common to both.

Firstly, here is his specification for the organ at Wallasey parish church, where he was organist, and which Willis built in 1861. It had 26 speaking stops.

Great 13 stops		Swell 9 stops		Pedal 4 stops	
Double diapason	16	Open diapason	8	Open diapason	16
Open diapason	8	Stopped diapason	8	Bourdon	16
Flute (open to middle C)	8	Principal	4	Trombone	16
		Harmonic flute	4	Bassoon	8
Gamba	8	Mixture	III		
Dulciana	8	Contra fagotto	16		
Principal	4	Trumpet	8		
Harmonic flute	4	Oboe	8		
Twelfth	$2\frac{2}{3}$	Vox humana	8		
Fifteenth	2				
Mixture	IV				
Trumpet	8				
Clarion	4				
Clarinet	8				

The scheme is remarkable for its economy of material, but most of all for the swell organ. It has been seen that Hill was putting a 16 ft. reed in the swell before the great, but never before a flue double on the swell itself, or before a clarion. At Wallasey Best did both, showing he appreciated the importance of full swell in a church organ, and the importance of a 16 ft. reed in the full swell effect.

He reasoned in quite a different way when designing a concert organ, such as at Bolton Town Hall, which Gray & Davison built to his design in 1874. The specification is specially interesting because Best's 'explanatory memorandum' has survived.

The organ had four manuals and 48 speaking stops.

Choir (lowest keyboard) 8 stops		Great (second keyboard) 11 stops		Solo (third keyboard) 7 stops	
Bourdon	16	Double open diapason	16	Concert open diapason	8
Violin diapason	8	Open diapason	8	Flute harmonique	8
Vox angelica	8	Viola	8	Flute octaviante harmonique	4
Lieblich gedackt	8	Claribel flute	8	Cor anglais	8
Flauto traverso	4	Principal	4	Clarinet & bassoon	8
Piccolo	2	Flute octaviante	4	Tuba mirabilis	8
Echo dulciana cornet	V	Quint mixture	II	Carillon (bells)	
Trumpet	8	Great mixture	V	Octave	
		Double trombone	16	Suboctave	
		Harmonic trumpet	8		
		Clarion	4		

Swell (fourth key-board) 14 stops				Pedal 8 stops	
Lieblich bourdon	16	Vox humana	8	Double open	
Open diapason	8	Corno di bassetto	8	diapason	32
Viol da gamba	8	Hautbois	8	Contra bass	16
Voix célestes	8	Trumpet	8	Bourdon	16
Lieblich gedackt	8	Clarion	4	Violon	16
Salicet	4	Suboctave		Clarabella bass	8
Nazard	$2\frac{2}{3}$	Octave		Violoncello	8
Flautino	2	Tremulant		Trombone	16
Mixture	III			Trumpet	8

Best said that stop-control should be by means of pedal-operated ventils 'instead of effecting the necessary changes of tone by means of composition pedals or other appliances which thrust the stop handles backwards and forwards with a clattering noise, as well as cause much fatigue to the player'. Interdepartmental coupling was also to be effected by pedals.

The following remarks were made concerning the stops in the various departments:

Pedal. The clarabella bass 'furnishes a soft octave tone to the 16 ft. stop and thus supplies organists with what they often complain of not being able to get, even on large instruments—a soft 16 ft. and 8 ft. pedal bass uncoupled'.

Choir. 'The Echo dulciana cornet is a very small scale mixture not often introduced even in large instruments. The idea of its inclusion in the choir division is to make the full choir a kind of Echo great organ. For the same reason a trumpet is specified.'

Great. The stops were 'selected so as to secure the greatest fulness and richness of tone'.

Solo (note its position on the third keyboard, usually occupied by the swell).

Swell. 'Perhaps the first point that will strike a reader who is initiated into the mysteries of organ stops will be the fact that here are five reeds and yet not one of 16 ft. It is the custom to put a double reed into the swell in preference to the great organ, but for concert purposes the plan pursued in the present instrument is obviously better.'

Best thus showed that he realised what so few have done since his time —that a 16 ft. swell effect is a vital part of a church organ, but it is of very little use in a concert instrument. The design as a whole, like Wallasey, is a triumph of economy, and shows that despite his orchestral arrangements, Best had a very lively conception of what a classical organ should contain. The presence of a nazard is particularly interesting.

Best had a very long career as a concert organist, pre-eminently the greatest of his day. He was appointed to the Panopticon of Science & Art in Leicester Square, London, in 1854, and he retired from St. George's Hall, Liverpool, in 1894.

Schulze & Lewis could see no more merit in the work of Willis than could he in theirs, and it was left for the new, illustrious, but short-lived firm of Michell & Thynne to bring the opposing ideals together in one organ. This they did in the instrument they showed at the Inventions Exhibition in 1885. In the following year it was shown at the Liverpool Exhibition after which it was acquired by a Mr. Grove who presented it to Tewkesbury Abbey where it stands, uncased, in the north transept and has always been known as the 'Grove organ'. Its specification is another triumph of economy. There are four manuals and 35 speaking stops as follows:

Great 10 stops		Swell 9 stops		Choir 7 stops		Solo 4 stops	
Violon	16	Open diapason	8	Spitz flöte	8	Harmonic	
Great open		Flauto traverso	8	Viole sourdine	8	flute	8
diapason	8	Viole de gambe	8	Gedackt, wood	8	Violin cello	8
Small open		Voix célestes	8	Gemshorn	4	Voix humaine	8
diapason	8	Geigen	4	Zauberflöte	4	Tuba	8
Claribel, wood	8	Mixture	III	Flautina	2	Tremulant	
Octave	4	Contra		Clarinet	8		
Flûte		posaune	16	Octave		Pedal 5 stops	
octaviante	4	Horn	8			Harmonic	
Quint mixture II		Oboe	8			bass	32
Great mix-		Octave				Great bass,	
ture	IV	Tremulant				wood	16
Trombone	16					Dolce, wood	16
Trumpet	8					Great flute,	
						wood	8
						Bombarde	16

Like Schulze's and Lewis's mixtures, these contain no tierces. The resonant acoustics of Tewkesbury Abbey are well able to accommodate the bold, Schulze-type diapason chorus and this, coupled with the Willis-type reeds produced an effect of great splendour which must be memorable to those who are so fortunate as to have heard it, since the organ has been almost unplayable for 10 years, at the time of writing this book, and there seems no immediate likelihood of its being put into order. Not only did this organ bring together the schools of Schulze and Willis for the first time, but in addition it incorporated the builders' own entirely new conception of organ string-tone, never surpassed, and very fine flutes. It may thus be regarded as the first fully developed English romantic organ and one which has seldom if ever been surpassed in that capacity. As such it is an instrument of the greatest artistic and historic importance.

Walkers developed along different lines. They sought a massive unison diapason, of nevertheless considerable harmonic development. This they achieved by enormous scales and the then fairly high pressure of about $4\frac{1}{2}$ in. This was their number one open diapason, the chorus being related to the second open, of more normal treatment. The large open could therefore be regarded as a special effect which did not have to be drawn with the chorus. For chorus reeds they used a moderate pressure of about $5\frac{1}{2}$ in., obtaining a brilliant and powerful quality of tone, of excellent attack, but falling off appreciably in the trebles. These stops serve equally well as chorus reeds or as solo stops in the French eighteenth-century style, and they have seldom if ever been surpassed. However, Walkers did not try to carry their reed choruses up to 4 ft. pitch, and instead of a clarion they used a brilliant compound stop called 'clarion mixture', which was treated similarly to the ordinary chorus mixture, but was higher pitched. The clarion mixture may thus effectively be drawn with the diapason chorus, which then takes on a degree of brilliance and dramatic quality approaching the German seventeenth-eighteenth-century school, and certainly unrivalled in England. The famous 1891 Walker at Holy Trinity, Sloane Street, London, has been substantially remodelled, suppressing the clarion mixtures, but a superb specimen, in original condition, survives at St. Mary's, Portsea. A later, rather more normal development of the same theme is at St. Margaret's, Westminster, built to the design of Lemare in 1897. This organ is still in its original state, unlike Holy Trinity, Sloane Street.

Finally, as a sort of *fin-de-siècle éminence grise*, came Robert Hope Jones; an electrical engineer by trade who unfortunately strayed into organ building, to which he first applied an electric action of more ingenuity than reliability and then a tonal system of tasteless vulgarity.

He took the heavy pressure reeds of Willis and developed them in two excessive directions; double-harmonic trombas of egregious scale for the great, more resembling fog-horns, and exiguously narrow trumpets, more like very loud orchestral oboes, for the swell. He took Walker's large-scale, heavy-pressure diapason, covered the upper lips with leather to cut out all brightness of tone, doubled the wind-pressure and called it a 'diapason phonon'. He took Thynne's strings and reduced them in scale to the proportion of stair-rods (an 8 ft. viole d'orchestre pipe scaled only

$1\frac{1}{16}$ in.). He took clarabellas and vastly increased their scale and wind-pressures and called the result 'tibia plena' or (if stopped) 'tibia clausa'. Finally, for the pedals he developed a device which he called a diaphone, in which reeds were replaced by a vibrating diaphragm which could produce a huge output of foundational tone. His organs contained no upperwork above a 2 ft. piccolo so that considerations of chorus or blend did not arise to hamper the development of these unsociable sonorities.

Whatever merits the thing might have been considered to possess, the fact remained that it was incapable of playing any music ever written for the organ, and no one ever wrote any music for it. The only exception is Elgar's organ sonata which is perhaps hardly a sufficient excuse by itself.

Hope Jones managed to sell one to Worcester Cathedral in 1896, but even this did not convince the generality of musicians that he had produced a musical instrument. In 1903 he removed to America, where he had such considerable success that it took 40 years for American organ building to recover from him. In 1914 he committed suicide.

1900-40. Arthur Harrison

If it took British organ-building 55 years to sink from William Hill's masterpiece at the George Street Chapel in Liverpool to the banality of Hope Jones at Worcester Cathedral, it took at least as long to regain a level where the British organ could claim to be on level terms once more with Continental progress. Yet even when at its nadir, Hills & Lewis could produce their greatest triumphs in pure classical style. Hills completed their *magnum opus* at Sydney Town Hall, Australia, in 1890. With five manuals, 127 speaking stops and a full-length 64 ft. reed it was in the pure classical tradition of William Hill. The great has four and the pedal three mixtures and the choruses throughout the instrument are as generously proportioned. The only stops it lacks are a proper variety of solo mutations. Even after 70 years the mechanism is still functioning, although at last becoming temperamental. The tonal effect is described by all who have heard or played it as magnificent. Then, in 1896, came Lewis's *magnum opus* at Southwark Cathedral, with fully developed light pressure choruses on great and swell and, to an extent, choir. Only the pedal organ was lacking in definition and upperwork.

Although Hope Jones had only a moderate success on this side of the Atlantic, his influence was considerable. For the first half of the century very few new British organs were to possess adequate choruses, and irreparable harm was done to innumerable ancient masterpieces. But for two men, Lt.-Col. George Dixon, T.D., and Arthur Harrison, the picture would undoubtedly have been a lot worse than it was. To some extent, they may be said to have taken the place of Henry John Gauntlett, and William Hill 60 years earlier.

The Durham firm of Harrison & Harrison was founded in 1861 and throve in a small way of business until the reins were taken over by Arthur Harrison. In 1904 he secured the contract to build a large, substantially new organ for the church of St. Nicholas, Whitehaven, followed in 1908 by Ely Cathedral, which set the standard for cathedral organ design for the next 30 years.

It is difficult to distinguish between Harrison's own tonal ideas and those of Col. Dixon, although there is no doubt that Dixon influenced and helped Harrison to a substantial extent. But as to the quality of Harrison's workmanship, voicing and fine regulation, there can be no doubt; in these he was the true follower of Father Willis and with them, like Willis, he swept all before him.

As might be expected of his generation, Harrison explicitly regarded the organ as an entirely 'romantic' instrument. To this outlook may be attributed the shortcomings of his organs as general-purpose instruments, but he never forgot the classical basis which every organ must have to be worthy of the name. Accordingly, every organ with over 30 speaking stops had a mixture on each of great and swell. Like Willis, he made the swell flue chorus much softer than that of the great, but he tried to advance from Willis by introducing a greater measure of tonal contrast between the two departments. Thus, the great upperwork contained the full harmonic series of 8 ft., including the seventeenth and flat twenty-first (12.15.17.19.♭21.22). The mixture (containing the last four) he in fact called 'harmonics' and usually carried it up for three and a half octaves without a break. The twenty-first, even more than the seventeenth, produces an acid, reedy effect and this was enhanced by the bright, almost 'edgy' tone of the individual ranks. Therefore, while Harrison's greats undoubtedly possessed a chorus and considerable brightness it must be confessed that the general effect was not particularly felicitous. The chorus was based upon the second open, the first being a powerful stop with leathered lips, although considerably less unsociable than those of Hope Jones. The important consideration was that they formed no integral part of the great chorus. For the great reeds Harrison used fairly smooth-toned, heavy pressure trombas to contrast with thin-toned trumpets on the swell. In three-manual organs he voiced the trombas as semi-tubas and made them also separately available on the lowest key-board, by means of a transfer coupler. In very large organs he introduced a second great mixture composed entirely of quints and unisons. This was first done at Ely, where Col. Dixon suggested that a mixture some-what on the lines of the Schulze stop at Armley (but with less crudely arranged breaks) would be a desirable addition. When a Harrison great contained one of these mixtures a very splendid and classical chorus was available, by omitting the No. 1 diapason and the harmonics. Considering the date, 1908, the Ely Cathedral great was a remarkable conception:

Sub-bordun	32	Octave	4
Gross geigen	16	Geigen principal	4
Contra clarabella	16	Wald flöte	4
Open diapason I	8	Octave quint	$2\frac{2}{3}$
Open diapason II	8	Superoctave	2
Open diapason III	8	Harmonics 10.17.19.21.22. V	
Geigen	8	Mixture 15.19.22.26.29 V	
Hohl flöte	8	Trombone	16
Quint	$5\frac{1}{3}$	Tromba	8
		Octave tromba	4

Harrison's swell was conventional, capped by a family of heavy-pressure trumpets of thin but refined tone, in which the attack inevitably suffered. The diapason chorus had a nice, silvery quality, but it was too soft for much except accompanimental use.

The choir organ in a four-manual organ he regarded as a miniature great, topped by a soft mixture. These departments had some accompani-mental uses, but if they were omitted from any of his organs it is doubtful if anyone but the player would have been any the wiser.

Harrison's solo organs were an advance upon what had gone before, although not an advance of a kind which is any longer regarded with favour. Instead of being a collection of unrelated voices, he sought to give it a cohesion by building it up with a family of strings, harmonic flutes and orchestral reeds. It was in fact an orchestral more than merely a solo

Contra viola	16	Clarinet	16
Viole d'orchestre	8	Orchestral hautboy	8
Viole céleste	8	Tremulant	
Viole octaviante	4	Tuba	8
Cornet de violes 10.12.15 III			
Harmonic flute	8		
Concert flute	4		
Piccolo	2		

department. Unlike most nineteenth-century solo departments it was always enclosed, except for the tuba. The Harrison solo organ emerged, already fully fledged, at Ely (p. 109).

Harrison was at his worst in the pedal organ. He relied upon a heavily blown open wood foundation of prodigiously booming tone, and a very powerful, smooth-toned, heavy pressure reed. These two stood apart from anything that might be drawn on the manuals and tended to obliterate entirely the lower manual voices. Where there was a pedal mixture, as often as not there was no metal diapason structure, so that it could only be drawn with the reeds; and thus served no very obvious musical purpose. He freely used extension, and the borrowing of manual doubles, in his pedal organs.

In three-manual organs Harrison usually treated the lowest manual in the Ouseley tradition, sometimes adding one or two accompanimental stops. He built a great many instruments of this kind, of 30 speaking stops and upwards. That in the Repton School Chapel, dating from 1930 containing 34 speaking stops, is typical:

Great 12 stops		Swell 10 stops		Choir 5 stops (enclosed)	
Double geigen	16	Violin diapason	8	Viole d'orchestre	8
Open diapason, large	8	Lieblich gedackt	8	Harmonic flute	8
		Echo gamba	8	Concert flute	4
Open diapason, small	8	Voix célestes	8	Orchestral bassoon	16
Hohl flöte	8	Gemshorn	4	Clarinet	8
Stopped diapason	8	Mixture		Tremulant	
Octave	4	15.19.22.	III		
Principal	4	Oboe	8	**Pedal 7 stops**	
Octave quint	2⅔	Tremulant		Open wood	16
Superoctave	2	Double trumpet	16	Subbass	16
Harmonics		Trumpet	8	Geigen (from	
17.19.21.22.	IV	Clarion	4	Great)	16
Tromba	8			Octave ⎫	
Octave tromba	4			wood ⎬ extended	8
Transfer coupler				Flute ⎭	8
Great reeds on				Trumpet (from	
Choir				Swell)	16
				Ophicleide	16

The basic soundness of Harrison's idea is clear from this specification. It failed because of the almost complete lack of balances available between the manuals, and the over-emphasis of contrast between them.

Arthur Harrison died in 1936 while working on the new Westminster

Abbey organ, first used in an incomplete state at the Coronation of King George VI. If his work is now seen to have certain artistic shortcomings, it must be judged against the background of the very poor taste prevalent when it was conceived. But what was commendably advanced at White-haven in 1904 or Ely in 1908, was badly out of date in 1936; for Arthur Harrison never advanced.

George Dixon was another north-countryman. He was born in 1870, lived, and died in 1950, in the remote Cumberland town of St. Bees. There, as a young man, he got to know Father Willis, who built one of his last organs in the Priory Church. At Cambridge he developed very clear ideas of what form the organ should take, and being a man of comfortably independent means and with a wide acquaintance in church and collegiate circles, he soon achieved a position of remarkable influence over British organ building. He saw in Arthur Harrison an artist both sympathetic to his ideals and very well able to put them into effect. As he was in most ways a very modest person, and Harrison a reticent one, it is difficult to determine quite where the ideas of the one ended and the other began; perhaps it is not even very important.

Dixon himself claimed to have been greatly influenced by Thomas Casson who was born in 1842 and died in 1910. Casson was a banker, but fairly early in life he was able to devote most of his time to organ building. In this, he was not particularly successful, but several of his ideas were sounder than his execution and advanced for their date. He advocated the use of extension on the pedal organ, and borrowing manual doubles on to the pedals. He was also in favour of having a section of the pedal organ under expression. None of these is now considered to be sound practice but they must have seemed sensible enough to Dixon and Harrison, seeking to hammer out a new sort of classical-romantic organ at the beginning of the century, to replace the excesses of Hope Jones. Casson also used the full harmonic series, including the flat 21st, and he even anticipated manual extension to an extent, obtaining a choir organ by octave duplication of selected stops on the great; and an echo by octave duplication from the swell. This questionable device was never taken up either by Dixon or Harrison. In console design he advocated the grouping of interdepartmental couplers with the speaking stops of the departments they affected. This convenient practice was carried out both by Father Willis and Arthur Harrison, and others after them.

Col. Dixon has been criticised for considering the choir organ as a miniature great and in his early days he certainly did so. But later he increasingly saw the importance of having a second manual chorus of comparable power to the great, but clearer and brighter in tone. This is apparent in his later writings and in the divided great organ in the last important instrument he designed, for Norwich Cathedral. To celebrate his 72nd birthday, in 1942, he sent to Cecil Clutton a scheme for a cathedral organ of three manuals, which would be advanced, even today. The great had two mixtures (one, needless to say, a 'harmonics'), only one unison diapason and no reeds. The choir was to be a boldly voiced unenclosed department with solo mutations, a high-pitched mixture and small chorus reeds. There was no fourth manual but the swell consisted of the conventional chorus of reeds and mixtures, together with a family of solo flutes, and wide-scale strings. The pedal organ was fully independent. For only 54 speaking stops, plus six entirely borrowed from manuals to pedals, bringing the total up to 60, it is a truly remarkable scheme, especially considering its date.

Dixon's shortcomings, as we can now see them, lay in his devotion to the open wood as the flue foundation of the pedal organ, and an absolute refusal to see the least merit in any reed voiced on light pressure (by which he meant less than $4\frac{1}{2}$ in.).

Taken all in all there is no doubt that Col. Dixon exerted a powerful influence for the good of British organ-building throughout the first half of this century.

However, not all the successes could be claimed by the powerful Dixon-Harrison team. Henry Willis III built two heroic organs in the early 'twenties, for Liverpool Cathedral and the Roman Catholic Cathedral at Westminster. These large resonant buildings suit his forthright voicing, in which some saw a welcome change from the extreme refinement of Harrison's work. In 1926 he also built (with some old material) an outstanding instrument for the Jesuit Church in Farm Street, London, in conjunction with Guy Weitz, the eminent organist there. This organ showed the way to an improved classical taste and it was not surpassed for 20 years at least.

Messrs. Walker also built some conservatively sound instruments, benefiting from the superb reed voicing of W. C. Jones, a great artist directly in line from the Willis tradition, who had also worked for Arthur Harrison.

John Compton pursued a line of his own, in the form of the extension organ. 'Extension' is a form of selective coupling. By planting a rank of, for example, 73 flute pipes on a sliderless chest it can be used independently as an 8 ft. or as a 4 ft. stop; and the principle can be extended further to take also a 16 and a 2 ft. stop and even (at slight expense of

1 *Fifteenth-century positive organ: Hugo van der Goes triptych,*
Holyrood House, 1476
Reproduced by gracious permission of Her Majesty The Queen

2 *St. Stephen, Old Radnor: case c. 1500, restored 1872*

accurate tuning) a $2\frac{2}{3}$ ft. The same rank can also be used on two or more different manuals. All this means a considerable saving of space and produces an impressive array of stops at the console, relative to the financial outlay; although in fact the cost of an extension organ, per pipe, is very much higher than that of a 'straight' organ. Compton was an undoubted artist, and produced some fine instruments, of which that at Holy Trinity Church, Hull, is perhaps the best. He enjoyed considerable success in the 'twenties and 'thirties, but it is now seen that the extension system is incapable of producing a really good artistic effect and that its economies are doubtful. Extension is now rarely used except for very small organs, of two or three units, which may be useful in very small churches where space is the prime consideration. One of these, produced as a standard instrument by Messrs. Mander, is illustrated in fig. 110. It may also be had in slightly enlarged form with two manuals and pedals; but for anything larger the clear advantage is with a straight instrument.

Such was the state of British organ-building up to the outbreak of war in 1939 and also in the early post-war years; but in 1939 one instrument already pointed towards what was to come 20 years later. In about 1937 the church of All Hallows, Lombard Street, became unsafe and a new church was built, called All Hallows, Twickenham, to house the Grinling Gibbons furniture and the Renatus Harris organ and case from Lombard Street. At a time when electric or pneumatic action and high pressure reeds were regarded as the *sine qua non* of every organ, this one was rebuilt by Messrs. Kingsgate Davidson & Co., to the design of Cecil Clutton, with tracker action, all on 3 in. wind. With only 26 speaking stops, plus three borrowed, it comprised two complete flue choruses of balanced power; a solo sesquialtera; a 16 ft. swell reed and a pedal 16 ft. reed and the essential 'romantic' voices under expression. At the time the organ was much criticised, but in the 1960s there is a marked return to tracker action, which has once more been recognised by nearly all the leading players as being essential for playing of the most sensitive kind.

The Post-War Revival

As has been related in Chapter I, a return to the principles of classical design had started on the Continent from about 1925 and from 1930 was firmly established. In England the movement caught on much more slowly, but the early post-war years saw some tentative, not very successful beginnings. The movement really took root only with the opening of the organ in the Royal Festival Hall, London, in 1954.

The organ was designed in meticulous detail by Ralph Downes and built by Messrs. Harrison & Harrison, who since 1945 have been under the management of Cuthbert Harrison, a nephew of Arthur Harrison and a grandson of the founder of the firm. Most of the reeds in the instrument were made and voiced in co-operation with the French builder, Louis Eugène-Rochesson. It must be confessed that it manifests certain short-comings for which it would not be fair to blame the British builders. As foreseen by many competent judges, the grafting of French reeds on to an Anglo-German chorus was not entirely successful. The specification of over 100 speaking stops is somewhat repetitive, and five complete manual diapason choruses seems wasteful in a concert instrument. There is, in effect, no string tone (being considered by Mr. Downes as inappropriate to an organ) with the result that it is not effective for a good deal of valid romantic organ music. Also, the scaling does not seem well suited to the non-resonant acoustics of the hall, which are, indeed, calculated to show up any organ in the worst possible light.

But despite all these defects the organ remains a grand concept, finely executed by the British builders and a tribute to those in authority who had the faith to go on backing it in the face of fierce criticism from the highest, but misinformed, musical circles. They have been rewarded by the remarkable success of the organ as a concert instrument, regularly performing to paying audiences of over 1,000. It has, moreover, introduced the organ as a musical instrument to a wide musical public who had not previously regarded it as such.

The effect of all this took about four years to make itself felt, since when it can be said without exaggeration that British organ building has taken a sudden and entirely new turn. Among the most eminent builders, the lead has been taken by Messrs. Harrison & Harrison, Messrs. J. W. Walker & Sons and Messrs. William Hill & Son and Norman & Beard. A fairly typical modern British specification is that of the Walker organ in the Italian Church in Hatton Garden, London, completed in 1959. It contains many older pipes but is in effect a new and extremely effective organ. It contains three manuals and 45 speaking stops. The manual stops are voiced on $2\frac{3}{4}$ in. wind and the pedal stops on $2\frac{7}{8}$ in. wind.

So far as the great, swell and pedal are concerned, the organ bears a remarkable likeness to many Hill specifications of 110 years earlier. The choir, however, is a notable advance upon anything done in the nineteenth century, conforming more closely to the eighteenth-century German model. It is loud enough to stand up to the great chorus and has nothing of the 'miniature great' about it. The organ is deficient in tierces

Great 10 stops		Swell 12 stops		Pedal 14 stops (plus 1 borrowed)	
Quintatön	16	Open diapason	8	Double open	
Principal	8	Gedeckt	8	diapason	32
Rohr flute	8	Viola	8	Open diapason	16
Octave	4	Céleste T.C.	8	Violone	16
Flute octave	4	Gemshorn	4	Subbass	16
Quint	$2\frac{2}{3}$	Melophone	4	Principal	8
Superoctave	2	Nazard	$2\frac{2}{3}$	Violoncello	8
Tertian 19.24.	II	Fifteenth	2	Bass flute	8
Mixture		Scharf		Twelfth	$5\frac{1}{3}$
19.22.26.29.	IV	22.26.29.33.	IV	Fifteenth	4
Trumpet	8	Bassoon ⎱ unit	16	Rohr flute	4
		Hautboy ⎰	8	Mixture	
Choir 9 stops (unenclosed)		Trumpet	8	19.22.26.29.	IV
		Tremulant		Bassoon (Swell)	16
Bourdon	8			Trombone	16
Fugara	4			Trumpet	8
Harmonic flute	4			Clarion	4
Octave	2				
Blockflute	2				
Larigot	$1\frac{1}{3}$				
Sesquialtera 26.31. II					
Mixture 29.33.36. III					
Crumhorn	8				
Tremulant					

available as melodic mutations, and the viola and céleste have in fact very little string quality at all. But subject to these limitations it is a truly all-purpose instrument capable of dealing with all types of legitimate organ music. To this extent it and its British contemporaries represent an advance upon the neo-Baroque instruments of Germany, Holland and Scandinavia, which have been deliberately cut off from any romantic attributes whatever as being unworthy of the true organ. The French have developed an instrument more like the British, as befits their extensive nineteenth- and twentieth-century repertoire of native composers. America for a time followed the same course, from about 1935, under the leadership of Donald Harrison, a Willis-trained English builder who obtained control of the Aeolian-Skinner company and did much excellent work. But since his death the tendency in America has been to go over to the most extreme type of German instrument.

In avoiding such extremes the authors believe that the British organ will prove to be of more enduring use. There are bound to be fluctuations in musical taste, sometimes towards classicism; sometimes towards romanticism, and the best organ is the one which is best able to meet all legitimate demands that can be made upon it.

There is a tendency to suppose that the modern classical organ must rely on mutations for its colouristic effects, but this was far from the practice of the sixteenth- and seventeenth-century German builders, who included an ample supply of highly-flavoured solo reeds (mostly of the regal family) in every organ of any size. It is therefore wrong to suppose that the classical must be lacking in 'warmth'. Entirely the reverse should be the case. Certainly, there is no place in the organ for mere copies of orchestral tonalities, but there are plenty of other ways of 'colouring' an organ, and the modern organ should be made as colourful as it can be without copying the orchestra. Organ string tone is an effect *sui generis* only nominally related to the violin family. When moderately scaled it is a genuine organ effect and it is one which goes back far into the eighteenth century. This is the belief, in particular, of Messrs. William Hill & Son and Norman & Beard who endow their organs with the most extensive tonal spectrum possible, compatible with a classical outlook.

Electric action continues to be generally used, but the leading players are increasingly coming to appreciate the greater merits of tracker action. Certainly in instruments of moderate size, and where the layout of the organ permits of its efficient application, tracker action gives a sensitive player a measure of control over the instrument which no other mechanism can equal. However, it is difficult to use tracker effectively for the pedal organ, and if direct mechanical action is used for the stop action (as it generally is in Germany and elsewhere) the player is inevitably denied any effective aids to registration. For playing early music such aids are not necessary, but for service-playing and playing the legitimate romantic repertoire, they are essential. It therefore seems likely that tracker action for the manuals, and electric action for the pedals and stop mechanism may become an increasingly usual arrangement. It was first used in the rebuild of a nineteenth-century organ, along classical lines, at St. Helen's, York. The work was carried out by Messrs. Walker to the design of Dr. Francis Jackson, the organist of York Minster. At the time of writing this book, only one new British tracker action of any size has been made during this century. This is for the three-manual organ installed in 1961 by Messrs. N. P. Mander in the London City Church of St. Vedast, Foster Lane. The pipework is mostly eighteenth-century, but the tracker action and the layout of the organ are new.

The increasing classical trends in British organ building have aroused a sense of the importance of preserving our few remaining historic organs that have not already been altered beyond recall and recognition. For this and other advisory purposes the Council for the Care of Churches (the Church of England central advisory body) has set up an Organs Advisory Committee, by which important work has already been done. Perhaps the most important case dealt with has been the University Organ in the Church of Cambridge, Great St. Mary. This organ stands in the west gallery and has a case and much pipework by Father Smith. It was conservatively rebuilt as a three-manual organ by Messrs. Hill in 1872. Following the recommendations of the Organs Advisory Committee it has been rebuilt by Messrs. William Hill & Son and Norman & Beard in its 1872 form without any mechanical alterations, while its tonal features will be altered only to the minimum extent necessary for performing the classical repertoire.

Looking back, it can be seen that the British organ has gone through five well-defined stages during the last 400 years, which may be summarised as follows:

(1) The original native school up to 1665.

(2) The post-Restoration school of Father Smith, continuing up to about 1820.

(3) The first classical school of Gauntlett & Hill continuing up to 1851.

(4) The development of the romantic organ by Schulze, Willis, Walker, Thynne, Hope Jones and Harrison, covering roughly the century 1851 to 1951.

(5) The second classical school stemming mainly from the Downes-Harrison instrument in the Royal Festival Hall. As this book is published this final school is still rapidly gaining ground. The authors have tried to foresee along what lines it may develop.

CHAPTER III

MUSICAL USE

This chapter is by no means intended as an organ tutor; it aims only to solve some problems of registration posed by the average British organ, especially in relation to the performance of early British, French and German music.

A very large and probably the best part of the solo repertoire of the organ was composed for the German and French organs of the seventeenth and eighteenth centuries. The British organ at what may be regarded as its most typical (between approximately 1600 and 1840) evoked a varied and interesting school of composition which, with the publication of modern scholarly editions, is now becoming appreciated in its original form. What may be described as the Royal Festival Hall school of English organ-building is almost perfectly adapted to the playing of all this music, but the average twentieth-century instrument certainly is not. The late seventeenth- and eighteenth-century British organs were fairly well adapted to playing much of the contemporary French music, much of which has no pedal part; but since few of these instruments survive, this is of little more than academic interest.

The nature of the seventeenth- and eighteenth-century German and French organs has been described in Chapter I, and typical British organs of the corresponding period in Chapter II. If these are compared with the Repton School specification (p. 110) it is not difficult to see how different they are. There are still some old-fashioned musicians of the 'Bach would have revelled in the modern organ' school who feel justified in sweeping aside all considerations of historical style (whether of registration or phrasing) in the playing of old music. In doing this they undoubtedly save themselves a lot of trouble, at the expense of doing grave injury to the music. Even five years ago it might have been thought necessary to put forward extensive arguments to discredit this school of thought and performance; but in the improved taste of the 1960s its adherents have amply discredited themselves and the topic no longer provokes serious discussion. For the conscientious student, however, the problem of how to get the best out of the average British organ likely to be at his disposal is not an easy one, and there is singularly little teaching guidance. It is therefore necessary to consider how British organs of the period approximately 1850 to 1950 can best be exploited to play music composed for earlier and different types of organ, so as to sound as nearly as possible as the composers intended.

The musical use of the British organ must be considered under various distinct headings.
 (i) The native schools of composition; and the adaptation of the average British organ to their requirements.
 (ii) The adaptation of the average British organ to the musical requirements of seventeenth- and eighteenth-century foreign schools of composition (notably the German and French).
 (iii) Church accompanimental purposes.
 (iv) Nineteenth- and twentieth-century solo music.

(I)

The first of these headings falls into two quite distinct subdivisions with very little overlapping.

By 1625 Byrd, Bull and Orlando Gibbons were all dead. Of the great Tudor keyboard composers only Thomas Tompkins lived on and continued for a time the great Tudor school. Up to 1625 the dividing line between music intended for harpsichord, virginals or organ is sometimes so slender as to be indistinguishable. Pure virginal music is usually not difficult to identify since the strong melodic quality of this instrument and its poor sustaining power—both in relation to the harpsichord—evoked a markedly secular, rhythmical and brilliant style of composition. Usually in variation form, it is quite unsuited either to harpsichord or organ (despite the elephantine attempts by some recitalists to play it on the modern harpsichord, which is anyway poles apart from the eighteenth-century instrument). The more serious sixteenth- and early seventeenth-century music may usually be played with equal propriety on harpsichord or organ, though it is fairly clear, for example, that the long pavanes and galliards of Gibbons were meant to be played on the harpsichord (then a single-manual instrument with one or two 8 ft. stops only), while his fantasias are organ-music.

In playing this highly intellectual, undramatic, but profoundly beautiful music on an average British organ, it is only necessary to remember that it was composed for a fairly small single-manual organ without swell box or pedals. If this is borne in mind the dictates of correct style and good taste can hardly be exceeded. Powerful stops and extreme sonorities are quite unsuitable.

The second group of native composers is more complicated in its musical requirements, and may be said to extend over two centuries from John Lugge to Samuel Sebastian Wesley. It was for these composers that the British organ at its most typical was available.

Before about 1600 British organ music of the great Tudor school consisted mainly of 'free' fantasias and voluntaries, hexachord fantasias, In Nomines and various pieces founded on plainsong *cantus firmi*. Shortly after the turn of the century when organs of two keyboards began to be made, the 'double organ voluntary' came into being. One of earliest known exponents of this type of composition was John Lugge, who was organist of Exeter Cathedral from at least 1602 until 1645, or later.[1]

The characteristic Lugge type of double organ voluntary consists of a series of solos for left hand on the great (or 'double') organ accompanied by other parts on the chaire (or 'single', 'tenor', 'little') organ, both hands being transferred to the great organ for the final section. The later double organ pieces of Locke and Blow follow a similar pattern, although there are to be found solos for the right hand and short antiphonal sections on alternate keyboards.

In considering how best to register early double organ pieces on a modern instrument, it is necessary to think of them first in terms of a 'complete' instrument of the period, such as Thomas Dallam's Worcester Cathedral instrument of 1613, the specification of which is given on p. 54. One thing must be certain: from the nature of the pieces the great or 'double' is intended to be somewhat louder than the chaire. It is possible to surmise the registration on the Worcester organ of one of Lugge's voluntaries which seems suitable for bold treatment (say No. 1

[1] John Lugge, *Three Voluntaries for Double Organ*, edited with a commentary by Susi Jeans and John Steele, Novello, 1955. There is a piece by Orlando Gibbons in Benjamin Cosyn's Virginal Book (No. 21) entitled 'A Fancy for a double Orgaine', but it seems very unlikely that this is intended for a double organ (one with two keyboards) in the sense that Lugge's voluntaries are. The Gibbons piece is not satisfactorily laid out for two keyboards, and it appears that someone has attempted, not very successfully, to adapt it for two keyboards by inserting manual changes; 'ten' meaning tenor or chaire organ, and 'base' meaning great organ. 'Double Orgaine' here probably has the earlier meaning of an instrument of long or 'double' compass.

3 *Gloucester Cathedral, east front: chaire case, 1579: main case, Harris, 1666*

4 *St. Michael, Framlingham: case* c. *1580*

of the set). The boldest possible treatment would be full great for the double, and full chaire (omitting perhaps the two-and-twentieth) for the single. If the voicing of later organs is anything to go by, it would be reasonable to suppose that rank for rank, the great organ would be voiced more boldly than the chaire. This, and the doubling of ranks, would produce a contrast of quantity (rather than of quality) between manuals, sufficient to give the 'double' the due amount of prominence, although the presence of 8 ft. open metal registers on the great would obviously add greater depth and profundity to that department.

Same sound — smaller

In terms of the modern organ, given a swell flue chorus of fairly bold quality, an appropriate registration might be:

Great (double):	Small open diapason	8 ft.
	Stopped diapason	8 ft.
	Principal	4 ft.
	Fifteenth	2 ft.
Swell (single):	Flute (or gedackt)	8 ft.
	Principal	4 ft.
	Fifteenth	2 ft.

If, as frequently happens, the swell is too weak, some choir stops can be coupled to the swell to add strength, or the great reduced proportionately.

A suitable *mezzo forte* treatment on the Worcester organ might be:

Great: One open diapason (or recorder if this was of 8 ft. pitch) and one principal.

Chaire: Stopped diapason and principal.

Here, no doubt, the great would be sufficiently louder than the chaire to give the 'double' part prominence without obscuring the 'single'. It is a simple matter to devise appropriate registration on the modern organ.

While there is no evidence to the contrary, it seems very unlikely, both from the undramatic character of the music and the unenterprising specifications of the organs, that sonorities of boldly contrasted tone were envisaged in this kind of music. Reeds, mixtures and solo mutations are quite inappropriate.

The double organ voluntaries of the Restoration composers, Locke, Henry Purcell and Blow, call for similarly restrained treatment. It has already been said that the pre-Restoration type of organ continued to be built for a time until it was superseded by the new school of Smith. When the more exotic sonorities of the new organs (cornet and sesqui-altera) are required by composers, they are usually specifically requested in the scores; and it therefore seems unlikely that such stops are called for in any piece by Blow, Purcell and their contemporaries headed 'Voluntary for a Double Organ' in which no registration instructions, other than manual changes, appear.

In the second half of the seventeenth century a few stop registration instructions began to appear in organ-music. For instance, in Blow's Complete Organ Works[1] we find *Voluntary for the two diapasons and flute*, and another piece called *Vers for the Cornett and Single Organ* in one source and *A Voluntary for the Cornett stop* in another. A voluntary in C attributed to Purcell requires 'Diapason and Flute' followed by solos for 'Cornet' in the treble and 'Sexquialtera' in the bass.[2]

In eighteenth-century editions of organ-music, registration instructions become really prolific, and leave little scope for doubt as to the composers' requirements. The following is a list of the terms more frequently found, taken from the works of Handel, Stanley, Greene, Walond, Travers, Bennett, and Samuel Wesley.

Full Organ (occasionally qualified by 'without the trumpet' or 'with the trumpet').	Diapasons.	Trumpet.
	Corno or diapasons.	Vox humana.
	Stop diapason.	Hautboy.
Mixture of diapasons, flute, principal, fifteenth and twelfth.	Flute.	Swell.
	Cornet.	Ecchos.
Diapasons and principal.	Sesquialtera.	

This registration terminology, although at first sight self-explanatory, in fact requires some elucidation. Some help is provided by the treatises of John Marsh and Jonas Blewitt, both published towards the end of the eighteenth century.[3] These two works are by no means as clearly expressed or as comprehensive as one would wish; but in conjunction with a study of the music and some practical experience of an organ of the period, they give a good indication of the conventions of registration current in the late eighteenth century, of which a summary is given below. If we remember the innate conservatism of British organists and organ-builders (of which there is evidence in the virtually static basic specification of the

[1] Edited by Watkins Shaw. Edition Schott No. 10595.

[2] Tallis to Wesley series, No. 10. Edited by Gordon Phillips. Hinrichsen Edition No. 1659a. Mr. Phillips' view that this piece is probably by John Barratt, a pupil of Blow, is confirmed by Franklin B. Zimmerman in *Henry Purcell, An Analytical Catalogue of His Works*, 1963, p. 426.

[3] John Marsh, *Eighteen Voluntaries for the Organ . . . To which is prefix'd an Explanation of the . . Stops etc.* Preston & Son, London, 1791.

Jonas Blewitt, *A Complete Treatise on the Organ to which is added a Set of Explanatory Voluntaries etc.* Longman & Broderip, London, ?1795.

British organ for at least a century after the time of Father Smith), we shall not be far wrong is assuming that these conventions applied for at least a hundred years before the publications of Marsh and Blewitt.

Most modern organists who have read the writings of Lt.-Col. Dixon and have given some thought to selective registration, think of the expression 'diapasons' as meaning only the 8 ft. stops of an open metal on which the 'diapason chorus' is based. But in eighteenth-century terminology 'diapasons' means both open and stopped registers. In fact the *stopped* diapason was regarded as being quite as much the 'foundation of the organ' as the *open* diapason, and it is significant that in small organs the stopped diapason was invariably the first 8 ft. stop to be introduced. With very few exceptions the stopped diapasons on all keyboards were always drawn. Blewitt says (and this is confirmed in similar terms by Marsh): 'let the Performer, when he sits down to the Organ, draw out the Diapasons on each set of keys, by which means he is sure of a foundation; and indeed this is absolutely necessary, because no Stop whatever ought to be used without one or both of these Stops, except the Flute'. An important function of the stopped diapason was to enliven the open diapason, and to cover up the slow-speaking bass pipes which were conveyanced off in the front of the case. While the open stop could on occasion be used alone in slow *sostenuto* diapason movements, both stops were needed for 'airs of a more sprightly nature'.

Of the solo effects listed above, the cornet, trumpet, vox humana, cremona and hautboy, although apparently self-sufficient, were not intended to be heard without the support of the stopped diapason, and possibly the open diapason as well. Only the solo flute (4 ft.) was drawn alone, and consequently solos for this stop are intended to sound an octave higher than written. In addition to this, the dulciana, as Marsh says, 'has a peculiar sweetness of tone, and may be used quite alone'. There are no other exceptions to the convention that qualifying foundation stops should always be drawn with all combinations.

The solo 'sesquialtera' was the compound stop of that name (containing the tierce) used in the lower part of the compass with the support of suitable stops of lower pitch. Blewitt remarks, 'where there is no Cornet, the Sesquialtera is a tolerable substitute'—advice which is valid to-day.

'Full Organ' is not meant to be understood literally, nor even necessarily as full great. It is simply a 'full' great effect, approximating to the Continental *organo pleno* or *plein jeu* except that reeds could be used. The cornet formed no part of the full chorus. Marsh says that 'being only a half, or treble stop, it ought never to be used in the Full Organ, but only with the Diapasons, in Voluntaries, giving out Psalm Tunes, Symphonies of Anthems, etc.'. He also gives five different kinds of full organ:

(i) Great up to sesquialtera.
(ii) The furniture added to the sesquialtera.
(iii) The trumpet added instead of the furniture.
(iv) The trumpet and furniture both added.
(v) The clarion added to the whole.

Dealing with lesser combinations, Blewitt says the principal 'should nevertheless never be used singly, in the manner of a Flute, because it does not answer quick to the finger; but when blended with the Stop Diapason in an airy style, it is shown to the greatest advantage'. He adds, 'this is the best mixture of stops on the Organ'. There is no suggestion that the twelfth, fifteenth or mixture should ever be added without a firm 8 ft. and 4 ft. foundation. Of the choir organ he says, 'When the Choir Organ is designed to be full, never use more than the Stop Diapason, the Flute, the Principal and the Fifteenth, because the Reed Stops, if admitted, are too predominant, and are the most liable to go out of tune, nor indeed, have these latter at anytime so good an effect as when used, singly with the Stop Diapason alone.' The combination of dulciana and flute is recommended which 'resembles the Cymbal'.

'Corno' refers to the French horn stops which began to appear in English specifications during the first half of the eighteenth century. These, as Sumner says, 'were stops of trumpet quality but with a certain stifling of tone caused by the use of thick metal tongues and partially closed tubes'.[1] Many volumes of eighteenth-century voluntaries contain movements with passages in sixths, fifths and thirds, imitating orchestral horns. When, as frequently happened, a horn stop was not available, 'diapasons' was considered to be an effective alternative—indeed the middle register of an eighteenth-century diapason is quite horn-like.

Although the swell organ developed from the earlier boxed echo organ, the terms 'Swell' and 'Ecchos' (which frequently appear in different movements within the same voluntary) are not synonymous. The old echo organ was primarily a short compass solo division on which, during trumpet or cornet voluntaries, phrases were echoed on the echo cornet or trumpet, as the case might be. When the echo box was turned into a swell box, composers began to write movements for the 'swelling organ',

---

[1] *The Organ*, etc. 3rd edition, 1962, p. 313.

taking care that, when both hands were intended to play on the swell, the left hand did not stray below fiddle G. When, as frequently happens, the bass part does extend below fiddle G, it was intended to be played throughout on the choir organ. In passages marked 'Swell' the use of the swell pedal is clearly implied, although *crescendo* and *diminuendo* markings do not appear until late in the eighteenth century. For echo passages use of the swell pedal is stylistically inconsistent,[1] indeed there is no necessity to play these on the swell rather than any other available keyboard.

Both Blewitt and Marsh are agreed that the swell cornet should only be used in the full swell (e.g. with the reeds) or as an echo to that on the great.

From the foregoing it will be gathered that British eighteenth-century registration was conservative in the extreme. Upperwork never seems to have been added without a full unison foundation. No one appears to have thought of using stops such as the twelfth, tierce and larigot as solo mutations; nor of colourful effects such as stopped diapason and fifteenth which, like many other *piquant* effects, is very pleasing if not overdone. The successful *grand jeu* combination, consisting of trumpet, clarion, principal and cornet, is never requested. Even so, the point about conventional eighteenth-century British registration is that when applied to a contemporary instrument (such as that at St. Mary, Rotherhithe, the greater part of which still sounds as when finished by Byfield in 1764) it is found to be entirely practical. The great organ stopped diapason adds much fullness to the front open diapason, particularly in the bass where it is most needed, as well as to the full great, which sounds somewhat thin without it. The practice of using qualifying flue stops with reeds, of course, is recommended by Dom Bedos and Mersenne. Used with the solo reeds, the diapasons cover up the slight irregularities of tone and attack which are inevitable in reed stops of that date. They also qualify the somewhat strident character of the mounted cornet.

This is not the place to go into the vexed question of whether any continuo style 'filling-in' is desirable in British late seventeenth- and eighteenth-century music. But it is worth pointing out that anyone who plays this music on an organ of the period, and conscientiously follows the indicated registration, will find singularly few opportunities for adding extra notes. Much of the time each hand will be engaged on a different keyboard. When both hands are occupied on the same manual,

[1] Voluntary I, 2nd movement, of William Russell's second set (1812) has the following instruction: 'As the Swell in this and the 3rd Voluntary is intended as an Echo to the Trumpet it is requested that the Pedal may not be used'.

they are usually playing preludes and fugues in a number of well-defined contrapuntal parts to which the addition of more parts, to say the least, presents considerable technical difficulties.

British organs built during the second half of the nineteenth century (particularly during the period approximately 1850 to 1880) are generally very well adapted to the performance of all this music. The average twentieth-century instrument, however, has two main deficiencies:

(1) The lack of a 'full organ' of sufficient transparency and vitality.
(2) The lack of appropriate solo tone colours.

Many eighteenth-century diapason choruses had no more upperwork in number of ranks than the average modern organ (St. Mary, Rotherhithe, for instance, has only twelfth, fifteenth and three rank mixture), yet they possessed considerably more brilliance and vitality. The main reason for this difference is that in the old organs, all the upperwork was scaled in proportion to the 8 ft. open diapason, all the ranks, whatever the pitch, being more or less alike in power. The trumpets and clarions were voiced on the same wind pressure as the diapasons, and they blended with and enriched the chorus without overpowering it. About a century ago, organs were still being built by Hill, Gray & Davison, Walker and Holdich with flue and reed choruses developed on these lines. These organs often had bright unenclosed choir organs, and solo reed stops which are a very effective substitute for eighteenth-century specimens. Should the organist be fortunate enough to play one of these instruments which has escaped 'modernisation' (and consequently ruination), he will find that eighteenth-century registration can be transferred to it virtually *in toto*, and that the tonal results will be entirely satisfactory. If the solo reeds are very prompt and regular, the qualifying flue stops can be dispensed with, but they will generally be found to be advantageous. A Willis organ of the same period (of which one survives at St. Peter's, Tiverton) will be found to be equally adaptable. Father Willis's reeds will be entirely self sufficient, and are best drawn alone in solo use. His unenclosed choir organs, and sometimes the great organs of his smaller instruments, usually contained a full blooded corno di bassetto. This is an excellent substitute for an eighteenth-century cremona.

The only real disadvantage will be the lack of a solo cornet. All Father Willis's three-rank mixtures, and those of many other nineteenth-century builders, contain 17, 19, 22 at bottom C and break to 12, 15, 17 at middle C. These make quite a useful solo cornet when combined with 8 ft. and

4 ft. flutes, or the 8 ft. flute and principal. Many of these tierce mixtures (Willis's excepted) are of larger scale than is really desirable for chorus purposes, and are therefore more effective in solo use.

The organist who has to contend with a typical organ of the period 1900 to 1950 will be less fortunate. It is very unlikely that transparency and vitality will be the predominant characteristics of the major chorus. The great organ will probably have as its basis a large open diapason; the principal will be related to the small open diapason in scale, and the upperwork reduced in power proportionately. The great organ chorus reeds, particularly if they be trombas, will probably be too powerful and smooth for prolonged use, besides being of a tone quality completely antipathetic to music written for clear and bright choruses. Here the remedy must be to select the clearest and brightest combination of stops from those available. The large open diapason must anyway be omitted since, being unrelated to the upperwork, it will add nothing but tonal confusion. It will generally be found that a fairly bright, clear chorus can be built up on the small open diapason. It may even be desirable to omit the second open, substituting an 8 ft. flute for it. It is surprising how often this will be found to supply an adequate, clear sounding foundation for the upperwork. If the mixture contains a flat twenty-first, the result will not be happy. In this case the mixture must be omitted, or the tuner be persuaded to stop off the rank, which he will probably be delighted to do, flat sevenths being a nuisance to tune. Use of the great chorus reeds being artistically out of the question, recourse must be had to coupling the swell 8 ft. and 4 ft. trumpets for very 'full' effects.

The modern hautboy, vox humana and orchestral clarinet will be too soft and sugary to be adequate substitutes for the more robust eighteenth-century solo reeds. The clarinet, particularly useless by itself, may with the addition of a piccolo or fifteenth serve for an eighteenth-century vox humana. Filled out by 8 ft., 4 ft. and 2 ft. flutes it can provide a tolerable substitute for a cremona. As the great 8 ft. chorus reed will probably be too loud for trumpet solos, these must be played on the swell trumpet. The latter may be too thin (if the organ is a Harrison) or too smooth (if it be by any other builder), but these disadvantages can be mitigated to some extent by the addition of 8 ft. and 4 ft. flue stops, or a mixture, as the case may be.

The two volumes of voluntaries by William Russell, organist of the Foundling Hospital, published in 1804 and 1812 respectively, and the compositions of Samuel Wesley indicate that eighteenth-century registration conventions were continued well into the nineteenth century. In

Russell's voluntaries, all the familiar indications appear together with some developments, such as more extensive use of the swell (with expression markings); solos for trumpet bass (which appear very infrequently in eighteenth-century pieces); and extensive solo passages for hautboy and cremona, occasionally with both reeds in duo.

Russell's voluntaries also contain an early, probably the earliest, appearance of an obbligato pedal part in British organ music. This seems a suitable opportunity to put forward some guidance on a problem which must be faced by all who seek to give an authentic performance of British organ music of this period: how best to adapt music written for a long GG or FF manual compass and 'old English' pedals for performance on organs of the German compass which gradually became established after the time of Gauntlett. The occasional GG or AA of the short octave compass required by seventeenth- or eighteenth-century music can easily be played on the pedals. But some of the requirements of composers such as Russell and the Wesleys are less easily met. The organs for which much of their music was written had a long manual compass down to GG or FF; a limited number of 'pull-down' pedals (permanently coupled to the corresponding manual notes); and the dubious assistance of 'pedal pipes', sometimes sounding 16 ft. pitch, sometimes returning to the octave above in the lower part of the compass. In the music we are now considering the pedal part (as will be seen from the examples which follow) is written at 8 ft. pitch—the pedal pipes being optional and, if indeed they were of the 'return' type, probably a downright hindrance. The pedals were regarded as a kind of 'third hand' confined mainly to sustaining bass pedal points, or to slow moving passages. Bass passages which require depth of tone, and which range beyond the limited pedal compass of the day, are occasionally given to the left hand in octaves. These frequently move above and below bottom C, and it is here that the main difficulties arise.

S. S. Wesley was a firm opponent of the German compass and all that it entailed, and his early compositions are laid out for the older type of instrument. At the beginning of his *First Set of Three Pieces for a Chamber Organ* (from which the well known *Choral Song* is taken) he says, 'On Organs of the German Compass, use a 16 ft. Stop and play an octave higher'. This works well enough for the pedal notes, but it cannot be applied consistently to some of the left-hand octave passages (Example 3).

During the first half of the present century there have been many attempts to 'arrange' this music for the modern organ. The method usually employed is to set out the bass on the pedal stave, transposing up

5 *St. Nicholas, Stanford-on-Avon: main case* c. *1580*

6 *West front*

KING'S COLLEGE CHAPEL, CAMBRI
main case Thomas Dallam, 160
chaire case, probably Pease,

7 *East front*

an octave where necessary, and to provide extra parts to occupy the otherwise unemployed left hand. All too often the results are the worst of both worlds; a thickened up travesty of the composers' intentions and a poorly laid out work in terms of the modern organ.

In the authors' opinion, the satisfactory solution is to regard the original text as sacrosanct so far as possible and to use the pedals only where they are necessary:

(*a*) for the original obbligato pedal part;
(*b*) to rectify the shortcomings of the 'German' manual compass, and at the same time to ensure consistency of tone quality throughout the piece.

In most cases this means following S. S. Wesley's dictum, and playing an octave higher with a 16 ft. stop coupled to the manuals. Three examples are given by way of illustration, two where this procedure is applicable, and one where it is not.

Example No. 1 shows that in order to ensure consistency and evenness of tone quality in passages originally set out for the left hand in octaves, it is necessary to play all such passages on the pedals, including those which lie within the manual compass.

Example No. 2 shows that all adaptation must be tempered with commonsense. The addition of octaves between X and Y is justified because the composer has used them elsewhere in the same fugue (example No. 1). The octave on the F sharp at Z was only omitted because this note would not have been available on the organs of the day. Here it is more logical to play the whole section on the pedals, and only the most rigid purist could object to this.

There are rare instances where the left-hand part moves above the compass of the average modern pedal board, and it is not possible to follow S. S. Wesley's dictum. His own *Choral Song* is one of them. While it would be possible to use a 16 ft. pedal only for the few manual notes which lie below bottom C, the result (apart from technical awkwardness) would hardly be a bass line of even tone quality. Probably the best solution here is to use a light 16 ft. pedal stop coupled to the manuals throughout, and to transpose only the offending passages an octave higher (Example No. 3).

This method was followed in the edition of E. H. Thorne, who was most scrupulous in preserving S. S. Wesley's original notes.

The inherent difficulties in performing British organ music of the period *c*. 1600 to *c*. 1850 on the modern organ, and the generally unsatis-

Musical Example No. 1. William Russell (1777–1813). Fugue from Voluntary XII (Twelve Voluntaries for the Organ or Pianoforte, 1804), bars 39 to 51

factory nature of arrangements, are undoubtedly major reasons why these compositions have been so unjustly neglected.

(II)

The requirements of the German and French seventeenth- and eighteenth-century composers are entirely different from each other, and the German will be considered first.

The main shortcomings of the average British organ are threefold, some of which have already been touched upon in considering the performance of British music.

(1) The lack of two complete and balanced manual choruses.

(2) The lack of independent pedal organs of well-defined quality.

(3) The lack of bold and colourful solo effects, particularly those derived from solo mutations.

The first of these is the most difficult to overcome, and the more recent the organ the greater the difficulty usually is. The organs built by Hill, Walker and Gray & Davison a century ago usually possessed a well-developed flue chorus on the swell manual which was able to do very fair justice to passages intended for a Rückpositiv or Oberwerk department. Even later, Walker organs, in particular, maintained this tradition, as unwittingly did Lemare, who for quite different reasons demanded a swell organ actually louder than the great. Willis was the first prominent builder who whittled down the power of the swell flue chorus from the early 1860s and this tradition was continued with even greater disparity in power by Arthur Harrison. For playing Bach's major works this shortcoming is crippling and often insuperable; but it can usually be mitigated to a substantial extent.

The manner in which the great Bach works were registered in the eighteenth century was described in Chapter I. The main requisites were two manual diapason choruses of roughly equal power, the positive being more penetrating in tone than the great.

Nineteenth-century English organs of the Willis type generally had a swell flue chorus very much softer than that of the great, and an unenclosed choir organ, fairly brightly voiced, but without any chorus upper-work. If the swell could have been coupled to the choir the result would have been strong enough to balance the great chorus, at least up to fifteenth, but this is seldom possible in organs with tracker action. When such organs have been rebuilt with electric or pneumatic action, but tonally unaltered, a better balance is therefore easily achieved, although the change is to be deplored from other points of view.

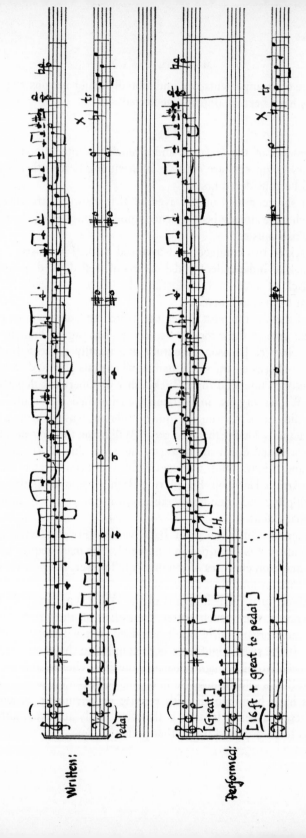

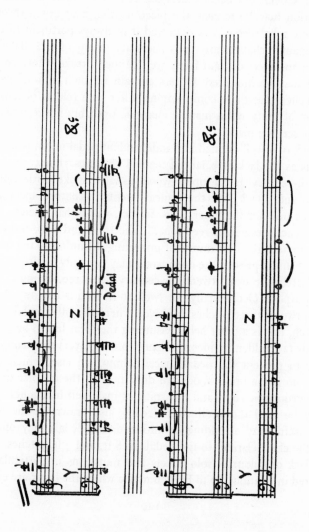

*Musical Example No. 2. Russell's
Fugue from Voluntary XII, bars
144 to 158*

When dealing with a typical twentieth-century organ of the Repton type there is no such easy solution, since the choir organ is in effect a solo department. The best that can be done is to draw the swell octave coupler with the full swell diapason chorus. In extreme cases the addition of the clarion may be helpful, if it is tolerable at all. The great must then be reduced in power so far as possible. This can be done by omitting the large open diapason and building up the chorus on the small open or 8 ft. flute as suggested above. According to the composition of the mixture, either it, or the twelfth and fifteenth, may be omitted until the final return to the great after the last episode.

When a satisfactory balance between choruses cannot be achieved, the best solution may be to play the piece on the great organ throughout. Even where a balance can be achieved it is always pertinent to consider whether manual changes are really necessary. Many of J. S. Bach's organ works, for instance, contain fairly well defined breaks where changes of keyboard may be indicated. Others contain no such indications, and it can be argued that these compositions suffer by a release of tension and disruption of unity when manual changes, probably never envisaged by the composer, are made.

The lack of a well-defined and independent pedal organ is usually not so serious as the lack of balanced manual choruses. The early and mid-nineteenth-century pedal open wood usually spoke with remarkable definition and attack, but the typical twentieth-century specimen does neither the one nor the other. It is, in fact, worse than useless for poly-phonic music. Mezzoforte reed tone, in the 16 ft. and 8 ft., and even 4 ft. pitches provides the best means of imparting definition to the pedal line, and where this is present the open wood may certainly be dispensed with. Unfortunately the usual twentieth-century pedal reed is much too loud for this purpose. Occasionally the swell 16 ft. reed is borrowed on to the pedals in two or three pitches, but even when it is only available there in 16 ft. pitch, this is a great help. Assuming the great has to be coupled to the pedals (a maddening inconvenience to the player) the main objective must be to prevent the pedals overwhelming all else, which they will certainly do if the open woods are drawn. With the coupler drawn, the pedal bourdons in 16 ft. and 8 ft. pitches may well be enough, and will certainly be so if the swell 16 ft. reed is also drawn on the pedals. A further useful way of adding definition to the pedals may often be to couple the choir clarinet to the pedals in 8 ft. and 4 ft. pitches.

The lack of colourful solo effects and mutations in particular is best considered in relationship to French music where the latter are even more

Musical Example No. 3. S. S. Wesley (1810–76). 'Choral Song', bars 1 to 9

indispensable than in German. Feeble little flute mutations began to appear in British organs from the mid-'twenties of this century, and although they are better than nothing, they are really of very little use. The classical French solo mutations were much more full-blooded affairs.

In nineteenth-century organs it often happens that the great twelfth tends towards flute quality and can be used effectively with the 8 ft., or 8 ft. and 4 ft. flutes as a solo nazard. Equally, in Father Willis organs it is always soft enough to be used in this way. As previously explained, many three-rank tierce mixtures can be used to provide a passable solo cornet. But what can seldom be produced is a solo twelfth and seventeenth in the tenor register, so necessary for the many beautiful French compositions for 'tierce en taille'. The player must either make do with his makeshift nazard solo, or couple a fairly smooth-toned clarinet to it.

Nineteenth-century reeds are usually voiced on a low enough pressure, and have a good enough attack to answer for the more dramatic French versions; and many an old cremona or 'clarionet' is sufficiently thin in tone to serve as an excellent cromorne. If, as is likely, the trumpet bass does not attack well enough for a solo 'basse de trompette', the addition of 8 ft. and 4 ft. flue stops and possibly a mixture will cover up the deficiency.

Thus, as is so often the case, a mid-nineteenth-century organ proves to be much more adaptable than its maker ever envisaged. The organist confronted with a typical twentieth-century Harrison instrument is by no means so fortunate. The twelfth is generally too loud to be carried by the flutes, and the mixture or (worse still) harmonics, too unsociable to go with anything at all. The alleged chorus reeds are singularly deficient in attack below middle C, and although the tuba usually attacks well, it is much too loud. The clarinet is almost always too sugary and unctuous to be of any value on its own in seventeenth- or eighteenth-century music; although, as suggested when dealing with British music, it has its uses in faking effects such as the old English cremona and vox humana, and these are comparable to the French cromorne and voix humaine.

In fact, a typical British twentieth-century organ is of remarkably little musical use except as an accompanimental medium, for which purpose it is remarkably good. But since there is no reason why a good accompanimental organ should not also be a first-rate solo instrument, this can hardly be adduced in mitigation of its glaring deficiencies.

8 *St. Mark, Old Bilton: Robert Dallam case, 1635-6*

9 *Tewkesbury Abbey, 'Milton' organ: case 1597 or earlier*

10 *Lincoln Cathedral, c. 1672*

11 (Below, Left) *St. George's Chapel, Winds[or], chaire organ facing east, probably Thomas Dalla[m], 1609*

12 (Below, Right) *St. George's Chapel, Winds[or], great organ facing west, probably Thomas Dalla[m], 1609*

(III and IV)

Sections three and four may be considered together, and briefly, since they represent a widely understood current idiom.

The great, but relatively few, nineteenth-century romantic composi- tions for the organ were conditioned to a considerable extent by the aids to registration then available. The organ, by its very nature, is really alien to the romantic idiom, and to a greater or less extent romantic organ music is orchestral in inspiration in its demands for rapid and often kaleidoscopic changes of registration. Thus, the German composers relied largely on the *Rollschweller*, being a general stop crescendo operated by a pedal in the form of a drum, which the organist turned with his foot. Long crescendos and diminuendos therefore figure in German music of the Max Reger type, and this encouraged the building of the very large German organs of the period. The French symphonic school, which produced the greatest number of significant composers, and which is still flourishing, was conditioned by Cavaillé-Coll's system of stop control by pedal-operated ventils and couplers. Although England produced no nineteenth-century composers of front rank, the Willis system of stop control has proved in the long run to be the most adaptable and generally useful. Bishop introduced composition pedals early in the century, but it was Willis who first made possible a really complete system of stop con- trol in his 1855 console at St. George's Hall, Liverpool, with its inclined stop-jambs, pneumatic stop mechanism, and pneumatic thumb pistons and composition pedals. These included even general pistons, and before the end of the century he had perfected a system of adjustable pistons which has not been materially improved upon.

However, the very ease of stop operation which the Willis system pro- vided, and the lightness of touch of pneumatic or electric action, regard- less of the number of couplers drawn, has led to lazy habits of registration. All too many modern organists rely entirely upon pistons for registration, and have the swell organ permanently coupled to the great. They seldom move a stop-knob by hand. As the pistons are often set in a most hap- hazard style, the resultant mash of tone, presented in greater or less volume, is not particularly flattering to the organ nor interesting to the audience or congregation.

The greatest variety of effect is provided by the use of individual stops and uncoupled manuals. When choruses are used it is again best to use the minimum number of stops. Great to fifteenth normally gains nothing by having the flutes drawn with it (modern flutes, unlike the old stopped diapasons, being bad mixers) and even less by having some or all of the swell coupled to it. It is a good general rule that not more than one 8 ft. flue stop need be drawn in any one combination. Equally, the full swell is much more effective if used as a contrast to the great diapasons and not merely as a background heard through them.

In playing German and French music it must be remembered that the Continental instruments have never possessed the large masses of unison tone (both flue and reed) to be found in so many British instruments, and these are therefore to be used only rarely and with circumspection. When César Franck stipulated 'Fonds 8 pieds' he was not thinking of three or four diapasons, but a combination of lightly voiced flutes, strings and diapasons which, on a Cavaillé-Coll organ, is a mellow and entirely satisfactory blend of foundation tone. However, since on British organs this amalgamation of tone is not particularly interesting, some fairly transparent *mezzoforte* combination must be sought instead, or possibly a medium open diapason alone. Equally, French trumpets are extremely fiery in tone, and a chorus of thick-toned trombas is no substitute even though there may be no available alternative.

There is a current tendency to decry the tuba, which is perhaps a pity, as it is a particularly British development. It is now supposed to be improper to use high wind-pressures for any purpose at all, and so far as the chorus sections of the organ are concerned this is correct. But except in buildings of the size of St. Paul's Cathedral the tuba never has been a chorus stop, and it is only its use as such, as a super-climax to full organ, that has brought it somewhat into disrepute. If it is used antiphonally in chords against the rest of the full organ, or as a solo stop in single notes heard through an appropriately powerful combination of chorus stops, the effect of a tuba can be extremely noble, and this is especially true in the accompaniment of congregational singing. It is an effect which can only be obtained upon a fairly high wind-pressure; certainly not less than 7, and preferably at least 12, inches. A very loud and fiery-toned trumpet, voiced to capacity on a lower pressure, is not at all the same thing, although it may be an acceptable substitute.

The modern classical organ is well adapted to playing twentieth-century romantic music, as well as pre-romantic music; especially when it has not been entirely deprived of moderate string tone of the kind much required by César Franck and to be found in any Cavaillé-Coll organ. It is also well suited to the emergent school of organ composition which recognises that the organ is essentially a polyphonic instrument *sui generis* and that the less it resembles an orchestra, the better.

CHAPTER IV

ARCHITECTURAL HISTORY

The architectural history of the British organ may conveniently be considered under two main headings: the position of the instruments in our buildings at various periods; and the appearance of the instruments themselves, that is to say, organ case work. The design of organ cases is a branch of architecture. From their inception, organ cases have embodied decorative features of the architectural periods in which they were made, and since about the beginning of the nineteenth century the designing of British organ cases has been largely undertaken by architects.

1 POSITION

For over a thousand years the British organ has been used primarily as an accompaniment to Christian worship, and its development is directly related to its position and use in our ancient churches. Our concern here will be primarily with cathedrals and parish churches, because in these the organ has occupied different positions at various times in accordance with the prevailing internal arrangements. The same considerations do not apply to college chapels, where the arrangements have remained fairly constant, and the organ has seldom deviated from its traditional position in a gallery or on the screen separating the chapel from the ante-chapel. Nor, obviously, do they apply to Nonconformist chapels, since organs were not commonly set up in these buildings until well into the nineteenth century (by which time the instrument had reached tonal maturity), and they were not affected by ecclesiological fashion as cathedral and parish church organs were from time to time.

The position of organs cannot be considered apart from their size. It has been shown that compared with Continental organs, British ones were for centuries small and tonally undeveloped. Not until the mid-nineteenth century did they catch up with the Continental instruments of about eighty years earlier both in size and tonal stature, at which time they were the best in the world. The smallness of the early British organs, and by Continental standards their retarded tonal development, may be attributed to two main causes—the comparative lowness of the buildings; and the tastes and requirements of British church musicians.

Most of our ancient churches have always been unsuitable for the siting of large organs. Freeman has given a good illustration of the generally inferior size of British churches compared with Continental ones.[1] St. Margaret's, Westminster, which is an average-sized parish church with a tower 85 ft. high, could easily stand under the near-by Abbey roof; but the seventeenth-century organ at s' Hertogenbosch in Holland would not stand in the west end of the Abbey unless taken out of its gallery, and even then it would be 2 ft. too wide for the nave. This may seem to be an extreme example. But it is a fact that organs of a size common on the Continent from quite early times could not be fitted into the average British church without much compression and rearrangement.

British organs, then, had necessarily to be smaller than those on the Continent; but in our big cathedrals they could have been considerably larger than they were without spoiling the architecture or the tone. That they were in fact no bigger must have been primarily because no one wanted them otherwise. Not until the early nineteenth century is there any indication that British organ building was influenced to more than a minor degree by Continental tonal ideals. Smith and Harris transformed the British organ, but they had to do so within its existing insular framework. Renatus Harris's attempt to interest the St. Paul's Cathedral authorities in a Continental size scheme came to nothing. Burney was impressed by the spectacular organ case at Haarlem, but unmoved by its tonal contents; and organ treatises before the 1855 edition of Hopkins and Rimbault show little appreciation or understanding of foreign organs.

C. F. Abdy Williams suggested that the real reason for the difference in size between British and Continental organs was 'to be found in a certain peculiarity of the national character, in the reserve of the average Englishman, in his intense dislike to the exhibition of any emotion or feeling, however deeply he may be inwardly moved. This feeling of reserve has caused him to be indifferent or hostile to all emotional or

[1] *English Organ Cases*, 1921, p. 19.

exciting or grand forms of music: and it is not impossible that the dislike to emotion, or its exciting causes, was at the bottom of the smallness of our organs.' After mentioning some seventeenth-, eighteenth- and nineteenth-century complaints of noisy music, he says: 'Until the German musical invasion of the nineteenth century, our countrymen preferred their music to be of a quiet and soothing, rather than an emotional, strenuous and grand character, and, whether this was the cause or not, our organs were for centuries far behind those of the Continent in size and completeness, while on the other hand they are supposed to have surpassed them in quiet purity of tone.'[1]

There may be something in this explanation, but it is certainly not the whole truth. It does not explain, for instance, why the reserved character of the average Englishman should undergo so extraordinary a change in the second half of the nineteenth century when the taste was for large loud organs, and massive Handelian choirs. Moreover, noise is a very relative thing. The big organs at Alkmaar, Haarlem and Weingarten do not seem unduly loud in their immense surroundings. And it is by no means certain that the old English organs were subdued and sweet, as the argument implies. The few surviving choruses of the late seventeenth and mid-eighteenth centuries give reason for believing that many of the older organs, although of sweet quality in individual ranks, were vigorous and strong in chorus, and the equal of anything on the Continent of similar size.

A more likely explanation (which can be no more than a theory in the absence of sufficient evidence) is that from quite early times British church musicians were more interested in singing than in solo organ playing, and the organ was accordingly given the subservient role of choral and liturgical accompaniment. Moreover, until the nineteenth century there were no large congregations to accompany. This being so, there would have been no need for large organs. The small positives or portatives known to have been available in pre-Reformation times would have been quite adequate. These had necessarily to be near the singers—to the side of the chancel, or on a screen—where much larger instruments would have been impractical.

British organists appear to have been very content with small, or moderate sized instruments until well into the nineteenth century. Only then was the need for larger instruments felt—to support the singing of the greatly increased congregations (for whose benefit the buildings were being adapted), and to sustain a flexible and expressive accompaniment

[1] 'The Evolution of the Choir Organ', *Musical Times*, Jan. and Feb., 1907.

to the 'romantic' Anglican choral services.[1] These were quickly provided, with unfortunate architectural consequences, as will be seen.

On the Continent, in contrast to this, the existence of large churches with spacious west galleries together with a greater emphasis on solo playing, encouraged the tonal development of the instrument during the sixteenth and seventeenth centuries. In the great churches of Calvinist Holland, organs were primarily secular instruments (comparable to the town hall organs of the nineteenth-century Britain) and the possession of a bigger and better organ than the neighbouring town was a matter for civic pride.

Writing in 1921, Freeman expressed the belief that before the Reformation only two west-end organs are known in English churches: Croyland Abbey (where there was a second one in the choir) and the Beauchamp Chapel of St. Mary's, Warwick.[2] There are grounds for believing that pre-Reformation cathedral organs were usually placed on the choir screen, although secondary organs were often in use elsewhere. There were screen organs at Exeter, Durham, Lichfield, Ripon and York, but these were not necessarily the chief instruments in use. There is plenty of evidence to show that in pre-Reformation parish churches, organs were frequently placed in the rood lofts, which would be quite roomy enough for small instruments. Churchwardens' accounts and Wills of the fifteenth and sixteenth centuries contain numerous references to rood organs and rood lecterns (for the lofts were put to other uses, such as preaching and singing, in addition to accommodating organs). There are several instances of a church possessing two or more organs (see p. 46). Organs began to disappear from rood lofts soon after 1500, no doubt as they began to outgrow this restricted position; but as late as 1528 at St. Mary Magdalene, Milk Street, London, four porters were paid 'ffor lefting up of the organ to the Newe loft'.

From the Reformation until the mid-nineteenth century the majority of cathedral organs were set up on the choir screens. In parish churches, as the result of an Order of 1547, all the roods in the country with their attendant images had to be removed. Another Order of 1561 finally brought down the lofts and with them the organs, although the screens which supported the lofts were allowed to remain *in situ*. Then followed a period of gradually increasing puritanism during which a great many

---

[1] In town halls they were needed to accompany large oratorio choirs, and for the performance of the orchestral transcriptions which were becoming a staple part of the mid-nineteenth-century repertoire.

[2] *English Organ Cases*, 1921, p. 20.

organs were taken down, or allowed to fall into disrepair. This culminated in the 1644 Ordnance of the Lords and Commons 'for the speedy demolishing of all organs, images and all matters of superstitious monuments in all Cathedrals, and Collegiate or Parish-Churches and Chapels, throughout the kingdom of England and the Dominion of Wales, the better to accomplish the blessed reformation so happily begun and to remove offences and things illegal in the worship of God'. After the Commonwealth, when organs were again freely admitted to Anglican worship, the most favoured parish church site (in parishes who could afford or obtain organs) was the west gallery together with the singers. This was particularly so in the many new town churches built during the eighteenth and early nineteenth centuries.

Choir screens, rood lofts and west galleries are positions where organs can be seen and heard to the best advantage. Long Gothic churches are improved by the presence of organ screens. They provide an intermediate feature on which the eye can rest, and avoid the unsatisfactory effect of long uninterrupted vistas where these were never really intended. Up to the middle of the nineteenth century, therefore, it can confidently be said that musically and architecturally the majority of British organs were well sited.

After about 1850 there came a considerable change for the worse. Even before the end of the eighteenth century there had been pressure to introduce vistas into mediaeval buildings by abolishing organ screens. But shortly after the beginning of Queen Victoria's reign, the Tractarian movement began seriously to upset the settled arrangements of nearly 200 years; and there followed a thorough-going revolution in the internal arrangements of our churches which, so far as it affected the organ, can only be described as disastrous.

By that time the population had greatly increased, and the internal arrangements of many cathedrals and parish churches (which were never designed to be used as a whole for the accommodation of large congregations) were found to be inadequate and unsatisfactory. Even so, the theories of the ecclesiologists might have had a far less disastrous effect on organ siting and church architecture if it had not been for the influence of Dr. John Jebb, and to a lesser extent his friend Dr. William Farquhar Hook, Vicar of Leeds Parish Church, where Jebb's ideas were first given practical effect in 1841.

Jebb romanticised the Anglican cathedral choral service, which he regarded as the ideal form of worship, and he urged the rearrangement of both cathedrals and parish churches after the manner of the early Christian basilica, in which the singers were placed between people and altar.[1] He particularly disliked the current cathedral practice of seating a considerably enlarged congregation in the choir together with the singers and clergy; and envisaged the cathedral as a single unit of worship with the congregation occupying the nave at one end, the altar at the other, and the surpliced choir forming a link between the two. Solid stone organ screens obviously had no place in such an arrangement. He therefore boldly advocated the removal of these obstructions, or at least the substitution of open screens of wood, or brass and marble, such as Sir Gilbert Scott provided at Durham, Ely and elsewhere.

Jebb's ideas were easier to realise in the parish churches than in the long mediaeval cathedrals. Here he advocated the introduction into chancels of surpliced choirs, and a cathedral-style choral service in which congregational participation was not encouraged.

These precepts gained such acceptance that during the second half of the nineteenth century many cathedrals were knocked into outsize parish churches, while parish churches tried to turn themselves into miniature cathedrals.

During this period many cathedral choirs were opened out by removal of the stone screens.[2] Organs were taken down and re-erected in transepts, or on one or both sides of the choir. Occasionally as at Rochester, the screen remained, but the organ was divided on either side in two cumbersome halves. Gloucester and Exeter Cathedrals are noteworthy exceptions, because the seventeenth-century organ cases still stand centrally on the screens, although slightly altered. At York Minster, the organ rebuilt in 1960 also stands on the screen in the case originally made for the famous Elliot and Hill organ, dating from 1829. The screen, one of the finest in the country, was only retained after a heated controversy, following the gutting of the choir and the destruction of the earlier organ by a fire in that year.[3]

---

[1] Jebb's attitude is effectively illustrated by the following colourful quotation from his *Three Lectures on the Cathedral Service of the Church of England* (Leeds, 1845), p. 109. 'In the constitution of her choirs the Church of England has made the nearest possible approach to a primitive and heavenly pattern. Her white-robed companies of men and boys, stationed at each side of her chancels, midway between the porch and the altar, stand daily ministering the service of prayer and thanksgiving.'

[2] Not necessarily the ancient screens. Scott in his *Recollections* says that at the time of his Hereford Cathedral restoration (1856–63) there was a 'violent agitation, first, for making, where practicable, the choirs more proportioned to present uses, so as to give no excuse for using them for congregational purposes'. He adds, 'I was so far influenced by this fancy as regards screens (be it right or wrong), as to have laid down a rule for myself to open out choirs in cases where no ancient screens existed, but not otherwise.'

[3] The fire was lit by Jonathan Martin, the lunatic brother of John Martin, the painter.

13 *Nettlecombe Court*

TWO LOOSEMORE CASES, *1665*

14 *Exeter Cathedral, double case,*
  east front

15 *St. Mary-the-Virgin, Oxford, west front: Father Smith case 1675-6, Gothicised by Plowman in 182*

16 *St. Lawrence Jewry, London: Harris double case 1684, as drawn by Norbury in about 1870*

Generally parish churches fared worse than the cathedrals. Organs were moved eastwards to accompany the newly robed choirs, and were re-erected, often considerably enlarged, in chancels or side chapels never designed to hold them. The results were often tonally and architecturally deplorable. Many parishes who had hitherto managed quite well without organs were encouraged to buy them. The old gallery bands were abolished and replaced by new organs in unsuitable positions. Even in many new Tractarian churches, the organ was given a position equivalent to a chantry or side chapel.

This movement unfortunately coincided with the demand for the larger and louder organs deemed to be necessary to lead the singing of the nave congregations, and to accompany in quasi-orchestral style the increasingly elaborate choral services. Jebb, to his credit, had no time for large organs, and to describe them he coined the term 'music mills' which was adopted by Sir John Sutton (see p. 97). The larger the organs became, the more difficult it was to dispose of their more cumbersome parts. Consequently the various departments were stowed away in triforia, behind choir stalls, over vestries, or in sundry odd corners quite regardless of musical or visual effect. The period was also one of well-meaning but ruthless vandalism. In both cathedrals and parish churches many fine organ cases were destroyed. Others were mutilated or expanded to suit the new positions and bigger instruments. Today this needless destruction of so much irreplaceable old material is rightly deplored. The only consolation is that the transition led to the building of many fine modern organs (some of which in turn suffered at the hands of twentieth-century vandals), and to the designing of some excellent new organ cases, several of which are illustrated in this book.

College chapels were not immune from the consequences of this fashion for larger organs, although generally they retained the traditional gallery or screen position.

The shortage of organ space in parish church chancels led to the invention of the organ chamber. At its best, such as provided by J. L. Pearson at St. Michael-and-All-Angels, Croydon (84), this was an elevated position on the north side of the chancel, with fairly wide openings and a brick or stone interior. Although inferior to a free standing position, such conditions did not make it impossible for an organ to be heard effectively. At its all too frequent worst, the organ chamber was a kind of brick box, built on to one side of the narrow chancel of a mediaeval church, with constricted openings and sound absorbent linings—a lethal chamber calculated to extinguish the most artistic voicing.

During the past half century or so there have been a few attempts to restore the parish church organ to its traditional rood screen or west gallery position. But the days of organ chambers are by no means past. They are likely to remain so long as church authorities are content to have unnecessarily large organs in the wrong places.

The principle of the organ chamber is open to two main aesthetic objections. The first is that it is absolutely incompatible with the classical conception of the free standing work-principle organ, upon which the great organ music of the seventeenth and eighteenth centuries can only be realised authentically. The second objection is that to hide the organ in a chamber or behind a screen is to throw away an opportunity of enriching the building with a decorative object of considerable dignity— one which can almost be regarded as an art form in itself—an organ case.

2 CASEWORK

PURPOSE, INGREDIENTS AND EVOLUTION

An organ case is a wooden enclosure around the pipes and machinery of the instrument, the front of which is left open and filled with pipes and woodwork in various formal arrangements. Its purpose when properly applied is both visual and tonal.

In the early stages of the organ's development simple instruments were made without any casework, the pipes being arranged in natural sequence with their tops uncovered. A positive organ of this kind is depicted in the 1476 triptych of Hugo van der Goes at Holyroodhouse (1).[1] As soon as larger organs were developed, great pains were taken to enclose the pipes and machinery with a case, no doubt because it was realised that unencased organs of any size but the smallest look unsightly. Almost from the beginning of the use of the organ in the Christian Church until about the middle of the nineteenth century it was accepted that the organ should please the eye as well as the ear, and the visual aspect was never stinted for the benefit of the tonal. The first organ case came into being when an unencased positive organ was given a canopy, back and sides. The case was completed by the addition of hinged doors, the upper part forming a cupboard enclosing and protecting the sound-producing part of the instrument.

From the tonal point of view a properly conceived organ case is as much a sound-producing part of the instrument as the sound-board of a

[1] A Flemish, possibly a Scottish, organ of the period. See *Musical Times*, January, 1920, for an article by C. Antrobus Harris.

pianoforte or the body of a violin. On the Continent of Europe, from Gothic times until at least the 'disintegration' of the Baroque organ in the first half of the eighteenth century, the organ case was frequently conceived as a resonating chamber within which the tones of the various stops were mixed and projected into the building by the hard interior surface. The enhancement in volume and impact of choruses sounding under such conditions is considerable. Organs designed on the work-principle (which has been explained on p. 26) usually had a separate box-case for each department. The effect of this is to emphasise directionally the contrast between choruses which is essential if the music of J. S. Bach and his contemporaries is to be heard at its best. As the Baroque organ gradually disintegrated into the 'Classical' and 'Rococo' schools (see p. 35) the work-principle was gradually abandoned, and with it the musical value of casework. Contrast is no less important for the British double organ music of the seventeenth century, and the old arrangement of great and chaire organs in separate cases (see p. 165), while not strictly analogous to the Continental work-principle cases, would have contributed greatly to its effect. In Britain this important musical function of the organ case was lost sight of with the decline of the old chaire organ cases during the eighteenth century, although there are occasional instances of its use in the nineteenth. The majority of British nineteenth- and twentieth-century organ cases are not really organ cases at all within the strict meaning of the term, but merely ornamental screens. A few modern British organ-builders are now adopting the work-principle case system following the lead of neo-classical builders in Europe and the U.S.A.

As a minimum background to a study of British organ case history, it is necessary to outline the elements of organ case composition, and to show how these have been manipulated by designers; in other words to show how the organ case developed from simple beginnings.

In Europe a fairly continuous history of case design can be traced in extant examples from the late fourteenth-century Gothic cases at Sion and Salamanca, through the Renaissance, Baroque and Rococo styles to the present day. But there are no British organ cases earlier than the transitional Gothic-Renaissance case at Old Radnor, which has been dated as early as *c.* 1500 but could be slightly later. Consequently it is not possible to draw on British organ-building history to illustrate the early evolution of the organ case. This can only be done by reference to foreign examples, or to British cases designed in the Gothic and Renaissance revival styles of the nineteenth and early twentieth centuries.

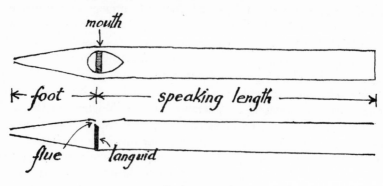

17 *Basic organ pipe*

The Basic Organ Pipe

The principal element of organ case design is the basic pipe of the normal open diapason or principal of metal. Wooden and stopped metal pipes are rarely displayed in organ cases, and although trumpet pipes arranged *en chamade* are a distinctive feature of Spanish cases, they are not often used in Britain. The basic pipe has two main parts, the foot and the body (*17*). The body or speaking-length is determined by the pitch of the note, but the length of the foot can be varied at the discretion of the designer. Centuries of established usage have given this basic pipe certain proportions which the designer can only violate at the risk of spoiling the scale of his design. The most fundamental of these is the ratio of the foot length to the body length. The latter decreases proportionately as the body length increases; in other words, the longer the pipe the shorter the foot must be in proportion. A long pipe with an attenuated foot will look out of scale, as will a short pipe with a chubby foot. It is likely that this body–foot relationship was originally based on function, because in the early organs the height of the mouths would have been determined by the level rackboards in which the pipes stood.

The tops of a row of pipes in chromatic sequence with a horizontal line of mouths assume a curve which is steep at the bass and flattened at the treble. In order to make possible other arrangements (for instance a straight line or a different sort of curve at the tops), designers have adopted at various periods one or several of the following expedients:

(*a*) Varying the foot lengths, so making the mouths follow a slanting or curved line instead of a horizontal one.

(*b*) False body lengths—providing extra length at the tops and cutting away (or 'slotting') the backs to give the desired pitch.

(c) Wooden grilles, partly concealing the pipe tops called 'pipe shades'.

(d) Sloping or curved toe-boards.

These methods will be discussed later in this chapter, particularly when the actual cases are considered.

The Form of the Organ Case

The early form of the organ case was determined by the functional shape of the instrument it enclosed. A traditional organ case has two distinct parts, divided by the impost which indicates the level of the windchest upon which the pipes stand. The part above the impost contains the pipes; the lower part the keyboards, bellows and mechanism.

In the earliest and therefore the simplest kind of organs where the pipes were planted directly over the keys, the upper part of the instrument was the same width as the lower. When at least as early as the fifteenth century the invention of the roller board made it possible to transmit the key movement laterally and so to extend the compass, the upper part of the case became wider than the lower part, and was made to overhang it. This elegant and entirely functional feature of 'overhang' or corbelling is immensely attractive on all the cases of which it forms part, and its undoubted beauty has led many designers to use it even after it had ceased to be functionally necessary. Early use can be seen in the cases at Old Radnor (2), Framlingham (4) and King's College Chapel, Cambridge (6 and 7). Its revived use where it was still functional can be seen in the Pugin cases at Jesus College Chapel, Cambridge (61) and West Tofts (82); and in the Jackson case at Brasenose College Chapel, Oxford (86 and 87). In modern times it has been used by S. E. Dykes Bower in the Andrew Freeman memorial organ at Standish (105); and by Noel Mander in his Denham organ (110) which is based on a contemporary Dutch model. Many of the organs of Smith and Harris possessed this feature originally, although most have since suffered alteration.

Pipe Arrangements and Pipe Shades

As mentioned previously, in the earliest organs the pipes were arranged chromatically directly over their respective keys. The pipes of the main stop would be in the front of the case, and those of the others in parallel rows behind. Soon it was discovered how to arrange the front pipes in any desired sequence, either by means of the roller board, or by tubing them off from the wind chest. Fig. 18 shows a simple case with the pipes in natural sequence. The West Tofts and Great Bardfield cases (82, 68) illustrate an obvious alternative arrangement.

18 *German Table Organ, 1627, showing arrangement of pipes in natural sequence* (*Drawing by Cecil Clutton*)

Up to this point cornices were continuous—either horizontal or in line with the tops of the pipes. The next step was to divide the front pipes into separate compartments and then to break the line of the cornice by grouping the larger pipes in separate compartments called 'towers', and the smaller ones in intervening compartments called 'flats'. The Theddingworth case (*62*) has a horizontal cornice with the pipes divided into three vertical compartments. The cornices of the West Tofts and Great Bardfield cases are gable-shaped. Irregular cornices and grouping into towers and flats are illustrated at Stockcross (*85*) and Weybridge (*77*) amongst others. All these cases, although made during the past century or so, are quite early in style, and will be considered in the true historical perspective later in this chapter.

All the cases so far considered have two main features in common:

compartments of single tiers and a straight impost plan. At least as early as the first quarter of the fifteenth century pipes were arranged in compartments of two or more tiers, and by the middle of the century the irregular impost plan made an appearance, probably because of the desire to plant more pipes in a front of a given width.

Double-storeyed towers are seldom found in Britain, but flats of two or more tiers may be frequently seen in British cases of all periods. Bodley's case at Cheshunt Parish Church has four double tier compartments—two on each side of a central tower (*80*).

The innovation of the irregular impost plan took the form of planting the larger pipes in projecting towers of rounded or pointed shape. At first the intervening compartments were 'flats' (that is, straight on plan), but from about the mid-eighteenth century they were sometimes curved on plan, too. The latter are known as 'curtains' or 'breasted compartments'. At Jesus College, Cambridge, is a simple example of an irregular impost case. Here there is a central pointed compartment of five pipes between two flats of seven pipes each. At Tewkesbury Abbey (*9*) the 'Milton' case has three semicircular and two pointed towers of varying heights separated by four single-storey flats. There are ogee shaped curtains with semicircular towers in the Harris-Byfield case at St. Vedast, Foster Lane (*40*), and double-storey breasted compartments may be seen in the Schwarbrick case at Birmingham Cathedral (*27*).

Very rarely in British organs, pipes are arranged in recessed compartments. Examples are at St. John's, Hammersmith (by J. F. Bentley) and Oriel College Chapel, Oxford (an old case rearranged by Sir Thomas Jackson).

Rounded towers may occasionally be larger than semicircles. Curved towers and curved case ends are not often seen in British cases, although they are a common feature of Continental cases in Baroque or Rococo style.

Pipe shades have already been mentioned as a means of adjusting the line at the top of a row of pipes. They also occupy decoratively the space between the pipe tops and the upper casework. At first they were merely fringes of tracery standing clear of the pipe tops, as at Stockcross (*85*). The pipes would be left their natural length, the resulting asymmetrical appearance within the symmetrical framework of the case being very pleasing. An example of natural length pipes is illustrated in the Temple Moore case at St. Peter's, Yaxley (*97*). It will be seen that here, as in the Weybridge case, the shades are 'engrailed' to follow exactly the rake of the pipe tops. This was the next stage of development. Finally, at least as early as 1413 (Zaragoza Cathedral) pipe shades were made to cover the tops of the pipes, which is how they are commonly used in Britain. Inverted shades around the feet of pipes are often found in German and Dutch Renaissance cases, but only very occasionally in British cases of the same period.

The line formed by the mouths of a row of pipes is an important element in the design of an organ case. At first, for reasons already given, all the feet were of equal length and consequently the mouths formed a horizontal line in each, or all, of the groups of pipes. For examples see Stockcross (*85*), Jesus College, Cambridge (*61*) and Yaxley (*97*). This is a feature of all the early Gothic cases, and of most of the cases of the Italian Renaissance. Soon, however, in both Gothic and Renaissance cases, designers began to vary the feet lengths inversely with the body lengths, thereby exaggerating the natural body-foot ratio already described, and causing the line of mouths to form a slant or a curve. This practice dates from at least as early as 1413 (Zaragoza Cathedral). Slanting use can be seen in the two upper tiers of the end towers of the Cheshunt case (*80*), and in the lower flats of the main case at St. James's, Piccadilly (*36*). Curved use is illustrated in T. Garner's Renaissance-revival case at St. Catherine's College Chapel, Cambridge (*88*). The origin of the practice was probably economic, since there would be no point in wasting valuable metal in providing unnecessarily long feet to the larger pipes, and the basic body-foot proportions would naturally tend to become exaggerated when open diapason pipes were arranged in the front of cases instead of on level rackboards. Less frequently in early organ cases, the foot lengths were increased proportionately with the body lengths (Amiens Cathedral, main case, 1429). It will be seen that this has been done at St. Catherine's College both in the choir case and the main case central tower. Many British designers of the revivalist schools adopted this practice almost as a matter of course, with a complete disregard for historical authenticity. Unless handled very carefully cases with compartments of pipes treated in this manner seldom look completely satisfactory, because the similar motion of the mouth and top lines tends to detract from the functional appearance of the pipes. It is probably most successful when combined with both the other treatments, as at Exeter Cathedral (*14*).

Sloping toeboards appeared at least as early as the middle sixteenth century (St. John's, Lüneburg), and curved toeboards appear in Britain in the Framlingham case about 1580 (*4*). Both these treatments are very common in British Renaissance cases, for example, King's College,

St. Mary, Dublin: Harris organ

20 *Newcastle-upon-Tyne Cathedral: Harris case, 1676: enlargements and chaire case by R. J. Johnson, 1891*

21 *All Hallows-by-the-Tower, London: modern copy by Seely and Paget of case attributed to Renatus Harris, 1675*

22 *All Hallows, Twickenham: Renatus Harris case, formerly All Hallows, Lombard Street, 1703*

Cambridge (6,7), St. Paul's Cathedral (32), and St. Margaret's, King's Lynn (24). It will be seen that the feet are all of equal length, and that the parallel lines of feet and mouths move in contrary motion with the line of the pipe tops which is determined by the pipe shades.

Double Cases

The development of the back-positive on the Continent of Europe as a feature of the work-principle layout has been described in Chapter I (p. 26). This combination of main and subsidiary organs was given visual expression in the double organ case, the main part of which contained the great organ and keyboards, a smaller secondary case behind the organist containing the positive organ. On the Continent, it sometimes happens that cases of the Gothic period (as, for instance, at Amiens Cathedral) have had later back-positive cases added of Renaissance design. In Britain, second keyboards do not appear until shortly after 1600, and it is then reasonably clear that the chaire organ was sometimes the counterpart of the Continental back-positive.[1] The arrangement is illustrated in the detail from an engraving (after Hollar) in Dugdale's *Monasticon Anglicanum* of the Lincoln Cathedral organ as it appeared in 1672[2] (*10*). Allowance must be made here for the artist's obvious inaccuracies in treating the details of the case. This British manifestation of the work-principle was common to many organs possessing great and choir departments until well into the eighteenth century. As the century progressed, however, it became increasingly the practice to dispose the choir organ in the main case together with the echos or swell, and double cases are less frequently found. Nevertheless a late example occurs at Sherborne Abbey in 1856 with the choir organ in the traditional back position[3] (*70*). Dr. A. G. Hill also included a functional choir organ case in his Chichester Cathedral design of 1888 (*92*). Case designers were not slow to turn the double case to good artistic effect, and the relationship of the two parts, one either echoing or offsetting the other, is one of the most charming features of organ case design.

[1] It does not follow that in pre-Restoration times the chaire organ was always given the back position. There is reason to believe that it was sometimes the practice of the old English builders to dispose both great and chaire organs on one level within the main case, as at Adlington Hall. If in fact the Old Radnor organ had two keyboards, this system would seem to have applied there.

[2] The date of Hollar's engraving, which shows the organ on the north side of the choir. In about 1702 it was removed to the choir screen.

[3] Case by R. C. Carpenter: organ by Gray & Davison.

Decoration and Appendages of Casework

An organ case can be decorated by carving; by painting, gilding or stencilling; by the addition of ornamental appendages; or by a combination of any of these methods. Very few of the cases illustrated in this book do not bear some degree of carving, whether of shades, cresting, supporting tower brackets or pendants, panelling or wings. The type of wood and its treatment varies. The Stanford-on-Avon case, for instance, is of plain deal, although there are signs of paint having been applied to it. The Finedon case (*39*), among others, is of fine oak darkened with age. The restored case at St. Mary, Rotherhithe (*41*), is a rich polished mahogany. Painting, with or without gilding, is more frequently applied to cases of Gothic style, and most of the Gothic-revival cases illustrated are highly colourful. Gold leaf can be applied to dark wood with magnificent effect as, for instance, at St. James's, Piccadilly (*36*).

Carved figures appear in Continental cases at least as early as the beginning of the sixteenth century. These, and various carved appendages, either symbolic or purely ornamental, have been frequently placed on towers to give a sense of completeness. Where tower cornices are vacant, it is usually safe to assume that ornaments have been removed. These tower appendages are too numerous to be fully classified here. In Gothic cases they were usually steeples (Palma Cathedral, Majorca, *c.* 1420 is probably the earliest appearance), modern examples of which can be seen in the A. G. Hill case at Beverley Minster (*95*). During the Renaissance period they were commonly in the form of crowns and mitres (representing the temporal and spiritual authorities) as for instance at St. Vedast, Foster Lane (*40*), and Birmingham Cathedral (*27*); or angels with trumpets as at St. James's, Piccadilly (*36*). Sometimes the spaces between the towers are filled by reclining figures (as in the case last mentioned), or by scrollwork, as at St. Mary-the-Great, Cambridge (*46*). Pointed and curved pediments appeared at St. George's, Nordlingen, as early as 1466. A later variation, in broken form, can be seen above the towers at Trinity College Chapel, Cambridge (*48*), and Finedon Church (*39*). Other examples of Renaissance tower ornaments are cupolas (St. Sepulchre's, Holborn Viaduct (*54*)); and kiosks, such as Sir Thomas Jackson placed above the main towers of his Renaissance revival case at St. John's, Hampstead (*91*). Supporting tower brackets are frequently devised as winged cherub heads (see most of the Smith and Harris cases illustrated). This motif sometimes appears elsewhere on the casework, for instance in the panels below the flats of the Milton organ at Tewkesbury Abbey (*9*). Heraldic devices are another common

23 *Adlington Hall,* c. *1670*

24 *St. Margaret, King's Lynn :*
Snetzler case, 1754

25 *St. Leonard, Shoreditch :*
Bridge case, 1754

form of ornament which have been worked into organ cases at various periods.

Doors can be ornamental as well as functional, particularly when pictures are painted on them as at Theddingworth (*62*), West Tofts (*82*) and Jesus College, Cambridge (*61*). The elegant effect of the doors hanging open, their silhouette mirroring the shape of the main front, is very pleasing, and amounts to an extension of the overhang effect mentioned previously. Doors were gradually superseded by carved wings, such as can be seen at Great Bardfield (*68*), St. Catherine's College, Cambridge (*88*) and Sherborne Abbey (*70*). These are increasingly found in Continental cases of the Renaissance period, towards the end of which they sometimes became very exaggerated in size.

Embellishment of Pipes

Fronts of organ pipes can either be left their natural colour, or be embellished by gilding, colouring, or embossing. These methods were all used in early cases, and were probably originated in that order.

The natural colour of pipe metal will depend principally upon the proportions of tin and lead in the alloy. Pipes of pure tin, or of a high tin content (as at Adlington Hall (*23*) and All Hallows, Twickenham (*22*)), have a bright silver colour which always looks extremely handsome, particularly when burnished. Alloys containing between about 33 per cent and 55 per cent tin produce a mottled appearance which is known as 'spotted metal', and pipes of more than two-thirds lead are pewter coloured. The greater the proportion of lead, the darker the colour. Zinc, which has a dull bluish colour, is the least attractive of all pipe metals as well as the cheapest, and for this last reason many modern organ builders use it for their larger pipes. Burnished copper has been used effectively in modern instruments.

Most of the Renaissance cases illustrated have gold leaf applied to their front pipes. Silvering is less frequently used, burnished tin being greatly superior. However, silvering has occasionally been used with good effect, as in the charming anonymous case at Harlton Church (*67*).

Embossed pipes can be seen in the Milton case at Tewkesbury Abbey and Old Radnor, the latter being made with all the other pipes and mechanism of the instrument in 1872 (see p. 175). In the main case at Stanford-on-Avon the pipes are both painted and embossed. More recently Bodley used embossed pipes in his case at the Church of the Holy Angels, Hoar Cross, and in a few other instances. Jackson incorporated them in a design for Blenheim Palace Chapel, following the precedent of the 1508 case at Gonnesse, where there is an early appearance of this form of pipe embellishment. The front pipes at Finedon (1717) still retain their original diapered decorations, and a later use of diapered pipes can be seen at Ely Cathedral by Sir Gilbert Scott (71) and Beverley Minster by Dr. A. G. Hill (95).

A subsidiary decorative feature of displayed organ pipes is the shape of the upper and lower lips. In the earliest pipes the lips were formed by pressing into shape the metal above and below the mouths. Later the lips were made separately and soldered into the rest of the pipe. At least seven different lip shapes have been used at various periods (26). No. 1, known as the *bay leaf*, is the most common in cases of all periods; the two French shapes, Nos. 5 and 7, are also frequently found. No. 7, which is normally reserved for large pipes, requires a special explanation: the extremities of the upper and lower lips are raised from the surface of the pipe, but the mouth is in fact recessed, not raised as appears at first. The type of lips used by an organ-builder will to some extent depend on the mouth width employed, but the purpose of the various treatments is largely decorative. Occasionally a boss is added to the upper tip of a pointed lip shape, such as can be clearly seen in the picture of the case at Jesus College, Cambridge (61). Many organ-builders have used two or more lip shapes in the same case. At Exeter Cathedral, for example, the east front end towers have No. 7, the middle towers No. 6, and the middle flats No. 5. Thomas and Renatus Harris were particularly fond of exhibiting their skill at metal pipe making in this manner (see p. 197).

With the preceding general background we can now undertake an historical survey of British organ cases. But before doing so, it may be

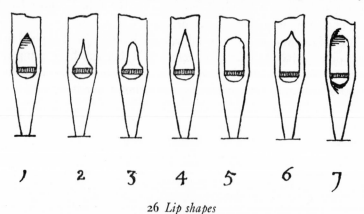

26 *Lip shapes*

helpful to the general reader to set out five principles of judgment as a guide to the assessment of an organ case. Some of these have been mentioned previously. They are all in some degree interrelated, and needless to say, they are not absolute. But there can be few serious critics of organ case design today who would regard any case where one or more of these rules had been broken as completely successful.

(1) *An organ case should be a balanced artistic entity, both in itself and in relation to its architectural surroundings.* Cases which have either been enlarged, or have had extraneous ornament added to them, seldom look right, no matter how skilfully this has been done. Ornamentation should never predominate at the expense of the functional aspect of a case.

(2) *The architectural scale of an organ case should be related to the size of the instrument it contains.* A complex case scaled down to enclose a modest instrument, and having as a consequence dummy display pipes of unrealistic proportions, is a non-functional absurdity. Several of Sir Ninian Comper's designs can be cited as offending in this respect. (See p. 271.)

(3) *Pipe tops should never project above the casework.* In no successful organ case of any period has this been allowed to happen.

(4) *Pipes should always look functional, even though they may be shams.* A case filled with pipes which are too thin, or nearly all the same length, will invariably look unnatural and false to anyone knowing the basic principles of pipe scaling and voicing.

(5) *The lines formed by the toes and mouths of a group of pipes should move in contrary motion to the line of the tops.* In an organ case the emphasis will naturally be on the vertical, and the three main lines across the front (those formed by the toes, the mouths and the tops) are the principal means of providing rhythm and variety. Parallel motion between toes and mouths is perfectly acceptable, indeed horizontal toe and mouth lines can give a feeling of solidity to a small front. But similar motion between either of the bottom lines and the tops will look unnatural, and parallel motion between mouths and tops absolutely nonsensical, since all the pipes would then sound the same note. Like good counterpoint, the best results come from contrary motion between parts.

EXISTING PRE-RESTORATION CASES

Only ten existing organ cases of British manufacture are known with certainty to have survived from the period *c.* 1500 to 1660. That there are so few is due to nearly a century of growing puritan antagonism to the use of organs in divine worship culminating in the notorious Ordnance of 1644; to the ravages of the Civil War; and to the 'improvements' and 'restorations' of subsequent centuries.

Freeman has pointed out that the destruction of organs during the Commonwealth was not so complete as once supposed.[1] In many instances the pipes only would have been taken and the cases not severely damaged. Some organs were allowed to remain throughout the Commonwealth; there was no objection to their use for amusement or recreation—only for divine worship. The instruments at the Cathedrals of St. Paul's, York and Lincoln, Christ's College and possibly King's College, Cambridge, were not disturbed. Of these only the King's College case now remains. The St. Paul's organ perished in the great fire of 1666.[2] Thomas Dallam's organ of 1632 at York survived, with alterations, until the fire of 1829; the Lincoln organ was superseded in 1826; and Christ's College in about 1705. An organ case with folding doors made by Robert Dallam in 1634 for Jesus College, Cambridge, survived in old All Saints' Church in the same town until 1864, when the church was destroyed and the organ presumably broken up. Many other similar instances could be given.

The few cases now left to us are all the more valuable because of their scarcity. A list is given on p. 175 together with the dates generally attributed to them.[3]

----

[1] *English Organ Cases*, 1921, p. 39.

[2] Hollar's engraving of the chancel of old St. Paul's in Sir Wm. Dugdale's *The History of St. Paul's Cathedral* (2nd edition, 1716) shows in one of the north bays of the chancel what appears to be a moderate-sized Gothic case with doors and a crocketed gable. There also appears to be a separate chaire case, but the detail is not clear.

[3] The following instruments in Britain of pre-Restoration date are excluded from this list either by reason of their foreign origin, or because they do not possess traditional organ casework:

Positive organ formerly in the Church of Santa Cruz, Madeira, c. 1540 (Victoria and Albert Museum).

German chamber organ, c. 1560 (Victoria and Albert Museum).

Remains of an organ-harpsichord by the immigrant Flemish maker, Lodowicus Theewes, 1579, formerly in the Chapel of Ightham Mote House (Victoria and Albert Museum).

Chamber organ of Flemish origin, made by E. Hoffheimer, 1602 (Carisbrooke Castle, I.O.W.).

Chamber organ, probably of Flemish origin, 1609 (Hatfield House, Herts.).

German Positive organ dated 1627 (Victoria and Albert Museum).

Positive-cum-regal by J. L. (John Loosemore), 1650 (Blair Atholl Castle, N.B.)

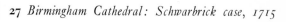

27 *Birmingham Cathedral: Schwarbrick case, 1715*

St. Magnus-the-Martyr, London Bridge : Jordan case, 1712

29 *Pembroke College Chapel, Cambridge:
Father Smith double case, 1708*

30 *St. Katherine, Little Bardfield:
Renatus Harris organ*

*St. Stephen's, Old Radnor, *c.* 1500 (*2*).

St. Lawrence, Appleby, Westmorland, pre 1571 .

*Gloucester Cathedral, chaire case only, 1579 (*3*).

St. Michael's, Framlingham, Suffolk, *c.* 1580 (*4*).

St. Nicholas, Stanford-on-Avon, Northants., *c.* 1580 (*5*).

Tewkesbury Abbey, Glos., 'Milton' organ, *c.* 1580 (*9*).

*King's College Chapel, Cambridge, 1605-6 (*6* and *7*).

St. Mark's, Old Bilton, Warks., 1635-6 (*8*).

Dean Bargrave's organ, Canterbury Cathedral, 1629.

Chamber organ by Christianus Smith, in the possession of Noel Mander, St. Peter's Organ Works, Bethnal Green, 1643.

Of these, only the cases marked * are in their original homes. Only the last-mentioned contains the original instrument, although at the time of writing it is not in playing order.

No organ cases have survived in Britain from the Gothic period, and the earliest case with any Gothic feeling about it is at St. Stephen's Church, Old Radnor. This is undoubtedly the oldest existing organ case in Britain. According to Rimbault, it was first brought to the notice of the Rev. F. H. Sutton (presumably some time in the 1860s) by Sir Henry Dryden, the historian and antiquarian. Sutton found the case in a derelict condition with pipes and mechanism missing, and in 1872 it was restored under his direction by J. W. Walker & Sons Ltd. The builders' estimate provided for 71 new front pipes, and for embossing the central pipe of each tower.

Sutton's monograph,[1] first published before the restoration of the case, contains some interesting but rather naïvely executed drawings, including one of the empty casework presumably as he found it (*31*), and another with front pipes showing how it may have looked originally. Comparison with the photograph of the case as now existing shows the considerable extent of the restoration. The organ is thought originally to have comprised a great organ of five stops controlled by levers attached to the right corbel; and a chaire organ of two stops, controlled by other levers working in the two vertical slots visible in the left-hand side of the lower case. But since no known English organ-music before the development of the double voluntary after 1600 calls for two manuals, it is reasonable to doubt that this organ originally had more than one keyboard. The old corbel stop levers, 18 in. long, which are shown in

---

[1] F. H. Sutton. *The Organ at St. Stephen's Church, Old Radnor* (1866). See also the same author's *Church Organs, Their Position and Construction*, London, 1872.

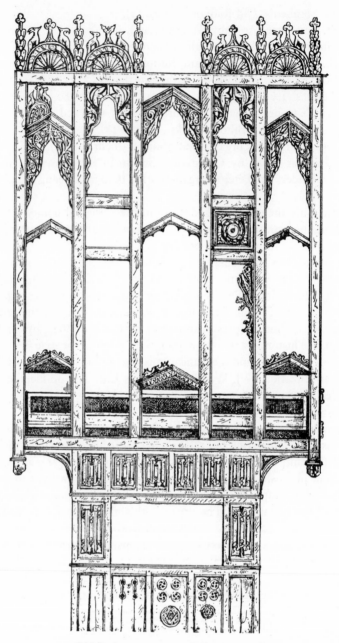

31 *Old Radnor organ case before restoration*
(Drawing by F. H. Sutton)

Sutton's conjectural drawing, were unforgivably removed when the organ was restored.[1]

The casework is of oak, and the design is a mixture of late Gothic and early Renaissance detail. Strong Gothic feeling is imparted by the generous corbelling, the intricately carved linenfold panelling on back and sides, and by the carving of the pipe shades. Renaissance feeling is provided by the panels between the flats (embodying a Tudor rose motif) and by the cresting along the top, consisting of a semicircular design, pinnacles and grotesque animals. The proportions of the case, and the interrelation of vertical and horizontal elements, are extremely satisfying. It is slightly marred by the horizontal bands across the towers (which are neither decorative nor functional), but since these are shown in the Sutton 'pre-restoration' drawing, they are presumably original.

The date of this beautiful and unique organ case is likely to be always conjectural. Sutton contented himself with the epithet 'mediaeval'. Hill attributed it to the reign of Henry VIII (1509–47). In his 1921 essay[2] Freeman thought it as early as c. 1500, but by 1946 had settled for c. 1520.[3] Blanton considers c. 1500 more likely for the reason that 'everything about it indicates that it was built in the reign of Henry VII and circumstantial evidence suggests that the organ was a gift of Henry VII or his mother, Margaret Beaufort. Not only is it in Wales where the Tudor family originated and where Henry VII was raised, but it bears the Tudor rose . . . a device which both Margaret and Henry used repeatedly'.[4]

The general acceptance of a date early in the sixteenth century is due largely to a well-founded belief in Freeman's integrity. Nevertheless, he gave no reasoned arguments in support of his view, and there is in fact nothing about the case which is inconsistent with a date much nearer the

---

[1] Sutton's drawings give a misleading impression of the proportions of the case. Its dimensions given by him are as follows:

Total height: 18 ft.
Width above windchest: 9 ft. 4 in.
Width below windchest: 5 ft. 9 in.
Height from floor to corbelling: 5 ft. 10 in.
Height of cresting and pinnacles: 1 ft. 8 in.
Depth: 2 ft. 6 in.

The hypothetical drawing of the case with front pipes shows the pipes with their natural, irregular lengths, the tops clearly below the pipe shades. In this respect it is probably more authentic than the restored front as now seen.

[2] English Organ Cases, 1921.
[3] Church Organs and Organ Cases, SPCK, 1946.
[4] J. E. Blanton, The Organ in Church Design, 1957.

middle of the century. The fact that the living was in the Royal gift from 1502 to 1534 supports Blanton's theory. Even so, the Tudor rose was a common decorative motif throughout the period, and the location of the organ in Wales is no especial reason to connect it with Henry VII any more than any other piece of Welsh church furniture of his reign. Hill wrote of the Framlingham case, 'It will be observed that old English organs generally appear to be of a considerably earlier date than is really the case ...',[1] and this can be applied to Old Radnor with equal logic. Stylistically it cannot be put later than c. 1550. All that can be safely said, therefore, is that while it could be as early as c. 1500, it could also be as late as c. 1550, and it is not possible to be more exact in the absence of more conclusive evidence.

The case and front pipes at St. Lawrence, Appleby, belonged to an organ presented to the church by the Dean and Chapter of Carlisle Cathedral in 1684. There are grounds for believing that this was the instrument mentioned in a Cathedral inventory of 1571. The front of the case has been shortened by about 2 ft. (and consequently ruined) in order to make it fit into a chapel on the north side of the chancel. This inexcusable mutilation probably took place in 1863 when the instrument was moved from the west gallery.

The chaire organ case at Gloucester Cathedral was dated by Hill at 1579, which Freeman considered to be a not unreasonable assumption. The style and treatment is considerably earlier than the main case which contained a new organ completed by Thomas Harris in 1666, and the two marry together very happily. In the chaire case (together with the next two to be considered, Framlingham and Stanford-on-Avon) can be felt a certain affinity with cases of the early Continental Renaissance, although the cresting above the towers, as well as other details of carving, are essentially English in character. The unusual treatment of the centre tower, with the singling out of the long middle pipe, is reminiscent of the design of two of the compartments in the monumental but sprawling case at Chartres.[2] Another unusual feature of the Gloucester case are the two compartments, concave on plan, between the three towers. The display pipes are almost certainly of a later date, having the typically Harris mixture of lip patterns. For a further discussion of the main case, see p. 213.

The organ case of Framlingham Church originally came from Pembroke College, Cambridge, in 1707–8, and is presumed to have belonged

[1] *Organs and Organ Cases*, etc., Vol. ii, p. viii.
[2] Built in Gothic style, 1542–51; enlarged in Renaissance style, 1615.

32 *St. Paul's Cathedral, London, north case: Wren-Smith, 1695–6*

33 *Compton Wynyates : Father Smith chamber organ*

34 (Below) *St. Peter's Organ Works, Bethnal Green : Father Smith chamber organ*

to an organ which, according to Hill, was built for the college by Thamar in 1674. The early style gives reason to believe that Thamar used the case of an older instrument, and Freeman's estimate of c. 1580 is entirely plausible. Both F. H. Sutton and Hill attributed the case to the reign of Henry VIII, although Hill, upon learning the dates given above withdrew from this position, and in the second volume of his *Organ Cases* made the observation about the deceptive appearance of old English cases which has already been quoted. Like the Stanford-on-Avon case (and to some extent the Gloucester one just mentioned) the naïvety of the composition of opposed vertical and horizontal elements is reminiscent of cases of the early Continental Renaissance. Features worthy of note are the graceful corbelling; the distinctive treatment of the cornices above the towers and the brackets below them; the three-sided central tower (comparable with the Stanford case) and the panels on each side of the console, which are carved to represent a perspective of an arched and paved interior. The undulating toeboards and the variety of lip treatment should also be noted. The front pipes have intricate diapering; but as long ago as 1919, S. W. Harvey [1] observed that the pipes had darkened with age and the diapering could not clearly be seen. A part of a former organ of unknown date, and consisting of an oblong panel of dummy pipes and interesting carving, is now fixed to the wall of the church. At one time it served as a screen to the organist, giving the effect of a kind of double case, and is so shown in Sutton's drawing.

In the west gallery of St. Nicholas Church, Stanford-on-Avon, is an unrestored double organ case of considerable dignity and charm. The original builder is unknown. As with so many of these matters, we are entirely dependent on the researches of Andrew Freeman, who had grounds for believing that the organ originally came from the Chapel Royal, Whitehall; that a choir organ was added shortly before 1638; and that after being diverted to other uses during the Commonwealth, the organ was reset in the Chapel Royal in 1660, and finally removed to its present home about 1663 together with the loft, to make room for the new organ by Father Smith. [2] The foregoing is consistent with a local legend that the organ was given to Sir Thomas Cave of Stanford by Charles II. Hill thought the case was made about 1625, but Freeman's date of c. 1580 has been accepted by other authorities, and is entirely in keeping with the early Renaissance style.

Even when Hill saw the case before 1891, all the internal pipework

---

[1] Illustrated article on the Framlingham organ in *Musical Times*, November, 1919.
[2] *Musical Times*, November, 1911.

(except one bass trumpet pipe) had disappeared and the mechanism was in a ruinous condition. The main case contained a typical post-Restoration one-manual organ of eight stops. The chaire case is a dummy, intended to serve only as a screen for the organist. It is certainly a later addition, possibly of the eighteenth century; and seems unlikely to be the chaire organ of c. 1638.

The deal casework still bears signs of original colouring and gilding. The pipes are richly embossed and gilded, some with patterns of gold on a dark blue background, and the lips are ogee, rounded and bay leaf in shape. Above the three-sided central tower of the main case are crown and mitre emblems on a supporting bracket decorated in blue, red and gold. Small cherubs with trumpets stand on the two semicircular end towers, which are supported by winged cherub heads; and the middle tower is supported by a bracket embodying two of these cherub motifs. Attention must be drawn to the 'engrailing' of the pipe shades of the end towers, and to the carved design of griffin-like creatures and foliage, features which appear also in variated form at Tewkesbury.[1] Blanton has remarked upon the feeling of French influence in the design of the cartouches in the panels below the main case flats.[2] The dummy pipes of the chaire case are painted to match those of the main case and the effective foliate patterns of the pipe shades are stencilled in cream. The balance of the double case composition is somewhat spoiled by the pseudo-chaire case being a little too large. Yet the scale of the whole is excellent in relation to the west end of the fourteenth-century church.

The history of the 'Milton' organ at Tewkesbury has been given in Chapter II (p. 55). It was sold to the Abbey in 1737, and stood upon the choir screen until this was removed in the 1870s. Upon the arrival of the 'Grove' organ in 1887 it was finally given its present position on the south side of the choir.

The strongly Elizabethan Renaissance character of the case indicates that it probably contained the instrument built or rebuilt by John Chappington in 1597. There is no need to date it earlier than this, although Freeman thought c. 1580 to be likely. It is unique amongst the few pre-Restoration cases in having both a nine-part composition (five towers, four flats), and a distinctive overhanging front with pendant

[1] This style of shade design is often found in cases of a design transitional from Gothic to Renaissance (e.g. Chartres), and its use at Stanford and Tewkesbury may be regarded as a 'hangover' from an earlier style.

[2] *The Organ in Church Design*, p. 293.

arches. All of the 37 front pipes (which contain 98 per cent tin) are gilt, and 10 are elaborately embossed. The lips (ogee and rounded in shape) are pressed into the pipes, not soldered. Above the flats the horizontal cornices are relieved by graceful scrollwork and, like the Stanford case, the pipe shades embody griffin-like creatures, those of the towers being 'engrailed' to fit each pipe. In its original condition the case would probably have been shallower than it is now. The Cromwellian inventory refers to a 'double organ', but it does not follow that it was ever a double case. The 'back front' facing the south aisle is quite plain, and probably no earlier than 1737.

The double-fronted organ case at King's College Chapel, Cambridge, possesses a considerable degree of sophistication which contrasts strongly with the other pre-Restoration cases. It can be faulted on a few details, but is undoubtedly one of the most beautiful organ cases of all time. It stands on what is generally regarded as the finest Renaissance screen in the land, which divides the chapel from the ante-chapel. The case has seen several instruments, and was first made by Chapman and Hartop of Cambridge for Thomas Dallam's organ of 1605–6. It is generally believed that this organ was taken down during the Commonwealth, although there is a tradition to the contrary. In 1661 Lancelot Pease added a chaire organ and presumably the existing chaire organ case. Subsequently the instrument was altered or enlarged by Thamar and Renatus Harris between 1675 and 1710; by Avery in 1804; and between 1859 and 1906 by Hill. The present instrument was rebuilt by Messrs. Harrison & Harrison in 1934. Apart from an increase of depth, the original proportions of the case are fortunately unspoiled by the various enlargements. Much of the added pipework is now tucked away inside the screen.

The case is of age-darkened oak, and the front pipes are gilded. According to Hill, the original front pipes were embossed, and decorated in blue and gold; Avery, or someone before him, remade them inside-out and the original decorations can still be seen inside. The carving is of very high quality.

Much of the graceful effect of the silhouette is due to both the corbelling and the upward curve of the cornice from the low centre to the well-proportioned end towers. This type of case was clearly a Dallam favourite. It appears at St. George's Chapel, Windsor (1609); also at Quimper Cathedral (1643) and Saint-Pol-de-Léon (1657–60)—two cases made by the Dallams during their sojourn in Brittany.[1]

[1] See 'The Dallams in Brittany', by H. Stubington, The Organ, Vol. XXX, No. 74; see also No. 167.

Of the two fronts the eastern is easily the best, being much stronger in design. Both chaire and main cases are of similar composition and are surmounted by similar ornaments, with the important distinction that the end towers of the main case are larger than semicircles and set corner-wise. They are also supported by brackets carved in the form of curious bird-like men. The splendid integration of the whole eastern façade is largely due to the manner in which the lines of the tower pipe shades (of both cases) are continued in a graceful curve along the pipe tops of the flat compartments; also, in the main case only, to the similar continuation of the line of the inverted shades along the mouths of the inner rows of pipes. The only dissonant feature is the obviously false lengths of the smaller pipes of the main case flats near the central small pointed tower. The chaire case is more successful in this respect.

The west front is extremely interesting, because it is a variation of the Dallam 'architectural perspective' type of front used at St. George's Chapel, Windsor, and Saint-Pol-de-Léon (see p. 189). The division into seven flats, the centre one slightly projecting, is altogether weaker and less satisfactory than the east front, and the overall design is not improved by the very unnatural look of the pipes of the three centre compartments. The outsize angels over the end towers are out of scale with the rest of the case. These are modern replacements of earlier figures which were supplanted in the eighteenth century by some incongruous pinnacles which can be seen in Ackermann prints of the chapel interior.[1] It must be remembered that the deepening of the case has given the western front a more prominent position than it would have had originally.

At St. Mark's Church, Old Bilton, is a dignified early Renaissance case which originally belonged to the organ built for the old chapel of St. John's College, Cambridge, by Robert Dallam in 1635–6. A chaire case had been added some time after 1660, presumably by Thamar, and the instrument was subsequently enlarged from time to time by Hill. When the enlarged instrument was removed to Sir Gilbert Scott's new chapel the old cases were discarded. The chaire case went to Brownsover Church (not far from Old Bilton) and the main case was acquired by the Rector of St. Mark's, who had it restored, fitted with a new instrument, and set up in his church. The Rev. F. H. Sutton supervised the work, and was

[1] An engraving in Valentine Green's *History of Worcester* shows Harris's Worcester Cathedral organ case of 1666 (which was based on Dallam's at St. George's Chapel, Windsor) standing on the screen with its end towers surmounted by similar horrors. The organs at Gloucester Cathedral and Christchurch Priory were similarly treated, among others.

35 *Bristol Cathedral : Harris cases.* Left, *original west front.* Right, *original east front*

36 *St. James's, Piccadilly: Renatus Harris main case, 1686–8; chaire case, 1852*

responsible, among other things, for the front overhang, the spirettes above the towers, and the restoration of the case to its original proportions. The case is painted a pale olive green, with gilded details, and the pipes are of plain metal with gilded mouths. Embodied in the shades are the Tudor rose and portcullis emblems of Lady Margaret, foundress of St. John's College. F. H. Sutton's restoration was carried out in admirable taste. Fortunately he did not see fit to 'Gothicise' this charming Renaissance case, a form of vandalism he seriously advocated in *Church Organs, Their Position and Construction.*

The casework of the instrument known as Dean Bargrave's organ (preserved in the Library of Canterbury Cathedral) is of little aesthetic interest, and is only mentioned here for the sake of completeness. It is a plain oak cupboard (about 4 ft. 7 in. high including a carved oak stand), with hinged doors bearing the arms of the Dean on the left and Christ Church, Canterbury, on the right. Pipes, keys and bellows are gone, but soundboard and some action remain. There were eight stops controlled by iron levers moving in horizontal slots, four on each side of the keys. These remains were found during the clearing of a room above the Cathedral Treasury in 1910. The organ is presumed to be the one bought by the Dean and Chapter for the use of the Dean, Dr. Isaac Bargrave, in 1629.

The chamber organ which is signed 'Christianus Smith' and dated 1643 (now in Noel Mander's organ factory in Bethnal Green) is of great historical importance, and its tonal significance has been dealt with on pp. 58–9. We are here concerned with the casework, of which the following description is given. The case is of oak (about 7 ft. 3 in. high, 3 ft. 9 in. wide and 1 ft. 9 in. deep), the original height having been slightly increased by the conversion of the action from 'pin' to 'backfall' and the provision of a new keyboard. The upper part of the case is enclosed by a pair of doors, the panels of which are now replaced by modern glass. Behind the doors, the upper case is charmingly painted in the form of a proscenium, within which is a picture of a semicircular arcaded chamber of Renaissance style, with a groined ceiling curving behind a central column in the foregound of the picture. The arcade consists of eight arches within which are arranged 30 decorated wooden pipes. Standing on the chequered pavement of the room are two male figures in seventeenth-century costume, one on each side of the column, playing the sackbut and the cornett respectively. On each side of this picture are narrow vertical openwork panels into which is carved the date '1643'. This precious piece of evidence of pre-Restoration British organ building could not be in more capable or sympathetic hands, and Noel Mander's restoration is eagerly awaited.

At the Restoration of the Monarchy in 1660 many church organs which had been damaged, taken down, or had fallen into disuse were hastily rebuilt and repaired.

It is not unexpected to find the Chapel Royal of St. George at Windsor amongst the first to be re-provided with an organ. The instrument made for the Chapel by Thomas Dallam in 1609 had been taken down during the Commonwealth. An entry in the Windsor Chapter Acts for October 22nd, 1660 says:

> Mr Dallame to make an organ for the Church and to have 600 li for it.

This refers to Ralph Dallam, and the organ was obviously in position by the date of the next relevant entry, November 29th, 1661:

> The Organ to be guilt. Mr. Doggerell is to guild the Organ and ye Organ case. He is first to begin with the Cheire Organ and if his workmanship in that be approved of, then he is to proceed on the great Organ, if not he is to loose all his labour and charges; but if he finish the whole (upon approbation of his guilding the Cheire organ) he is to have all for 120 li if men judicious in ye art shall judg yt he serves it.

Evidently men judicious in the art did judge that Doggerell had deserved his £120, because on November 15th, 1662:

> Ordered that where as there remains due fifty shillings to Mr. Doggerell of the residue of his bargain for guilding the Organ it shall be made up of five pounds for guilding the Angells.[1]

According to Hopkins, Ralph Dallam's organ consisted of only a great organ of one manual (five whole and four half stops), a typical 'new style' Restoration specification. Assuming Hopkins to be right (we do not know his authority), the absence of a chaire organ is puzzling. Some light is thrown on this question by two Hollar engravings from Elias Ashmole's *Order of the Garter*, published in 1672 (*11, 12*). The arms of Charles II as well as the date of publication, indicate that these are intended to depict the situation existing after 1660. It seems clear that as hinted by Sumner[2] there were at that time *two* independent organs on the screen at Windsor; a *great* organ facing west (*12*) and a *chaire* organ facing east (*11*), each being a quite separate and distinct instrument, even at that comparatively late date.

[1] W. St. John Hope, *History of Windsor Castle*.
[2] W. L. Sumner, *The Organ, Its History*, etc., p. 127.

The early style of these two cases as illustrated (especially of the chaire organ) together with a description of the organ case of 'Windsor Church before the Wars'[1] makes it reasonable to suppose that Ralph Dallam had re-erected the cases of his father's organ of 1609. The arms of Charles II could have been added in 1660. Alternatively it is possible that Ralph did not use his father's cases and that Hollar's engravings were based on sketches made before the Civil War (he came to England in 1637), and were subsequently doctored to meet the new situation.[2] Wherever the truth may lie, it seems very likely that these two pictures provide a rare glimpse of two cases dating from the early seventeenth century, which survived until the first few years of the Restoration period.

The great organ case has the characteristic Dallam curved cornice, and a front divided into five arched compartments, giving the impression of an architectural perspective. The Dallam case at Saint-Pol-de-Léon is very similarly treated. But there the three-dimensional effect is enhanced by the painting of the space between the impost and the pipe arcade as a Vermeer-style chequered pavement. Both these fronts are so reminiscent of the 1643 Christianus Smith design that it is interesting to speculate whether more pre-Restoration British organ fronts were devised in this singular style. From the engraving it is evident that the Windsor case, as at King's, was finely carved, and with the details picked out by Mr. Doggerell's gold leaf both cases would have looked very handsome. It will also be seen that individual pipes appear to be mounted on the dividing columns on each side of the middle compartment. It seems likely that these extraordinary features were not speaking pipes, but wooden dummies attached to the casework, and presumably gilded.

RENAISSANCE CASES OF THE RESTORATION AND AFTER (1660 to c. 1800)

The period now to be considered begins with the British Renaissance organ case at the height of its development, and ends with it in a state of weakness and decline.

[1] Hopkins & Rimbault, *The Organ*, 1877, p. 121.

[2] This being so, it is *possible* that the case on the screen at Windsor in 1660–1 could have been that now existing at St. Peter-in-the-East, St. Albans, in mutilated form. If Hopkins' specification is authentic, there is evidence that Dallam's Windsor organ was moved to St. Martin-in-the-Fields in about 1674, and thence to St. Peter's in about 1727. The case within which the instrument was then contained was *not* that depicted in fig. 12, but one of later style, not unlike the present case at All Hallows, Barking, in general outline. Whether this case came from Windsor is open to doubt, although Freeman thought it likely. For further details and an illustration, see 'The Organs of St. Martin-in-the-Fields', by A. Freeman. *The Organ*, Vol. i, No. 1 (1921).

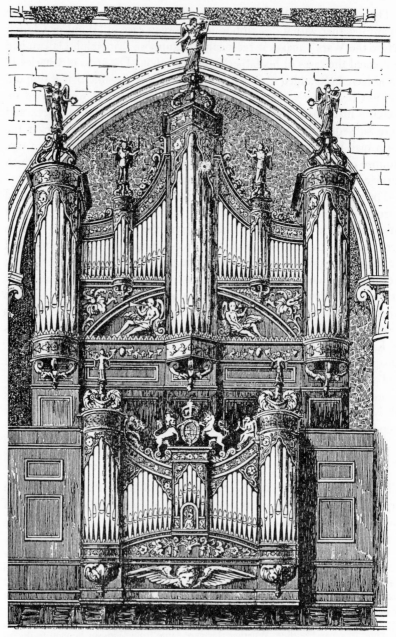

37 *Canterbury Cathedral. Case of Lancelot Pease's organ,* 1662–4,
reconstructed by H. T. Lilley from original designs

Between 1662 and 1664 Lancelot Pease built a new organ for Canterbury Cathedral (see p. 64) in a new case designed by George Woodroffe. This is one of the few instances where the actual designer of an old case is known. The drawing of the case by H. T. Lilley (*37*) is an imaginative reconstruction based on Woodroffe's original drawings of the great and chaire organ cases, which were attached to Pease's agreement with the Dean and Chapter. The drawing of the chaire case had become separated from the other documents and was presumed lost. But in 1915 it was discovered among the effects of the late John W. Warman by S. W. Harvey, was acquired by him, and eventually returned to the Cathedral, where both drawings may now be seen. Pease's organ was placed on the north side of the choir above the stalls. Illustrations of the organ after erection indicate that Woodroffe's design may have been modified in execution (although illustrations of organ cases by artists who do not understand them are notoriously unreliable as to details). But despite subsequent tonal alterations by various builders, the case remained *in situ* until it was finally superseded by one of Green's less attractive 'Gothick' constructions in 1784. Dimensions of the Pease case were: great 16 ft. wide by 23 ft. high to the top of the cornice; chaire 7 ft. wide, 9 ft. high, and 3 ft. deep. If one did not know the date, it would be reasonable to guess that this beautiful and, so far as is known, unique design had been made up to half-a-century earlier. As Freeman observed, it may be cited in support of Dr. Hill's remarks on the survival of older architectural styles in English organ case design.

Loosemore's famous Exeter Cathedral organ has been mentioned on p. 67. The case, bearing the inscription 'JOHN LOOSEMORE MADE THIS ORGAN 1665', still stands in its original position on the choir screen. The pipes of the unique double diapason were arranged in two towers of seven each, one on each side of the columns to the north and south of the screen, and were capped by cornices similar to those of the main case. These towers survived various reconstructions until 1876 when the organ was rebuilt by Speechly under the direction of the Rev. Sir Frederick Gore Ouseley. A shocking piece of vandalism then took place. Loosemore's original front pipes, of tin and richly embossed, were melted down and replaced. The double diapason towers were removed and their pipes recast in spotted metal for the main case, which was deepened to accommodate an enlarged instrument. Although the new pipes are stylistically in perfect keeping with the old casework, the destruction of the originals was inexcusable. About this time under the pressure of 'Jebbism', the choir screen was pierced in order to provide a view of the choir from the nave. This was a compromise more happy than in other instances where the organ screens were swept away. The provision of a virtually new instrument by Father Willis in 1891 necessitated raising the case, further deepening, and the construction of a duplicate chaire case on the west front to accommodate the new solo organ.

Even as it stands today, perched a little too high on the choir screen, the case with its overhanging sides is a noble and satisfying composition. The east front is the most distinctive and the least altered (*14*). It differs from the west front principally in having a flat centre tower with the middle pipe slightly projecting on plan. The two end towers are larger than semicircles, whereas all the west towers are semicircular. The small round compartments in the upper part of the east front are the weakest points of the composition, giving a feeling of falseness and undue fussiness. There is also a feeling of awkwardness about the circular caps of the main case towers which, as Freeman observed, would have been avoided if the cornices had been carried back as at King's College, Cambridge. Among the details which contribute greatly to the beauty and interest of the façade is the threefold variety of lip shapes; the variation of feet lengths (both inversely and proportionately); and the careful and consistent engrailing of the pipe shades. The case is remarkable in being entirely without figure carving, the decoration consisting almost entirely of flowers and foliage.

Through the kindness of Roger Yates it is possible to publish, probably for the first time, a picture of the Loosemore organ at Nettlecombe Court (see p. 67) (*13*). The front, which is recessed beneath a single horizontal cornice, has a very unusual plan (the figures indicate the number of pipes):

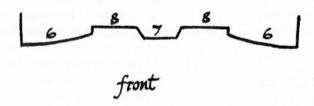

front

The casework is black with gilded details. The front pipes are of tin, and are alternately plain and richly embossed. The feet of the pipes in the two flats are abnormally attenuated. The two stars rotate when the bellows are filled, serving as an indication to the player. Unlike the

38 *St. Peter, Tiverton: Christian Smith case, 1696*

39 *St. Mary, Finedon: Shrider, 1717*

40 *St. Vedast, Foster Lane, London: Harris and Byfield, 1731*

41 *St. Mary, Rotherhithe: Byfield, 1764*

cymbelsterns of the German seventeenth-century organs, they have no bells, and their purpose is purely visual.

The half-century or so immediately following the Restoration is almost entirely dominated by the work of Smith and of Thomas and Renatus Harris. Owing to damage in the last war the number of their surviving cases is less than when Freeman's analysis was published in 1921; nevertheless at the present time there are at least three dozen authentic examples in existence (not, of course, all in original condition) of which just over half are in their original homes. Visually as well as tonally the

work of these two rivals invites comparison. One was made in 1847 by Sir John Sutton in his much quoted little book *A Short Account of Organs*. Sutton was an almost solitary enthusiast who admired and valued the organs of the old English builders in an age when they were being supplanted by larger, louder and uglier instruments. The value of Sutton's opinions, and the information he has given us is not diminished by the fact that he is often very prejudiced and occasionally wrong. His tonal opinions have been quoted previously. He held equally decided views about casework and (since his book is rare and not easily obtainable), they are given here fairly fully, together with the delightful illustrations.

The vignette at the head of the chapter represents the Organ case generally adopted by Schmidt, and is one from which he seldom deviated in general arrangement. The Organ of St. Paul's Cathedral, which he built, was designed by Sir Christopher Wren, to be in keeping with the Stalls, &c., and executed by Gibbons. It differs entirely from the example given, but it is the only exception of Schmidt's with which the writer is acquainted.[1]

The cases which were built by Schmidt, in the latter part of the seventeenth century, are far better than anything that has been built since, for

[1] *A Short Account of Organs*, etc., p. 17.

although the detail is not ecclesiastical, still the old form is kept up, and the general appearance is the same as those erected in Germany and Flanders, from the latter end of the sixteenth century, and the carved work is bold, and consists only of open work panelling in imitation of foliage and flowers, with large angels' heads, and at the present time, with the assistance of a hundred and sixty years, they really look very venerable, especially when they have diapered pipes, which is the case in the Durham Cathedral organ, and some others. . . .[1]

The etching at the head of this Chapter represents one of Renatus Harris's Organ cases, but he does not seem to have been consistent, like Smith, to

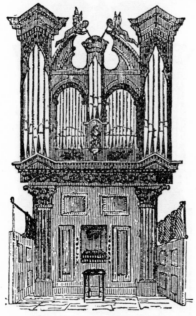

any one particular form, so that his organs are not so easily recognised at first sight as those of his rival. The Organ cases of St. Sepulchre's, Holborn, and St. Nicholas, Newcastle-upon-Tyne, resemble the example given, and they were built before the death of the elder Harris. But the instruments of this builder may be readily ascertained by examining the mouths of the front pipes, which are not sunk, as is usually the case, but are raised above the surface of the pipes, so that the mouth is more prominent than any part of it.[2]

The cases of Harris are much more elaborate than those of Schmidt, and many of the details are those which were in common use in fitting up the apartments of the court and nobility of France, during the reign of Louis the Fourteenth; wreaths of flowers and indelicate fat cupids, by way of angels, with drapery used for every purpose but to cover their nakedness. It is needless to comment further on such ornaments, as it must be evident to everyone that, to say the least of them, they are very much out of place in a Church, and offensive to the feelings of right-minded persons.[3]

Although Sutton's judgment here contains an element of truth, he is less than fair to Thomas and Renatus Harris, whose cases do not particularly reflect their sojourn in France. And although many of their cases were graced with naked babes and reclining figures, Smith's were

[1] Ibid., p. 96. [2] Ibid., p. 58. [3] Ibid., p. 97.

too at the Temple Church, and St. Paul's Cathedral. Sutton's views were highly coloured by the purist Gothic-revival (just getting under way under the inspired but fanatical influence of A. W. N. Pugin) which could see little value in anything which was not 'correct' Gothic, and where all angels appeared decently clothed. It is significant that in spite of this, Sutton found so much to admire in the Restoration cases, although his admiration of the overhanging sides of Smith's cases (the 'old form' which incidentally many Harris cases possessed too), is coloured in this respect by their resemblance to Gothic examples.

Sutton's account of the types of case favoured by Smith and the Harris firm is a considerable over-simplification of the facts. A detailed examination of their known work reveals a remarkable diversity of treatment on both sides. By considering only the basic outlines (the number and shape of the towers, and the shape of the intervening cornices) and disregarding the more subtle details of composition and decoration—at least 24 distinct types are found to have been used. Considering only the known work of these two builders, and disregarding cases of doubtful attribution, not less than 13 types appear to be exclusive to Smith; at least nine to the Harrises; and two further types were used by both builders in common. Their cases are considered below under these three distinct headings.

Generally, the cases of Smith and the Harrises were in some respects alike. 'In all but their very smallest instruments they used from two to four towers, separated from each other by flats, and so arranged that there was always a tower at each end and never a flat. Moreover their flats were invariably real flats and not curtains. . . .'[1] On the other hand Smith generally tended to favour horizontal cornices over his flats, whereas the Harrises did not. The caps of the latter's towers are often more elaborately moulded than Smith's, and they were generally more disposed towards figure work.

The greatest difference on a point of detail between the cases of these two builders is in the treatment of the lips of their front pipes (see p. 170 and fig. 26). Smith was generally content with the normal bay leaf shape (No. 1), although he occasionally seems to have used two shapes, for instance Nos. 1 and 2 at Pembroke College, Cambridge (main case). Harris organs frequently have three or more shapes in one case, for example at St. James's, Piccadilly, and St. Andrew Undershaft, where the towers have No. 7, the lower flats No. 4 (bossed), and the upper flats No. 5. His pipe mouths were generally wider than Smith's. Sir John

[1] A. Freeman, *English Organ Cases*, p. 44.

Sutton's remarks about the lips being raised, quoted above, is inaccurate. As previously explained, only the upper and lower extremities of the French shape (No. 7) are raised; the mouths are actually sunken. Moreover this form was normally restricted to the larger pipes, and not applied to all of them as implied.

Types of Case Exclusive to Smith (as opposed to the Harrises)

The type of Smith case illustrated in Sutton's vignette is composed of four semicircular towers, the two tallest in the centre, with horizontal cornices over the single-storey intervening flats. Smith appears to have used this obviously favourite design more than any other; but since the known examples are easily outnumbered by his other designs, it can hardly be described with accuracy as 'the Organ case generally adopted by Smith'. The following examples were all of this kind.

1. Christ Church Cathedral, Oxford (double fronted), 1680. This case, probably the first of its kind, was enlarged in 1870 by the addition of flats at each end, under the direction of Sir Gilbert Scott. A chaire case, also by Scott, which looks too large and out of scale with the main one, was added later.

2. St. Mary-the-Great (University Church), Cambridge, 1697 (46). This case still stands in the original west gallery position and, except for the front pipes, retains its original appearance. An important difference from the other cases of this design is the coupling together of the two central towers. The oak case is almost black, and the front pipes (which may have been originally gilded or diapered and were subsequently covered with ugly Victorian stencilling) are now seen as plain metal. (See p. 119 for mention of the restoration of this historic instrument.)

3. Banqueting House Chapel, Whitehall, 1699. Removed to the Chapel of St. Peter ad Vincula, Tower of London, by order of Queen Victoria in 1890, where it stands to the east of the northern aisle. It no longer has the overhanging sides which are shown in the print of the organ in its original home in Ackermann's *Microcosm of London.*

4. St. Michael's, Bridgetown, Barbados, 1699. Apparently damaged by a storm and earthquake in 1780 and subsequently replaced.

5. St. Margaret's Church, Leicester. The date and original home of this organ are unknown. It was removed to St. Margaret's by Crang and Hancock in 1773, and in 1858 the case, which by then had a new organ

42 *St. Mary Magdalen, Holloway Road, Islington: G.P. England, 1814*

43 (Below) *Our Lady of the Assumption, Warwick Street, Westminster: Byfield case c. 1790, extensions by Mander*

44 *Wooden pipework*

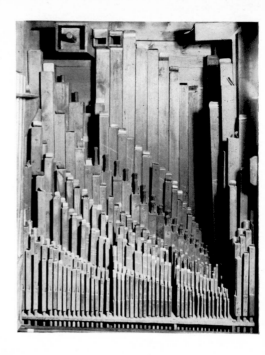

DINGESTOW COURT,
FATHER SMITH CHAMBER ORGAN

45 *Case provided in 1773 by Robert Gray*

inside it, was sold to
Bishop Street Wesleyan
Chapel in the same town,
where it still remains,
having undergone slight
alterations.[1]
6. *Eton College Chapel*
(*double fronted*), c. *1700*.
The case is now in
the Dominican Church,
Rugeley, Staffordshire.[2]

Another case by Smith
(1697), originally of similar
type to the six mentioned
above, belongs to the war-
damaged church of St.
James's, Garlickhithe. At
the time of writing the case
is taken down, but is to be
re-erected in the restored

46 *St. Mary-the-Great, Cambridge. Father
Smith case, 1697* (*Drawing by H. T. Lilley*)

building. About 1718 John Knopple ruined the scale by adding a very
heavy pediment and some ornamental emblems above the two centre
towers, and by providing upper storeys to the flats of somewhat weak
design. The overhanging sides remain, together with much original pipework.

Smith occasionally varied the four-tower type of case described above
by making the cornice above the flats in the form of single concave
curves, and dividing the flats into two storeys. Only two instances are
now known.

1. Durham Cathedral main case (*double fronted*), *1684–5* (*47*). This organ
originally stood on a seventeenth-century screen, and is so shown in
the reconstructed drawing by H. T. Lilley. In 1847 it was moved to
one side of the choir, and was finally taken down to make way for the
new divided Father Willis organ in 1876. The front pipes were
diapered. The old main casework and front pipes were preserved
in the Cathedral for some years, and are now erected on the

[1] See 'The Organs of St. Margaret's Church, Leicester', by W. L. Sumner. *The
Organ*, Vol. xxxvi, No. 144, April, 1957, where an illustration is given.
[2] See Hill's *Organ Cases*, Vol. ii, p. 95, for an illustration.

south aisle wall. The chaire case, of similar outline to the Temple Church case (see below), found a home in University College Chapel, Durham.

2. *St. Clement Danes, London, c. 1690.* Destroyed in 1941 when the Wren church was gutted during an air raid. The cornices were decorated by carving in the form of palm leaves, and the towers were surmounted by vases. The original proportions of the case had been ruined by considerable widening in 1893—additional towers and flats at each end, and an unsightly swell box protruding above the top. The restored church now has an excellent reproduction of the original case by the architect, W. A. S. Lloyd. It contains a neo-classical organ by Messrs. Harrison & Harrison.

47 *Durham Cathedral (East Front before 1847)*

A third variant of the Smith four-tower type is the main case at Trinity College Chapel, Cambridge (*48*). This was Smith's last organ: he died in 1708 before finishing it, and the work was completed by Shrider. The Lilley drawing shows this dignified case in all the beauty of its original proportions—extensions consisting of a large tower and flat at each end having been added in 1870 by Sir Arthur Blomfield to accommodate the particularly large 'music mill' then considered necessary. The main case differs from those previously discussed principally in having flat end towers, surmounted by broken segmental pediments. The charming chaire case, with only a single semicircular middle tower, has more elaborate mouldings than the main one. These, together with more subtle differences led Freeman to conclude that it was the older part of the double case—perhaps a part, or even the whole, of Smith's earlier

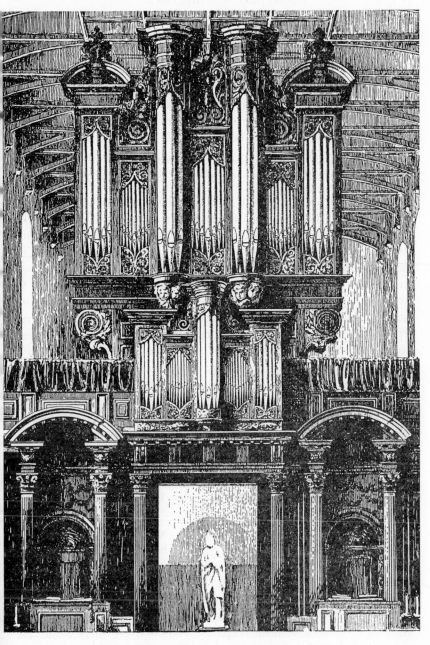

48 *Trinity College Chapel, Cambridge. Father Smith case, 1708, before enlargement*
(Drawing by H. T. Lilley)

organ of 1694. A 'back front' duplicate of the main case, similarly enlarged, faces west.

At least seven different types of case consisting of three towers separated by two flats are peculiar to Father Smith as opposed to the two Harrises. Of these the chaire case at Trinity College, Cambridge, has just been mentioned. The combination of two outer pointed towers, a taller semi-circular central tower, and horizontal cornices over the intervening flats, can only be found in two instances:

1. Christ's College Chapel, Cambridge, 1705.
2. Pembroke College Chapel, Cambridge, main case, 1708 (29).

Both of these are very similar, and only the Pembroke College case is illustrated. The Christ's College case was not improved by alterations carried out during the present century. It differs from the Pembroke main case principally in the carving of the pipe shades, and the treatment of the flats, which follow the pattern of the Pembroke chaire. The only criticism of the Pembroke main case (one which can also be applied to Christ's) is a feeling of weakness about the acanthus-leaf supporting brackets of the end towers. The chaire case, a rare example of twin towers separated by twin flats with horizontal cornices over, is another Smith variant. The relationship of the two contrasting parts of this delightful double case is entirely harmonious and complementary. Until Hill rebuilt the instrument in 1880–1, the chaire case had its own stop levers which the organist had to turn round to work. There are grounds for believing that the front pipes were originally diapered. They were silvered in 1903, and finally gilded when the instrument was recently rebuilt by Messrs. Hill, Norman & Beard.

At Emmanuel College Chapel, Cambridge, is another double organ case by Smith which dates from 1686 (49). The main case, which is quite small, is an isolated instance of another Smith variant—three semi-circular towers, the tallest in the middle, again with horizontal cornices between. The chaire case is similar to a few cases built by Smith and the Harrises with continuous concave cornices between twin outer towers (see p. 220), except that at Emmanuel College the central feature is a short pointed tower. The design is very much like the King's College east front with which it has several virtues in common. As at Pembroke, it originally had its own stop levers. The Lilley drawing shows the Emmanuel case much as it must have been originally. Although the small main case makes the balance less happy than at Pembroke, the dual composition is very pleasing, and much interest is derived from the contrary motion of

49 *Emmanuel College Chapel, Cambridge. Father Smith case, 1686*
(Drawing by H. T. Lilley)

the crossing lines. The front pipes of spotted metal replaced earlier gilded ones in 1871, and the general appearance of the organ is not improved by ugly pipe tops (not shown in the illustration) which now protrude from behind the main case cornices.

The main case of Smith's Chester Cathedral organ, subsequently removed to St. Paul's Cathedral, Valetta, Malta, is of similar outline to the Emmanuel College chaire, except that the curve of the cornice is broken by a short semicircular middle tower.

Four examples can be found of the use by Smith of three semicircular towers with concave cornices over the intermediate flats rising to a high centre.

1. St. Mary-the-Virgin, Oxford (University Church), west front, 1675–6 (*15*). This organ stands on a screen dividing the chancel from the nave. The nave (west) front was 'Gothicised' by Thomas Plowman in 1827 (see p. 238), but the east front facing the chancel, hardly more than an ornamental back to the case, was less altered. The latter is an instance of the use by Smith of three *flat* towers, two storeyed intervening flats, and concave cornices. The pipes are flattened wooden dummies.

2. Durham Cathedral, chaire case, 1684–5 (*47*).

3. Temple Church, London, 1683–7 (*50*). The case of Smith's famous instrument, the survivor of the 'battle of the organs' was replaced by a Gothic case in 1843, which in turn perished during the bombing of 1941. The illustration is a reconstruction by H. T. Lilley. It is based on a poor woodcut in Macrory's *Notes on the Temple Organ* and an engraving in Godwin's *London Churches*. The latter gives a very imperfect view of the organ, and the end towers appear to be rounded (that is, larger than semicircles). Artists who do not understand organ cases are notorious for getting them wrong, and Lilley's drawing is almost certainly authentic. The Harris-like feature of reclining figures between the towers has already been mentioned.

4. St. Nicholas, Deptford, 1697. This was an extremely dignified single case with overhanging sides, which was destroyed when the church was gutted in the Second World War. The flats were of two storeys. Unusual features were heavy inverted pipe shades at the feet of the towers, of equal size to those at the tops. A small case was made out of remnants of the damaged one to contain part of the new organ by N. P. Mander Ltd.

As stated by Sir John Sutton, the famous case of the organ built by

Father Smith for St. Paul's Cathedral in 1695-6 was designed by Sir Christopher Wren and carved by Grinling Gibbons (*32*). It is one of the earliest, if not the first, of British organ cases to be designed by an architect. Basically the design of the main case (which is largely echoed by the chaire) consists of two flat end towers separated by an intermediate flat compartment, the cornice of which is a graceful double ogee curve. Smith used this design only on one other known instance, at West Walton, Norfolk, which was considerably less ornate than St. Paul's, and no longer exists. The St. Paul's case was originally double fronted, and until 1860 stood in the choir screen with the chaire case facing east. Until 1826 it had some ugly glass shutters across the front pipes to keep out the dust.[1] Wren would have preferred to put the organ in one of the north choir bays, as at Old St. Paul's, but was overruled. In fact he did not allow for the organ screen initially, and had to strengthen the

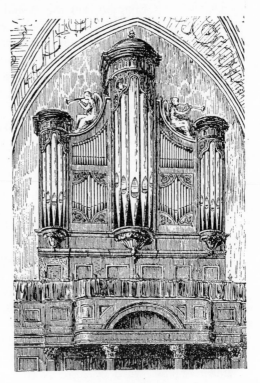

50 *Temple Church*
(*Drawn by H. T. Lilley*)

crypt vaulting to take the extra weight. In 1860 the influence of 'Jebbism', as well as more practical considerations of suitably accommodating large numbers of people, brought about the removal of the organ screen, and the instrument, temporarily shorn of its chaire case, was partly buried behind the north choir stalls. 'Having discovered in the archives of the Cathedral an original drawing by Sir Christopher Wren which showed the organ in one of the bays of the choir (as in Hollar's engraving of Old St. Paul's),

[1] Drawings of the organ case as it then stood can be found in *The Organs of St. Paul's Cathedral*, W. L. Sumner, 1930 (by H. T. Lilley); and *The Box of Whistles*, John Norbury, 1877. See also *The English Musical Gazette*, January, 1819.

Mr. Penrose (the architect) was glad to feel that at last he could carry out the wishes of the designer of the building.'[1] In 1872 the organ case was divided in its present position, and furnished with the existing superb instrument by Henry Willis. The idea of dividing the organ was claimed by Dr. Sparrow Simpson, but this would scarcely have been feasible without Willis's mechanical genius. The original east front and chaire case were placed on the north side of the choir, and were balanced on the south by the original west front (of identical design) together with a facsimile of the original Gibbons chaire case. At the same time the sides of the main cases were tastefully provided with speaking pipes, so that each case now has three speaking fronts.

The St. Paul's cases have been greatly admired; but although they are undeniably well proportioned and sumptuously carved, they lack the elegance and refinement of other seventeenth-century work where the 'old form' (the overhanging sides) 'is kept up'. There is an abundance of carved figure work—no less than 14 angelic figures on each half (cherubs, caryatids and otherwise), to say nothing of the string of cherub heads along the lower frieze. The altars and attendant figures above each of the main towers were added by Wren to hide the projecting pipes of Smith's long compass stops. The upper part of the chaire case takes the form of carved drapery supported by cherubs. This, together with the profusion of carved ornamentation, and the general tendency to blur or break the formal outlines of the structure by various devices, makes these cases interesting examples of the Baroque style in the comparatively mild form in which it influenced British organ case design.

At this stage may be mentioned the cases of the two Father Smith chamber organs owned by Lord Northampton and Mr. Mander (see p. 74 and figs. 33 and 34). Each front is differently disposed, but both are recessed and covered by single horizontal cornices. Both are excellent examples of case-design on a small scale, and are successful because care has been taken to use only real pipes of appropriate size. In Mr. Mander's organ these belong to the fifteenth—the largest metal stop in the instrument. The two fronts differ mainly in the treatment of the small end 'towers': in Mr. Mander's organ they are flat, whereas Lord Northampton's are semicircular. Both instruments have similar keyboards, with reversed colour, and ogee designs cut into the ends of the naturals—the same, incidentally, as at Adlington Hall. Both cases are of oak with tin front pipes, and both have doors, although those of the Compton Wynyates organ are replacements. The preservation of these two valuable

[1] W. L. Sumner, ibid., p. 18.

51 *Dulwich College Chapel: George England case, 1760*

52 *St. Mary, Stafford: Geib case, 1790*

53 *Down Cathedral: case of Green organ, erected* c. *1800*

organs must be largely due to the fact that for many years they were in the possession of the Sutton family. The Suttons also owned another Smith chamber organ with a flat recessed front, and *chinoiserie* decorations which were almost certainly added at a later period. This was known as 'King James II's travelling organ', and was bought by an American in 1925.

Types of Case Exclusive to Thomas and Renatus Harris (as opposed to Smith)

No four-tower cases are known to have been made by Thomas or Renatus Harris.

The type of Harris case illustrated in the Sutton vignette consists of two semicircular end towers, a shorter pointed middle tower, and single-storey intermediate flats, each of which is topped by a cornice in the form of half of a segmental pediment. Although this is a characteristic Harris design, it does not seem to have been a particular favourite. Three examples can be found, not one of which survives in original form.

1. St. Sepulchre's, Holborn Viaduct, c. 1670 (54). Originally a double case in the west gallery. The chaire case (of similar design to that at St. Lawrence Jewry) disappeared many years ago when the main case was moved eastwards and ruined by widening. The illustration is a reconstruction by H. T. Lilley of the case as it originally appeared, based on a picture in Norbury's *Box of Whistles* and photographs of the present case. It would have been reasonable to suppose that there were overhanging sides as at Newcastle-upon-Tyne Cathedral (see below). If Norbury's drawing is accurate, the Harris front pipes appear to have been replaced before 1877. The end towers are surmounted by cupolas, a species of ornament also used by Harris at St. Bride's, Fleet Street, and Christ Church, Newgate Street.

2. St. Nicholas, Newcastle-upon-Tyne (now the Cathedral), c. 1676 (20). The original case still exists as the centre piece of an enlargement carried out by R. J. Johnson, the Cathedral architect in 1891, when the organ was rebuilt by Lewis, and re-erected in the north transept. Two outer 16 ft. towers were added, set cornerwise, and connected to the original centre by weak flats of three pipes each. The chaire case added at the same time is charmingly done and in good scale with the old case, but looks absurdly small in relation to the enlargements. The case as it now stands illustrates the folly of tampering with what cannot be improved. The original overhanging sides have been retained, and by

54 *St. Sepulchre, Holborn Viaduct. Harris case, c. 1670,*
before alteration and removal from West Gallery
(Drawing by H. T. Lilley)

ignoring the additions one can gain a clear impression of this beautifully proportioned case as originally conceived. Although the case has a low centre by reason of the short middle tower, the graceful angelic figure with uplifted trumpet actually makes the centre of the (original) case the apex of the composition.

3. Chichester Cathedral, 1677–8. A double case, on the screen, destroyed by the collapse of the Cathedral tower in 1859. Fragments were incorporated in the present Gothic case by A. G. Hill.

In 1666 (when Renatus would have been about 16 years old) Thomas Harris finished his first known new organ at Gloucester Cathedral (*3*), using the chaire case of an older instrument (see p. 178). The east front of the new main case is of similar style to the three mentioned above which plainly derive from it, although there are sufficient variations to place it in a different category. The half pediments are straight, not segmental, and the short middle tower is placed high so that its cornice is level with the end towers. Another difference is that the short tower is flat except that the centre pipe projects on plan as at Exeter Cathedral. Generally the design is less sophisticated than those just considered, but the effect is dignified and restrained. Many years ago Freeman drew attention to the bad effect of daylight shining between the pipes—a defect which could only be rectified by the use of opaque material. The west front is much plainer, and is another example of a 'back front' not designed for the prominent position it now occupies. Harris's organ stood in a south choir loft until 1718 when it was put on the screen. The present organ screen dates from 1819. In 1878 Sir Gilbert Scott would have had it removed, but fortunately it was retained on the good advice of G. E. Street and Father Willis.

Only one type of case can be said to be characteristic of the style of Renatus Harris, in the limited sense in which the four tower cases are characteristic of Smith. This type consists of three semicircular towers, the tallest in the centre with convex (round shouldered) cornices over the intervening flats. Ten examples can be cited, all but the first two and probably the seventh being constructed after the death of Thomas Harris.

1. St. Lawrence Jewry, London (main case), 1684 (16). This was a double case with a chaire organ of the type used at St. Sepulchre's. It was considerably enlarged in 1875 and completely destroyed by enemy action in 1940. The Norbury drawing shows the organ in 1870, looking very much as it did originally, except that the original Harris front pipes had obviously been replaced. Very unusually for Harris there is a complete absence of figure carving. At the west end of the restored church there is now a dignified copy of the original main case by the architect Cecil Brown, in which some of the less happy features of the 1875 enlargement (flanking towers and fan trumpets above the cornices) are reproduced.

2. *Bristol Cathedral (east front), 1685 (35)*. Originally erected on the choir screen, but rearranged in two bays of the north side of the choir following removal of the screen in 1860. The overhanging sides, and some elaborate superstructures which formerly stood above the towers have now gone. Unlike the other 'round shouldered' Harris cases considered here, the east front has only single storey flats, the spaces below the cornices being plain expanses of wood. The former west front with segmental pediments above the flats on supporting pilasters is more architectural in feeling and falls in a completely different class. It is of similar type to the Father Smith case at St. Catherine Cree, mentioned later.

3. *Christ Church, Newgate Street, London, 1690*. This case was bereft of much of its original carving and widened by an extra tower and flat to accommodate Dr. Gauntlett's famous German compass organ for Mendelssohn's Bach recitals of 1837. It was destroyed by bombs in 1940.

4. *St. James's, Piccadilly (main case), 1686–8 (36)*. This organ was built for the 'Popish' Chapel, more properly the Queen's Chapel, in Whitehall, and was given by her to St. James's in 1691. The carving is by Grinling Gibbons. The slightly Rococo chaire organ case was added in 1852. Before the Second World War, during which church and organ were damaged, the front pipes were diapered. As now restored by Sir Albert E. Richardson the case is the most sumptuous example of Renatus Harris's work to be seen. It has a full complement of carved figures, which together with the front pipes are beautifully gilded. Details of the dark woodwork are also picked out in gold. The only criticisms are a slight foreshortening of the main case due to an elevated second gallery position for which it was never intended, and an inexcusably hideous swell box which has been allowed to protrude above the upper casework. The instrument is the pre-war one by Rothwell.

5. *St. Andrew Undershaft, London, 1696*. An engraving in Godwin's *London Churches* (1838) shows this organ standing in a west gallery with (in addition to the usual carved angels) a very singular superstructure above the central tower. Since 1875 the case has stood on the

55 *Bryceson barrel organ, c. 1805*

56 *Bates chamber organ, c. 1805*

57 *York Minster : case of Elliot and Hill organ, 1829*

south side of the chancel, shorn of its ornaments. The overhanging sides remain.

6. *St. Bride's, Fleet Street, London,* c. *1696.*

7. *St. Mary's, Dublin, date unknown* (*19*). These two cases differed from the 'round shouldered' cases mentioned above in that the pipe compartments in the lower storey of the flats were elliptical. The former was destroyed by bombing in 1940. The latter still exists in its original home but contains pipework by Flight and Robson, which is not at present in playing order.

8. *St. Mary, Lambeth, 1701.* Unrecognisably mutilated, although some carving remains.

9. *St. Andrew's, Holborn, 1699.*

10. *St. Nicholas, Newcastle-upon-Tyne* (*now the Cathedral*), '*back front*', *not provided until 1710.* The former was made out of part of Renatus Harris's rejected Temple Church organ (other parts going to Christ Church Cathedral, Dublin), and was replaced during the nineteenth century. The latter now faces east into St. George's Chapel. Like St. Mary's, Dublin, it has elliptical flat compartments.

The following four cases illustrate a type which, judging by known examples, seems to have been a secondary Harris favourite. Its basic elements are the standard three semi-circular towers, but with gable shaped cornices between them. It is a design which (disregarding two cases of doubtful authenticity—St. Giles-in-the-Fields and St. Peter's, Liverpool) does not appear to have been used by Father Smith. But it was very popular with the successors of Smith and Harris: John Harris and John Byfield, Bridge, Jordan and Schwarbrick, all of whom used it from time to time (see p. 226).

1. *St. Botolph, Aldgate, 1707.*

2. *Salisbury Cathedral, main case, 1710* (*58*). The former still exists in the west gallery with the inevitable added swell box protruding above. The Salisbury case, which stood on the screen, was one of the most exuberant productions of Renatus Harris, and perhaps the only one which, by reason of its excessive ornamentation, came within meriting the strictures of Sir John Sutton. Although only of average width (20 ft.) it was 40 ft. high to the tip of the extraordinary central tower superstructure. The Salisbury chaire followed the triple tower and ogee cornice pattern of the other Harris chaire cases at St. Sepulchre's and St. Lawrence Jewry, but differed from these by having the intermediate compartments arranged concave on plan. This is the only known

instance of such treatment in the work of Harris or Smith. The Salisbury organ was supplanted in 1792 by a Samuel Green organ in a Gothick case, presented by George III in his capacity as a 'Berkshire country gentleman'.

3. St. Peter Mancroft, Norwich, 1707. The case was removed to Great Yarmouth Parish Church in 1875, and destroyed by enemy action in 1941 (see the footnote to p. 228).

4. St. Dionis Backchurch, 1724. Renatus Harris's last organ, and where Dr. Burney was organist from 1748 until he went to St. Margaret's, King's Lynn, in 1751. In 1878 the organ was removed to St. Mark's, East Street, Walworth. In 1881 the Harris pipework was taken to Darenth Training College, Kent; but the case remained, and was eventually destroyed by hooligans after damage in the Second World War.

The modern organ case in the rebuilt church of All Hallows-by-the-Tower (*21*) is in all essentials a reproduction of the old case destroyed in the last war. This was generally believed to have been made by Renatus Harris for his organ of 1675. But Freeman thought it more likely to have been supplied in 1720 by Gerard Smith, who is mentioned in vestry minutes as providing a new case, 'very large, ornamented with fames, and surmounted by two carved figures, with trumpets'. The design, with the flat centre tower, and the gracefully curved lower flats, was apparently unique; although in outline it was not unlike the St. Peter's, St. Albans, case, formerly at St. Martin-in-the-Fields (see p. 189). There were enough Harris-like features to make it probable that Gerard Smith re-used and adapted Harris's earlier case. The front pipes, of narrow scale and with bay leaf mouths throughout, were certainly Smith replacements. The modern case is further discussed on p. 272.

Three more Renatus Harris cases must be mentioned here by reason of their individual treatment.

1. All Hallows, Twickenham (formerly at All Hallows, Lombard Street), 1703 (22). In its original home, the organ stood for many years at the eastern end of the northern aisle. In the west gallery of the Twickenham church, designed by Robert Atkinson, it can now be seen in something of its former glory. The appearance is unchanged, except that some unsightly Victorian pipe decorations have been removed, revealing plain tin. The most individual feature of the case is the large circular compartment in the lower part of the front. Pipes treated in this manner invariably have an unnatural look, and these are no exception. Also the shades of the upper flats are somewhat heavy, and their concave

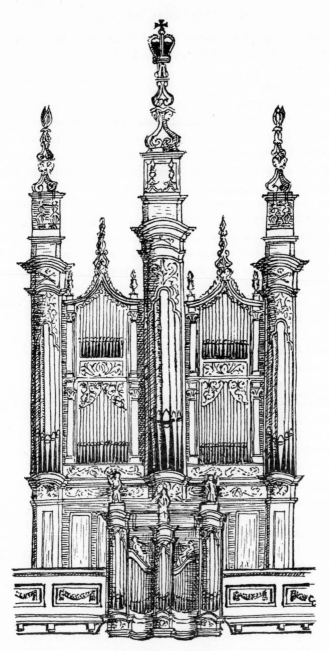

58 *Salisbury Cathedral. East front of Renatus Harris's case on
choir screen, 1710
(Drawing by Cecil Clutton)*

cornices are not particularly happy in the way they meet the short middle tower. This is a fine case, which must nevertheless be faulted in these few details.

2. *St. Clement's, Eastcheap, 1695*. Similar to the All Hallows case, but far less satisfactory. The front is in three stages, the middle one consisting of two small circular flats, one on each side of the short middle tower, and the lowest stage of a wide oval flat compartment containing 33 pipes. Viewed quite dispassionately the façade has an unhappy resemblance to a grotesque human mask, which no doubt did not occur to its designer.

3. *St. Edmund-the-King, Lombard Street*. A small case consisting of a central flat of 17 pipes bounded by a semicircular tower of five pipes at each end. These three compartments are covered by a curved pediment, the base line of which only extends far enough to cap the two towers, so that the latter appear as supporting columns. The pipes of the central flat are of painfully false lengths. The original case stands in the west gallery. A modern facsimile of it, containing part of the present instrument, stands on the north wall.

Types of Case Common to Smith and Harris

The following examples can be cited of Smith and Harris cases which are similar in general outline.

If Noel Mander is right in attributing the Adlington Hall organ to Bernard Smith (see p. 66), we have yet another type of Smith case to consider. The organ stands in a gallery at one end of the Great Hall which dates from the late fifteenth century (*23*). The lower case is older than the part above the impost, and almost certainly belonged to an earlier instrument. The three compartments of pipes in the 'Brustwerk' position are capable of speaking although they are not connected to any wind supply. So far as the upper part of the case is concerned, there is more than a superficial resemblance to the chaire cases of Renatus Harris at St. Lawrence Jewry (*16*) and St. Sepulchre's, Holborn Viaduct (*54*). The architectural treatment with fluted pilasters, as well as the treatment of the upper flats, is also very Harris-like. The arms and semicircular canopy above the case were mounted in 1693 on the occasion of the marriage of John and Lady Isabella Legh. The case is almost certainly earlier than this, because the whole does not have the appearance of being conceived as an entity.

A type of case consisting of a continuous concave cornice between two semicircular outer towers appears in the following instances.

59 *Royal Naval College Chapel, Greenwich : Green, 1789*

St. John, Waterloo Road, Lambeth : double case, 1824

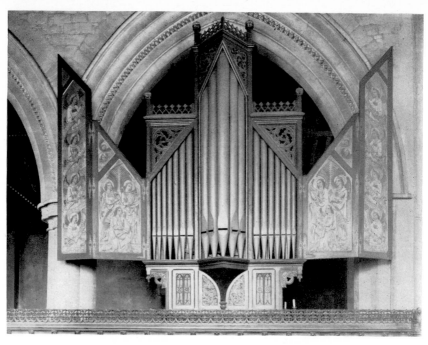

61 *Jesus College Chapel, Cambridge : case by A. W.N. Pugin, 1849*

62 *All Saints, Theddingworth : case by F.H. Sutton, c. 1870*

By Smith:

1. Emmanuel College Chapel, Cambridge, chaire case, 1686 (49), (see p. 204).

2. Manchester Cathedral. A small organ, destroyed by enemy action in 1940. The central feature was a short flat, projecting slightly on plan.

3. Bishop's Palace, Chapel, Auckland Castle, Co. Durham, 1688. A small case, in which the outer towers are separated by a single flat compartment.

By the Harrises:

1. Worcester Cathedral, main case, 1666. The contract between Thomas Harris and the Dean and Chapter required the design to follow Thomas Dallam: 'after the manner of Windsor Church before the wars'—see p. 189.

2. St. Katherine, Little Bardfield, Essex (30). A beautiful small organ, very little altered, which is attributed to Renatus Harris and said to have come from Jesus College, Cambridge. It is very similar to the Emmanuel College chaire organ case; the only real difference being that the latter has a small pointed middle tower.

One of the most beautiful of all Father Smith's triple tower cases is at St. Catherine Cree, made in 1686 *(63).* The provision of segmental pediments over the single storey flats places it in the same 'type class' as the Harris west front at Bristol; although details of the two cases are dissimilar, the latter being more architectural in treatment.

The foregoing account and comparisons of the score or so cases illustrated should make it quite clear that there is really no such thing as a 'Smith type' of organ case as distinct from a 'Harris type'. Apart from the repetition of certain favourite patterns (such as at Smith's St. Mary-the-Great case and Harris's St. James's, Piccadilly) it is difficult to point to any particular example as being 'typical' of either builder. To speak of a Smith or Harris *style*, however, has more meaning. 'There are . . . certain predilections of treatment—mostly in matters of detail—peculiar to each builder. Should one or more of these be present we should be quite justified in speaking of a case as being in Smith's or Harris's "style". Style, however, is a subtle and rather intangible thing, so that when none of the distinctive features appear—as often happens—and documentary evidence is lacking, it is often difficult, even impossible to say that a particular case was the work of this builder rather than that, or even that it was not the work of one or other of their immediate successors.'[1]

[1] A. Freeman, *English Organ Cases,* 1921, p. 56.

A very fine case of the late Restoration period can be seen at St. Peter's, Tiverton, Devon (*38*). Snetzler (who rebuilt or repaired the organ) said the original instrument contained work by Bernard and Christian Smith, but there is evidence that it was actually made by Christian in 1696. Originally in the west gallery, the case now stands on the north side of the nave and contains an exceptionally fine specimen of the early work of Father Willis. The proportions have not been spoiled by the slight

63 *St. Catherine Cree. Father Smith case, 1686*
(*Drawing by A. G. Hill*)

widening effected presumably at that time. Particularly distinctive are the richly carved cornice mouldings of the towers, the unusually deep shades of the lower flats, and the abnormally elongated upper lips of the lower pipes. Ogee-shaped lips in the upper flats can be clearly seen.

Before leaving the Smith-Harris era, the 1717 Shrider case at St. Mary's, Finedon, must be mentioned (39). The historically important pipework has been referred to on p. 81. The beautiful case is fully in the older tradition, and is effectually a triple tower version of Bernard Smith's main case at Trinity College, Cambridge. Enlargements and internal rearrangements carried out by Holdich in 1852 necessitated a slight forward extension of the Finedon case to the edge of the gallery. But apart from this it retains its original appearance, including the diapered pipe decorations and the overhanging sides.

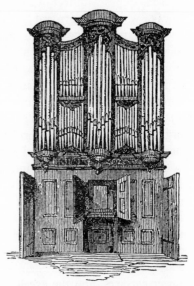

Sir John Sutton says, 'After the time of Smith and Harris, organ cases became plainer and meaner every year, and the old form was entirely defeated. Snetzler, Green and others in the middle of the last century enclosed their Organs in cases as much like a square box as possible, the sides being quite as broad as the front, and the tryptic like form, which was kept up by Smith by making the front overhang on each side, was discontinued'.[1]

Sutton's words may be taken as applying to the period 1724 (when Renatus Harris died) to 1847 (when *A Short Account of Organs* was published). He rightly saw that the 'old form' is perhaps the most important single feature in organ case design, and that the general run of cases following the time of Smith and Harris were poorer by its loss. His assessment holds good today with an important qualification. Looking back from over an extra century, during which the outward appearance of the British organ sank to unprecedented depths, Sutton appears less than fair to the work of the immediate successors of Smith and Harris.

[1] *A Short Account of Organs*, p. 98.

Mid-eighteenth-century cases may be adjudged inferior to the best Restoration work for reasons including the absence of corbelling, a tendency towards meanness of cornices and shades, and the more overt use of false pipe lengths. Yet the majority to be seen today are dignified, tastefully conceived and of good architectural scale. Many are richly decorated and carved. The style of carved work is different, but the quality of craftsmanship is beyond reproach. In the authors' opinion these cases are preferable to much Continental work of the same period, where the extravagances of the late Baroque and Rococo can be seen in full swing.

The vignette reproduced on p. 225 shows a type of triple tower case used by Snetzler for several of his instruments, of which the example at Peterhouse College Chapel, Cambridge (1765), is amongst the few surviving. The most characteristic feature is the treatment of the lower pair of flats—pipes with feet of equal length planted on curved toeboards, the lines of which are mirrored by the contrary curve of the shades above. At St. Margaret's, King's Lynn (24), there are single storey flats only; and here similar treatment is applied to a triple tower case with the shortest in the centre. This organ was made in 1754 by Snetzler at the instigation of Burney, and is a late instance of the use of overhanging sides. The flat front of the chamber size Snetzler organ at Sculthorpe Church, made in 1756, is similarly devised (64). This is one of the most charming of small organ cases. It has some Rococo ornamentation, and presents a virtually perfect blend of richness and simplicity.

Cases of the three-tower and gable type used by Renatus Harris at St. Botolph, Aldgate, have already been mentioned as being popular with certain of his successors (p. 217). Probably the finest example to be seen is at St. Leonard's, Shoreditch, made by Richard Bridge in 1754, and restored after war damage by Noel Mander (25). The casework is of mahogany of which details, as well as the front pipes, are freshly gilded. False lengths are very evident in the lower flats; but the finely moulded tower cornices, and the excellent scale of the various elements, both in relation to each other and to the stately west end of the elder Dance's church, make this case one of the best examples of the mid-eighteenth century. It can be imagined how the scale would be ruined by the removal of the bracketed church and state emblems from the towers, which add greatly to the feeling of completeness and dignity. Other existing cases of similar design are:

1. St. Helen's, Abingdon, by Jordan, 1725.

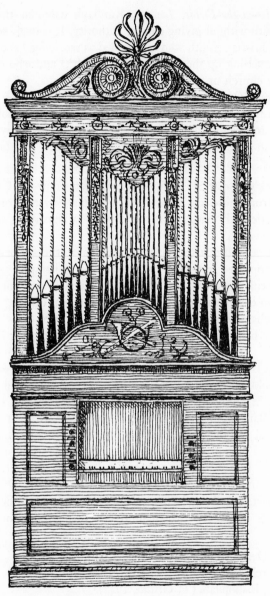

64 *Sculthorpe Church. Snetzler case, 1756*
(Drawing by Cecil Clutton)

2. St. Giles-in-the-Fields, London. Rimbault ascribed this organ to Father Smith without giving date or authority. It is likely to have been made by Christian Smith who is recorded as receiving £200 in 1699 for 'making & setting up the organ in the church',[1] and who re-erected it in the new church in 1734.

3. St. Luke's, Old Street, London, by Jordan and Bridge, 1733. This church became unsafe in 1960 and had to be partly demolished. The organ case and its instrument, containing fine work by Gray & Davison and Willis in addition to that of the original builders, is to be re-erected in St. Giles', Cripplegate, by N. P. Mander Ltd.

Schwarbrick's case at St. Philip's, Birmingham (now the Cathedral) of 1715 differs from those just mentioned in having breasted compartments (27). It is particularly fine, and is one of the few remaining cases of this kind now to be seen.[2]

During the second quarter of the eighteenth century a very individual type of case appeared in and around London, consisting of the standard three semicircular towers, but with ogee-shaped intervening compartments both on elevation and plan. This arrangement of pipes in graceful 'curtains' is characteristic of some Continental Rococo cases of the same period. Of the half-dozen surviving examples, the one in the rebuilt City church of St. Vedast, Foster Lane, is in the most perfect state of restoration (40). This organ was built by John Harris and the elder Byfield for St. Bartholomew-by-the-Exchange in 1731, where it can be seen in an engraving in Godwin's *London Churches* (1838). About 1841 it was moved to St. Bartholomew, Moor Lane, Cripplegate. In 1904 that church was demolished and the organ was presumed lost. In fact it had survived in St. Alban's, Fulham, jammed in a most unsatisfactory position behind a chancel arch. In 1961 it was restored and re-erected in St. Vedast by Noel Mander under the architectural supervision of S. E. Dykes Bower, where the effect, tonally and architecturally, is truly magnificent.

Similar cases of this type which survive in their original homes are as follows:

St. Paul's, Deptford (Richard Bridge, 1730).
Christ Church, Spitalfields (Richard Bridge, 1731).
St. Helen's, Bishopgate (T. Griffin, 1742).

[1] Parton's *History of the Parish of St. Giles.*
[2] A similar case with breasted compartments was made by Jordan for Great Yarmouth Parish Church in 1733. For many years this, together with Harris's case from St. Peter Mancroft, Norwich, served to screen the backs of the divided Binns organ. All were destroyed by enemy action in 1941.

St. Margaret Patterns (T. Griffin, 1749).
St. Andrew's, Enfield (Richard Bridge, 1753).

Another specimen, by Jordan (formerly in St. George's, Botolph Lane), can be seen in St. George's Church, Southall, Middlesex.

The Deptford example is the smallest of these; and the Spitalfields one of the largest and perhaps the most opulent, as befits its west gallery location in Hawksmoor's vast building. Something must be said here about Mr. Griffin. He was no organ builder, but a barber by trade who, although devoid of musical qualifications or ability, managed to hold the office of Gresham Professor of Music from 1762 to 1791. He entered into an arrangement with a number of London parishes, whereby in consideration of a life annuity he provided an organ, and engaged an organist so long as his own annuity was regularly paid. It is likely that he obtained his instruments from the Byfield, Jordan and Bridge combine.[1]

The case of the organ built for St. Mary, Rotherhithe, by the second Byfield in 1764 (see p. 83) is a good example of the weaknesses which by that time were beginning to creep into case design (41). All the front pipes belong to the original Byfield open diapason. The use of false lengths is extremely apparent in the flat compartments (the pipes seem too long for their scale), and this is not improved by the insubstantial feel of the curved cornices above, with their narrow Rococo shades. The case is a rich mahogany and much detail is picked out in gold leaf. The cornices of the towers are finely moulded and strong and the general effect of the case in its west gallery is very fine, despite the few faults which have been mentioned. Freeman says this case 'has much Rococo ornament not a little of which is plaster work'. A close examination of the woodwork makes it difficult to understand what this means, unless possibly the ornaments which top the towers are cast in plaster.

George England's case of 1765 in the west gallery of St. Stephen's, Walbrook, has considerably more Rococo ornamentation than the

[1] Hopkins and Rimbault (1877 ed.), p. 145 says, 'In consequence of the many new churches that were erected at the commencement of the eighteenth century an equal number of organs was required, which induced many persons who were totally unskilled in the art and mystery of voicing organ pipes to become builders. To prevent, therefore, the sad consequences which must have naturally followed, a coalition was formed between the three eminent artists of the day, Byfield, Jordan and Bridge, who undertook to build organs at a very moderate charge, and to apply their united talents to each; the result of which was a fair, though moderate, compensation to themselves, and superior instruments to our Churches. The organ in Yarmouth Parish Church, Norfolk, 1733, and in St. George's Chapel in the same town, were made in this way.' The case of the latter instrument was also of the type mentioned above.

Rotherhithe case, and is one of the best of the period (65). It is a pity that open wood pedal pipes can now be seen on either side. The use of the same general pattern by George Pike England, in a plainer and more flattened form, can be found at Warminster (1792), Blandford Forum (1794), and St. Margaret, Lothbury (1801). The last-mentioned case was enlarged in 1862 and 1881.

During the first half of the eighteenth century a few cases appeared

65 *St. Stephen, Walbrook. George England case, 1765*
(Drawing by H. T. Lilley)

showing a complete break with traditional form. The case of Abraham Jordan's organ at St. Magnus-the-Martyr, London Bridge (1712), still retains its original appearance, although all signs of the original tone have been long since obliterated (28). Here the decorative has completely overpowered the functional. There is some Baroque feeling, particularly in the broken and undulating pediment, and the draped foliate pipe shades. The pipes of the flat within the pediment are manifestly shams. The case of the Harris–Byfield organ at St. Mary Redcliffe, Bristol, made in 1726, was another fanciful, although undeniably spectacular construction (66). It was supplanted in 1867. Another case by the same builders (1728) can still be seen at St. Thomas's, Bristol, but deprived of its original west end position, and consequently seen to less advantage. Both cases were conceived on the same general pattern, the predominant feature being the broad, three-part, central tower.

From about the third quarter of the eighteenth century, the weak elements which had begun earlier to appear in Renaissance style cases became more pronounced. Church authorities either could not or would not pay for quality of style, and the tastes of the day did not demand it. By the end of the century meanness of design and sparseness of carving had become commonplace. False lengths and blatantly sham pipes are increasingly found in organ fronts. Pipe shades had withered down to the merest fringes, and eventually disappeared altogether, contributing greatly to the appearance of falsity. About this time many cases were being made in the Gothick taste. A discussion of these belongs to the next section of this chapter.

It must be stressed that even in those decadent times, all organs were properly encased, and no one would have dreamed that they should have been otherwise. Not until the 1850s were uncased organs deemed a virtue.

Although made as late as 1814, the case of the splendid George Pike England organ at Islington Chapel of Ease (now St. Mary Magdalen, Holloway Road) is typical of many Renaissance style cases of the end of the century (42). It is beautifully constructed of Spanish mahogany, but there is little carving. The cornices of both flats and towers are stringently devised, the shades appear as a series of pendants of equal length, and there is far too much parallel motion between the vital lines.

The case of the Smith chamber organ at Dingestow Court, Monmouthshire, made by Robert Gray in 1773 (45), is handsomely constructed of mahogany, and the front pipes are gilded. There is nothing wrong with dummy pipes provided they look real. But no attempt has been

The East Prospect of the Stone Gallerie & Magnificent Organ of S.t Mary Redcliff Bristol the Musical part perform'd by Messieurs Harris & Byfield

66 *St. Mary Redcliffe, Bristol. Harris–Byfield case, 1726*

made to give these a functional appearance, and comparison with the two original Smith cases illustrated in figs. 33 and 34 shows the inferiority of this admirable piece of furniture as an example of organ case design.

About this period, pipe shades frequently assumed the form of carved drapery. John Geib's case at St. Mary, Stafford, 1790 (52), is an example of 'good' debased design in which this feature appears, together with other weaknesses mentioned above. It is also a rare instance in a British case of a double storey tower.

Another 'bare' case of the period is at the Roman Catholic Church of Our Lady of the Assumption, Warwick Street, London (formerly the Chapel of the Bavarian Embassy) (43). It was made by John Byfield in about 1790. The illustration shows it after rebuilding by N. P. Mander Ltd. in 1960. Mr. Mander removed some large flats which had been added at each end, and substituted 'pavilions' to contain the parts of the instrument which overflow the case. The result is a good example of how an old case can be tastefully enlarged without destroying the scale. The actual case is about as plain as can be, yet the proportions are so good that the effect is pleasing. The pipe shades (of red and gold) are modern and were devised by Mr. Mander. Their presence has removed one of the main weaknesses of the original design.

A comparison of the last two cases with, say, Smith's case at Trinity College, Cambridge, or Harris's at St. James's, Piccadilly, will show the deterioration of design which had taken place over a period of about 100 years.

REVIVALISM AND THE CASELESS ORGAN
(1750 to 1950)

Samuel Green was probably the most prolific producer of organ cases in the 'Gothick taste'. At this point the story may be given over again to Sir John Sutton.

Early in the reign of George the Third, attempts were made to restore the Gothic style, at least in the restorations made in old Churches; with what success may be seen by examining the stalls at Westminster Abbey, the Altar and organ screens at St. George's Chapel, at Windsor, and other works executed about the same period. Green, who was at that time at the height of his popularity, and was very much patronised by King George the Third, was obliged to conform to the prevailing taste, and began to engraft innumerable pinnacles and incorrect Gothic details upon his taste-less boxes. And their effect was, if possible, worse than the plain ones which had preceded them. Many of our Cathedrals, College Chapels and Parish Churches, are disfigured by these unsightly organ-cases, which became every day larger and more heavy looking, and the ornamental parts resemble the barley sugar ornaments we see about Christmas time in pastry-cooks' windows, displayed for all their glory on a twelfth cake. From time to time slight improvements were made in the details, though they were injudiciously applied. Every part of a Church has been copied for the organ-case, and attempts have been made at one time to make the organ look like a tomb, at another like a screen, at another the canopies of

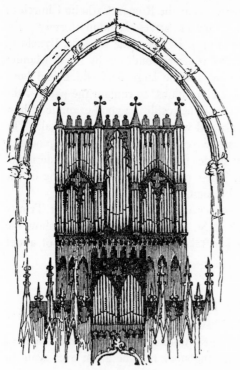

the stalls have been placed on the top of the organ, and latterly, as if in despair of producing anything decent, the organ has been put out of sight altogether.[1]

The conscious revival of Gothic as distinct from the survival of traditional forms can be traced to the first half of the eighteenth century, even earlier. By 1742 Batty Langley had published his *Gothic Architecture Improved*. The idea of that principal landmark of early Gothic revivalism, Horace Walpole's Strawberry Hill, was born about 1749, although the actual transformation covered a period of several years. The reappearance of Gothic in British organ cases occurs at least as early as the 1750s. In the *Dictionary of English Furniture* is illustrated a chamber organ, probably by Richard Bridge, c. 1755, with applied Gothick decorations. By 1762 the third and enlarged edition of Chippendale's *Director* included a number of designs for Gothick organ cases. A principal landmark in the revival is the case of George England's Dulwich College Chapel organ, erected in 1760 (51). Freeman regarded this case as an example of the survival

[1] *A Short Account of Organs*, p. 99.

67 *Assumption of Our Lady, Harlton :
very probable Sutton design, 1869*

68 *St. Mary-the-Virgin, Great
Bardfield : Pugin-Sutton
influence, c. 1860*

69 *St. Bartholomew, Armley: Schulze organ. Case by Walker and Athron, 1877*

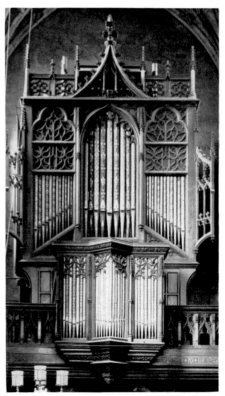

70 *Sherborne Abbey; case by R. C. Carpenter, 1856*

of traditional Gothic, 'born out of due time'. The spirettes above the three towers 'are not mere gables, but proper four-sided spires of pierced work quite in the tradition of such early cases as those at Zaragoza and Palma (Majorca) which date from the fifteenth century. The pinnacles, too, which stand on the top of the six buttresses, have the same affinity with the past. No revivalist would have tolerated them, nor would anyone before the time of Pugin have bettered them.'[1] Whether we regard this interesting case as 'survival' or 'revival', it is probably the earliest major instance of the use of Gothic forms in a British organ case for over 200 years.

The Sutton vignette reproduced on p. 234 is a fair indication of a type of Gothic case made by Green. Many of these merited Sir John's condemnation, but, as previously, his judgment must be qualified from the outlook of the present day. Sutton was writing from the earnest aesthetic-moral viewpoint of a member of the Cambridge Camden Society, which identified Gothic art with Christianity, and anathematised everything which did not fit into a preconceived notion of ecclesiological correctness. The Georgians did not see it this way at all. 'Earlier the Gothick (to continue to give it a Georgian spelling) has been for the most part a whimsical or a pedantic or sometimes merely an economical alternative to the dominant classical modes, little more serious than the concurrent Chinese or Turkish fancies'.[2] Viewed in this non-serious light, with full awareness of their stylistic absurdities, many of the Gothick cases of the late eighteenth and early nineteenth centuries can please and amuse by reason of their uninhibited superficiality. Their weaknesses become part of their charm. In this way they can be said to succeed artistically where many of the debased Renaissance cases fail. Only when the Gothick style is pompous does it become dull.

An excellent Gothick case containing an organ by Green[3] is at Down Cathedral, Downpatrick, Northern Ireland (53). It was set up in the Cathedral about 1800, but was probably made some years earlier. Another fine specimen can be found at Wymondham Abbey, Norfolk. This contains an organ built by James Davis for Longman and Broderip in 1793, which was restored and rebuilt with great artistry by Messrs. Hill, Norman & Beard in 1954. Figure 56 shows a chamber organ by Bates of Ludgate made in about 1805. It has a formal case with Gothick

[1] A. Freeman. Article on George England in *The Organ*, Vol. xx, No. 88, p. 141,
[2] Henry-Russell Hitchcock, *Early Victorian Architecture in Britain*, 1954, Vol. I. p. 13.
[3] Very sympathetically rebuilt by Messrs. Harrison & Harrison in 1914.

fripperies which, when it first came into the possession of Noel Mander, was painted a dirty chocolate brown. Mr. Mander restored the organ, and had the case repainted predominantly green, with details in red and gold. It now looks extremely charming. The case of the Bryceson barrel organ of about 1805 (55) is an absolute nonsense so far as any resemblance to a real organ is concerned. But what could be more delightful of its kind and period? The more pretentious Gothic cases of the late eighteenth and early nineteenth centuries are less successful. In considering, for instance, the case of Green's organ of 1776 at New College, Oxford (an extraordinary erection with a Gothic arch in the middle to allow a vista to the Reynolds west window)[1]; Blore's existing case at Winchester Cathedral, made in 1819; and the existing York Minster case (57), made for the Eliott and Hill organ of 1829, it is possible to feel more at one with Sir John Sutton. The York case illustrates a feature of many others of the period—the separation of individual pipes by wooden 'divides'—a device which is as ugly as it is non-functional.

Cases of the York type have earned the epithet 'prickly Gothic' by reason of the abundance of pinnacles and cresting. Another well-known example is E. J. Willson's case of 1826 which still stands on the choir screen at Lincoln Cathedral.

During this period, well meaning but misguided attempts were made to 'Gothicise' Renaissance organ cases by the substitution of Gothic shades, caps, tracery and panels for the original Renaissance work. As previously mentioned, this procedure was seriously advocated by F. H. Sutton, although he would have preferred a more scholarly kind of Gothic. The results were felt to be more in keeping with mediaeval architecture, a view with which we may now disagree. One of the earliest organ cases to receive this vandalistic treatment, and one which still survives, was the west front of the 1675-6 Father Smith case at the University Church of St. Mary-the-Virgin, Oxford (15). The alterations were carried out by Thomas Plowman in 1827. Several other cases received similar treatment, and among them the 1689 Renatus Harris case at Norwich Cathedral. This was first 'Gothicised' in 1833, further altered in 1899 and 1914, and finally burnt in 1939 (see p. 271).

For those who did not want the Gothick style, the Grecian provided a fashionable alternative. The case made for Samuel Green's organ of 1789 in the chapel designed by 'Athenian' Stuart and William Newton at the Royal Naval Hospital, Greenwich, is an outstanding example of super-lative craftsmanship wasted on a weak and tenuous design (59). An

[1] There is an illustration in Ackermann's *History of Oxford.*

71 *Ely Cathedral, 1851*

CASES BY SIR GILBERT SCOTT

72 *St. Mary, Nottingham, 1871*

73 *Selby Abbey, north case, 1909*

CASES BY J. O. SCOTT

74 *St. Albans Cathedral, 1908, eastern aspect (before addition of central positive case by Cecil Brown, 1963)*

excellent double case in the Grecian style can be seen in St. John's Church, Waterloo Road, Lambeth (60). Originally made for a Bishop organ in 1824, it was severely damaged in the Second World War, but the remains were re-composed into a likeness of the original design by N. P. Mander Ltd. in 1951. The present design differs from the original in a few details, but notably through the absence of pipe shades. The style is completely in harmony with Bedford's Greek Doric church. Another Grecian-style case, which appears to have been enlarged, can be seen in the Nash church of All Souls', Langham Place.

The early Victorian organ case reached its lowest ebb at Leeds Parish Church in 1841, where the organ was contained in a kind of Gothic shrine. The famous Bishop organ of 1844 in St. Giles, Camberwell, is also hidden behind a pipeless screen. Seventeen years previously Green's organ at Canterbury Cathedral had been completely pushed out of sight in the triforium. These things were but the forerunners of worse to come during the next hundred years.

Round about the middle of the century there were attempts by a few architects to produce some original designs both in keeping with classical buildings and suitable for the larger instruments then being made. The results were generally rather ponderous, but not entirely devoid of merit. Probably the best known existing specimen is at St. Martin-in-the-Fields, Westminster, by T. Allom, 1854 (75). This is another late example of a double case. The instrument, by Bevington, had an exceptionally complete tonal design. The front pipes are now gilded.

From about 1850 onwards two main divergent streams become apparent in the external appearance of the British organ. Both had their origin in the Tractarian movement of the Anglican Church. One led rapidly to the almost complete abandonment of the organ case as such; the other to the revival of its traditional form and design, albeit imbued with romantic mediaevalism.

The eastward migration of parish choirs to chancels, and organs to chantry chapels or other equally unsuitable places has been explained earlier in this chapter. It often happened that there was no room for the old organ case in the new position, and the tops of the casework were lopped off to make it fit. Thus the 'bare topped' organ came into being, not by design but by accident. From this it was a short step to the fronts of bare pipes, painted or plain, which disfigure so many of our churches. Church restorers thought that in discarding the traditional organ case they were returning to 'true principles'. In fact 'true principles' amounted to little more than an excuse for getting rid of old

75 *St. Martin-in-the-Fields. Allom case, 1854*
(Drawing by H. T. Lilley)

76 *St. George's Hall, Liverpool. Organ design by C. R. Cockerell, 1855*

casework which did not conform to current fashion, and for saving money.

The caseless[1] organ, or the ornamental arrangement of a front of un-covered pipes, is perhaps the only really characteristic contribution of the Victorian age to the external appearance of the British organ. All the Gothic and Renaissance revival cases shortly to be considered are derived from styles of an earlier age. The caseless organ is blatantly and un-ashamedly Victorian. It came particularly into its own in the large town hall organs which municipalities were providing for the enjoyment of their citizens. William Hill's Birmingham Town Hall organ of 1834 had a very respectable case, embodying large pipes, but conceived on tradi-tional lines. Twenty years later C. R. Cockerell designed a 'case' for

[1] So called to avoid confusion with the modern *unencased* organ, in which all or most of the instrument is 'functionally' displayed (see pp. 275–6).

Willis's historic organ at St. George's Hall, Liverpool, in which even the pretence of surrounding casework had been completely abandoned (76). The only acknowledgments to tradition were the fairly obvious arrangements of pipes into towers and shorter groups. Like Gilbert Scott (see p. 256) Cockerell discerned that there was something inconclusive about bare pipe tops, for he felt obliged to finish them off with crowns. The very blatancy of the composition has its own peculiar fascination. Many less attractive designs are to be found in public halls throughout the country, among them the Royal Albert Hall and the Alexandra Palace. Another imposing caseless town hall organ of the period can be seen at Leeds Town Hall. Here the designer, Cuthbert Broderick, thought it desirable to place incongruous caps above the two large 32 ft. towers while leaving the intervening flats uncovered. The Leeds organ, very famous in its day, was built by Gray and Davison in 1858 to the design of Henry Smart.

The origins of the revival of traditional form and design can be found in a handful of lovely little Gothic cases which appeared around the middle of the century. Their designs can be attributed directly or indirectly to Sir John Sutton, his younger brother, the Rev. Frederick Heathcote Sutton, and to Augustus Welby Northmore Pugin. By this time, largely as the result of Pugin's burning enthusiasm, Gothic architecture was being properly studied and taken very seriously. The Suttons were rich and influential, and members of the Cambridge Camden Society (later the Ecclesiological Society), with whom lies much of the responsibility for the internal rearrangement of Anglican Churches which took place during the second half of the century. They fully accepted the interior rearrangement of churches advocated by Dr. Jebb, but parted company with most of their fellow tractarians by insisting that the organ be given proper treatment. Sir John became a Fellow of Jesus College, Cambridge, and in 1847 published anonymously *A Short Account of Organs*, to which Pugin contributed a set of model Gothic case designs. F. H. Sutton was responsible for the sympathetic restoration of the cases at Old Bilton (see p. 184) and Old Radnor (p. 175) at a time when they were just as likely to have been chopped up for firewood. His book *Church Organs* (incorporating his 1866 monograph on the Old Radnor case) expresses the Sutton view on parish church organs. Briefly—the organ should be in the chancel; it should have a traditional case in the 'old form'; and it should be Gothic. Pugin had become a Roman Catholic in 1838. He died in 1852, mentally and physically worn out, having 'crammed into his forty years of existence the work of a hundred years'. It is generally assumed that Pugin provided the case designs and the Suttons the money.

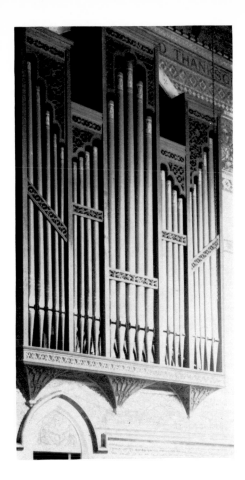

77 *St. James, Weybridge, c. 1865*

CASES BY J. L. PEARSON

78 *Westminster Abbey, north case, restored and decorated by S. E. Dykes Bower, 1959*

CASES
BY
BODLEY

79 (Above, Left) *St. Mary-the-Virgin, Pulham*, c. *1885*

80 (Above, Right) *St. Mary-the-Virgin, Cheshunt*

81 (Right) *All Saints, Danehill, 1890*

The Suttons were men of taste, widely travelled, and almost certainly knew more about organs than did Pugin. The actual extent to which one side influenced the other is likely to remain obscure, although the scales seem to be evenly balanced. Only two of the group of seven cases now to be considered are known to be Pugin's—but all reveal his influence.

The two undoubted Pugin cases are at Jesus College Chapel, Cambridge; and the one formerly at St. Mary's, West Tofts, Norfolk, now in the near-by parish church of South Pickenham.

The Jesus College organ faces into the chapel from a loft over the north stalls (*61*). Between 1846 and 1849 the chapel was restored under the direction of Salvin and then of Pugin. The organ was given by Sir John Sutton, and built by Bishop in conformity with Sir John's idea of what a perfect church organ ought to be—a two-manual pedal-less organ on the lines of a Father Smith. In fact it consisted largely of genuine Smith wooden pipes, which can still be heard today. In 1927 the instrument was enlarged by Messrs. Harrison & Harrison in such a way as to leave the original case and tonal scheme unimpaired. Figure 61 shows it before 1927, with the old console (which still remains) at the northern end of the case. The case is fully in accord with the spirit of fourteenth-century Gothic, and is as near perfection as anything to be found. Like all Pugin's work, and the best work of his successors, it is no mere copy of Gothic models, but rather a re-thinking in Gothic terms. It is fully in the old form, with corbelling; the top is covered, and there are winged doors which enhance the beautiful 'tryptic like form' so beloved by Sir John.

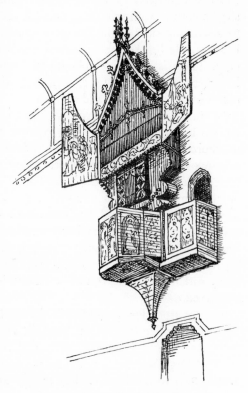

82 *St. Mary, West Tofts, Pugin case* (*Drawing by Cecil Clutton*)

In its original home, the West Tofts case was suspended, together with a cul-de-lampe, on the north wall of the chancel (*82*). It was provided during the incumbency of the Rev. Augustus Sutton (another of the Sutton brotherhood), the cost being borne by the Sutton family. Pugin restored the church in 1849, but since the chancel was not added until after his death, the case may also have been made posthumously. Both case and tribune formed a singularly charming composition. According to Freeman, the tribune was 'painted a light grey colour and decorated with light green, red and gold. Seven of the thirteen panels which compose its front and sides bear painted figures of angels with musical instruments. The remaining six are covered with stencilled patterns.'[1] The case was, and still is, decorated in green and red, with stencilled designs and gilding. The paintings on the doors are said to be by old Italian masters. As at Jesus College, the top is covered. The small Brustwerk conceals a diminutive short-compass swell organ. The gable-shaped cornice with crowning pinnacle, the flat front of pipes with their tops standing clear of the fringes of tracery, and the shape of the over-hanging side brackets, are features which indicate early German influence. There is a considerable affinity between this small case and the larger one, dating from 1492, at St. Valentin, Kiedrich. The latter is the oldest case in Germany, and also has associations with Sir John Sutton. Sir John is supposed to have first seen the Kiedrich organ in 1857, and he later had it restored at his own expense, spending no less than £20,000 on church, organ and choir school. The resemblance makes it tempting to suppose that he knew the German organ at an earlier date, and that his knowledge influenced the West Tofts design. It is difficult to imagine anything more perfect than the West Tofts case. St. Mary's Church is in a battle training area, and has been closed since 1941. In 1950 the organ was rescued from neglect and deterioration by the Rector and parishioners of South Pickenham, and set up in their church, where it now stands on the ground floor in the south-west corner of the nave.[2] It is a sorry sight without its gallery; but one must be thankful that it had been preserved.

Not far from Jesus College, in the small church of St. Andrew-the-Less, Cambridge (known as the Abbey Church), is another delightful little case which (judging by style and circumstantial evidence) is the work of Pugin and Sir John. It stands on the north chancel wall, and is very similar to the Jesus College organ, except that the central tower is

---

[1] *English Organ Cases*, p. 24.
[2] *Musical Times*, April, 1956, p. 201.

83 *St. John-the-Evangelist, Oxford: case by Bodley*

84 *St. Michael-and-All-Angels, Croydon: case by Bodley*

semicircular (the middle pipe being embossed), and the front overhangs but not the sides. There are hinged doors, and the top of the case is surmounted by cresting.

It seems likely that one of the Suttons had a hand in the design of the case at the Church of the Assumption of Our Lady, Harlton (a few miles to the south east of Cambridge), both in view of its style, and the fact that the living is under the patronage of Jesus College (67). It stands, a little off centre, in a bay of the north aisle—the reason for this curious site being the position of a former door which the organ now occupies. The date given on the impost inscription is 1869. Whoever designed this captivating little case must have been influenced by the early sixteenth-century case at Tirlemont, the oldest in Belgium. The Harlton case is of oak, with some gilt detail, and the front pipes are silvered.

The influence of the late fourteenth-century case at Notre Dame-de-Valère, Sion, can clearly

85 *St. John's, Stockcross. Case probably by F. H. Sutton, c. 1870*
(*Drawing by Cecil Clutton*)

be seen at St. John's, Stockcross, near Newbury (*85*). The living was formerly in the gift of the Sutton family, and almost certainly one of them was responsible for the ornate design. The Stockcross case lacks the doors, overhanging sides and elaborate colour scheme of Sion. There are other minor differences of treatment, but the pipe pattern and the silhouette of the cornices are similar.

At All Saints' Church, Theddingworth, is a simple covered case with doors designed by the Rev. F. H. Sutton during his incumbency of 1864–73 (*62*). Both the pipes and casework are decorated in colours and gold. A plain but picturesque little case with overhanging sides and folding doors can be found at Bolnhurst Church, Bedfordshire. F. H. Sutton was probably the designer, and it is very similar to one of the model designs in his book.

The Pugin-Sutton style is very evident in the organ at Great Bardfield, Essex, although no one has yet produced any documentary evidence (*68*). The flat-fronted gable design invites comparison with West Tofts. The main differences at Great Bardfield are the covered pipe tops; division of the front into three compartments; and the substitution of wings for doors. The casework is predominantly brown with lighter stencilling, and the carving has green, red and gold embellishments. Tonally the organ is outstanding. Everything about it points to the work of G. M. Holdich not long after 1860.

Among Pugin's many beautiful but unrealised projects is a sketch for the interior of Ushaw College Chapel, showing a screen organ with doors incorporating a rood and attendant figures (*90*). It is preserved in the print room of the Victoria and Albert Museum. One can imagine how charming this case would have been if worked out in detail.

After Pugin and the Suttons, the most outstanding designers of organ cases are Sir George Gilbert Scott (1811–78); his younger son John Oldrid Scott (1842–1913); John Loughborough Pearson (1817–97); George Frederick Bodley (1827–1907); Sir Thomas G. Jackson (1835–1924); and Dr. Arthur George Hill (1857–1923). With the exception of Jackson, and to some extent Hill, their cases are all predominantly Gothic in style.

Of the principal Gothic revival architects who followed Pugin, only G. G. Scott, Bodley and Pearson took any serious interest in organ case design. Of the others, G. E. Street, so far as is known, produced nothing. William Butterfield contributed designs for a couple of naked pipe racks to *Instrumenta Ecclesiastica* (A Series of Working Designs for the Furniture, Fittings and Decoration of Churches and their Precincts), which

86 *West front*

BRASENOSE COLLEGE CHAPEL,
OXFORD: *case by Jackson*

87 (Below) *East front*

88 *St. Catherine's College Chapel, Cambridge :*
    double case by Garner, 1895

89 (Below) *Sheldonian Theatre, Oxford :*
    case by Jackson, 1877

indicates fairly clearly the extent of his interest in the subject. That very 'tough' Gothicist, William Burges, produced a fantastic castellated design for Lille Cathedral, which together with one or two other similar designs never came to fruition.[1] R. C. Carpenter's solitary contribution seems to have been the 1856 case at Sherborne Abbey (70). This has a functional choir organ case, and despite a few obvious faults is exceptionally good for the date.

At this point the case which encloses the famous Schulze organ at St. Bartholomew's, Armley, may be mentioned (69). It was designed in about 1877 by the architects of the church, Messrs. Walker and Athron, and appears to have been their only con-

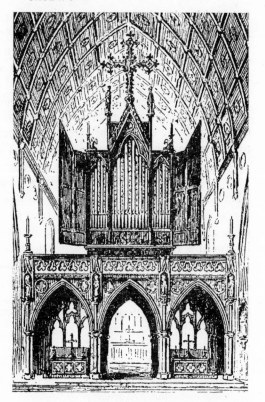

90 *Proposed interior of Ushaw College Chapel by A. W. N. Pugin*
(*Copy of Pugin sketch by H. T. Lilley*)

tribution to the art. Walker had studied with Scott, but the Armley case is far better than anything Scott ever did. Writing in 1883[2] F. H. Sutton described it as undoubtedly 'the grandest example of a modern Gothic organ in England'. Freeman said it was the first really successful attempt at massing large pipes without in any way departing from the true principles of organ case design. Beyond expressing agreement with these two authorities on the merits of this outstanding case, there is nothing more to be said.

Sir Gilbert Scott, the prime restorer and rearranger of our cathedrals during the nineteenth century, designed organ cases for those at Ely

[1] The Lille design is illustrated in G. A. Audsley's *Art of Organ Building*, Vol. i, p. 149.
[2] *Church Organs*, 2nd edition, 1883.

(1851), Manchester (1872), Bangor (1873), St. Mary's, Edinburgh (1874), Rochester (1875), Chester (1876), Ripon (1878) and Worcester, together with several lesser churches. Scott must have known some of the work of Pugin and the Suttons, and he had certainly studied foreign cases, for he tells us in his memoirs that at Ely 'I placed the organ partly in the triforium and partly overhanging the choir, founding its design upon those of mediaeval organs, e.g. Strasburg'. Yet in spite of this, most of his cases reveal one or more of the following main faults—uncovered pipe tops; pipes protruding above casework; and undue use of false lengths.

It is generally agreed that Scott's best case was at St. Mary's, Nottingham (1871) (72). Unfortunately it was recast and ruined by Temple Moore in about 1915. The illustration is Scott's original drawing, which is preserved in the church. Like Ely it is a free adaptation of the Strasburg case. Freeman has pointed out that it would have been enormously improved if the pipe feet had varied inversely with their body lengths, but the greatest fault was surely the protruding tops.

Freeman also said, very aptly, that if the Ely case was in some respects a failure, it was a glorious failure (71). There are enough false-looking pipes and uncovered tops to condemn it on purist grounds. Yet the scale is good and there is plenty of movement about it. Scott obviously felt there was something unsatisfactory about uncovered tops, because here (as at Worcester) he completed them with little tin hats. It is interesting to note that these do not appear in his original drawings of the case in the Victoria and Albert Museum.

Sir Gilbert Scott's other cathedral cases are much less pleasing than the two just mentioned. Their main fault is dullness. The Manchester case, which stood on a choir screen, was destroyed in the last war. The east front was rather better done than the west, which was marred by protruding pipes. The worst offender in this respect is at Chester. At Rochester, the organ is divided on the narrow screen in two rather chunky halves, which are not improved by wooden bands around the groups of larger pipes. The Ripon case also stands on the screen. It is rather squat and wide, although the removal of some side wings from the western front a few years ago improved it a little.

Most of Sir Gilbert Scott's parish church organ cases are marred by protruding pipes. A notable exception is at Holy Trinity, Littlebury, Essex (1852)—probably his most successful small case. It is flat-fronted, with generous side corbelling. Two end towers are surmounted by deep cresting, and are joined by a threefold compartment with a low-centred curved cornice.

In all, Scott must be given credit for designing cases far better than the general run of his day, at a time when interest in the subject was re-awakening. But one cannot help feeling that, with his knowledge and experience, he ought to have done better.

J. O. Scott's cases are more mature than his father's, and free from most of their blemishes. His cases show a close study of early German and Spanish Gothic models. In a sense they are the kind of designs Sir Gilbert might have produced had he completely absorbed the lessons of traditional examples. John Oldrid's work is best known at the Cathedrals of Lichfield and St. Albans (1907 and 1908), St. John's College Chapel, Cambridge (1889), and Selby Abbey (1909). A design for Canterbury Cathedral was unfortunately never carried out. The Selby organ has twin cases on either side of the chancel, which differ slightly in details of carving. The north case is illustrated as an example of this architect's best work (73). The effect, although good, would be much better if the length of the pipe feet varied inversely with the body lengths. At Lichfield there are two cases facing the choir and north transept respectively. Both are quite lavish in treatment. The choir case has two central pointed towers with intervening flats connected to flat end towers at a slightly lower level. The transept case has a single pointed tower between two flats. The fronts of both cases overhang. As at Selby the choir case is slightly marred by the incorrect treatment of the pipe mouths. The transept case originally had a cluster of Spanish trumpets under its tower, but these were removed many years ago. At St. John's College Chapel there are also twin cases, but they are placed in adjoining north bays. The design of each case is in the form of a pseudo-chaire organ, with overhanging front and sides, which screens the lower part of a larger case behind. The design fails because of the resulting sense of incompleteness. The eastern case is now adorned by the projecting pipes of Messrs. Hill, Norman & Beard's trompète réal. The St. Albans organ is divided in twin cases above the screen (74). Its scale is better than Sir Gilbert's design at Rochester; but it is an illustration that such an arrangement has no chance of success unless the cases are fairly shallow, as at Westminster Abbey.[1]

The spirit of Pugin and the Suttons is more strongly felt in the organ cases of Pearson and Bodley than in any others of their generation. J. L. Pearson is remembered mainly for his beautiful Gothic revival churches at Truro, St. Augustine's, Kilburn, St. John's, Red Lion Square, and

[1] In 1963 the St. Albans organ was rebuilt by Messrs. Harrison & Harrison, and a charming positive case, designed by Mr. Cecil Brown was erected on the eastern side of the screen. The Scott cases were provided with side grilles to allow egress of sound.

St. Michael-and-All-Angels, Croydon. But none of these contain his organ cases. The Father Willis organ at Truro Cathedral is without case-work, although the front pipes are arranged formally as though for its reception. St. John's, Red Lion Square (destroyed in the last war), had a good, but not faultless case by C. J. Hare, Bodley's one-time partner. The St. Michael's cases are Bodley's (see below). There are Pearson cases in the parish churches of Chiswick and Boothby Pagnell; at St. James's, Weybridge and Westminster Abbey. The last two are illustrated as examples of simple and complex designs by this architect (77, 78). St. James's, built in 1847-8, was Pearson's first church. It was enlarged in 1864, and the organ case probably dates from soon afterwards. The flat front, the diversion into vertical compartments, the horizontal line of mouths, and the engrailed pipe shades are all early Gothic characteristics. Freeman was no doubt correct in surmising that Pearson modelled his design on the cases in Salamanca Cathedral (c. 1380) and San Petronio at Bologna (1470-5). The pair of cases at Westminster Abbey, made for the divided Hill organ of 1884, were erected in 1899. When the organ was rebuilt in 1936 by Messrs. Harrison & Harrison, the cases were replaced by zinc fronts arranged in such a way that no casework would have looked satisfactory. These unsightly horrors remained until 1959, when the Pearson cases were superbly restored under the direction of S. E. Dykes Bower. Mr. Dykes Bower has rectified the only real defect of the cases as originally set up—lack of colour—by applying a rich decorative scheme of colours and gilding to which no description could do justice. The design of both fronts is extremely complex, and shows great variety and ingenuity. The north front is shown in the illustration. The south one follows the same broad pattern of three large towers, but differs greatly in the disposition of the other parts and details. Viewed from the screen it could be said that the cases look somewhat stiff and a little too rectangular. But they were obviously never intended to be seen from that privileged position. From the floor of choir or nave their width becomes an advantage. Both cases look quite gorgeous, and it is difficult to imagine anything more fitting for the building and position.

Of the three dozen or so cases which can be accredited to Bodley, it is only possible to mention a few which illustrate some of the many facets of his style.

The lovely little case at St.-Mary-the-Virgin, Pulham, Norfolk (79) is almost certainly Bodley's. The inscription records that it is in memory of a former Rector who died in 1885, and the church was restored about that time by Bodley during his partnership with Garner. The design is

91 *St. John, Hampstead : case by Jackson*   92 *Chichester Cathedral : double case by A. G. Hill, 1888*

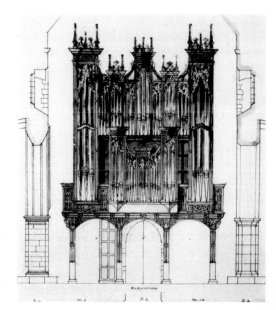

93 *Double organ case design for Hythe Parish Church by Nicholson, 1934*

94 *Peterborough Cathedral, 1904*

CASES BY HILL

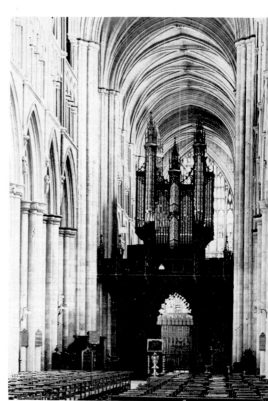

95 *Beverley Minster, 1916*

fully in the tradition of Pugin and the Suttons, and illustrates Bodley's indebtedness to them. Unlike so many of Bodley's more complex cases, the pipe feet are correctly treated.

At All Saints Church, Danehill, Sussex (built to the design of Bodley and Garner in 1890), the organ stands in the pre-Reformation position on the screen (*81*). The case is fairly small—only about 8 ft. from impost to top—and overhangs on all four sides. Its architectural scale, both in relation to the screen and the space above it, is quite admirable. The pipes are correctly and naturally treated. Both east and west pipe fronts are identically disposed, but there are minor variations in the decoration of the casework. The colour scheme is predominantly dark red, with stencilling in black and gold; pipe mouths and details of the carving are gilded. Part of the organ at St. Matthew, Chapel Allerton, Leeds, is also placed in a screen case. This consists of three single-storey compartments, the effect of which is rather heavy, and generally less prepossessing than the lighter and more varied arrangement at Danehill. There is also a screen organ by Bodley in the chapel of Queens' College, Cambridge. This is conceived on a far grander scale than the parish church cases just mentioned. But it is somewhat overpowering in the by no means large chapel, and is further marred by the unnatural look of many of the front pipes.

An irreproachable example of a flat-fronted Gothic case by Bodley is at Cheshunt Parish Church (*80*). Here the pipe feet are properly treated. This design obviously owes much to early Spanish models, such as St. Pablo, Zaragoza (*c*. 1420).

There can be little doubt that Bodley's design for the charming little hanging organ at St. John the Evangelist, Cowley Road, Oxford (the Cowley Fathers' Church) (*83*) was inspired by the early sixteenth-century 'swallow's nest' case at Freiburg-im-Breisgau Cathedral. The Bodley case is decorated in green, blue and gold, with some stencilling. The pipes are said to have been silvered; now they are a dull shade of gold, due possibly to gold paint or tarnished lacquer. There is a similar hanging case by Bodley at St. Mary's, Eccleston, near Chester.

At St. Michael-and-All-Angels, Croydon, can be found what must be a unique combination of period artistry—one of Father Willis's best instruments, a Pearson church with superb acoustics, and a double-fronted case by Bodley (*84*). It will be seen that the transept case is flat, and divided into five compartments. The chancel front, which overhangs the organist's tribune, has two semicircular towers and a number of apparently double tiered flats. Both the cases and the tribune are richly decorated, predominantly blue, and there is some gilding, particularly on the mouths of the pipes. There are, however, two blemishes which cannot be overlooked. One is Bodley's common habit of giving the longest pipes the longest feet. The other is the division of long pipes into double storey compartments. It always looks wrong to break the vertical lines of long pipes in this manner. The double tier flats in the chancel front would look better if they were filled with small pipes of appropriate scale. Here, as elsewhere, Bodley may have been at the mercy of the organ builder. A few words must be said about the St. Michael's instrument. In 1955 a rebuild was carried out by N. P. Mander Ltd. in memory of Dr. George Oldroyd, for many years organist of the church. The Father Willis work was carefully preserved, and there were some judicious additions, including a positive division, fully in character with the original tonal conception. The organ is now one of the best all-round church and recital instruments in the country.

Dr. A. G. Hill was a rare combination of scholar, organ architect and organ-builder. He made an exhaustive study of early Gothic and Renaissance cases, which he brought to public notice in his two volumes *Organs and Organ Cases of the Middle Ages and Renaissance* published in 1883 and 1891 respectively. These richly illustrated books undoubtedly did much to influence case design for the better.[1] Hill knew what an organ front should look like. In this way he had the edge on Bodley, and some others of his day, even though his cases may not equal theirs in picturesqueness.

With the exception of Hill's *magnum opus* at Sydney Town Hall (described by Freeman as the finest 32 ft. front that ever emanated from England) together with one or two others which are in Renaissance style, most of his cases are Gothic.

Two of Hill's best cases can be seen in the Cathedrals of Chichester and Peterborough. The Chichester case was made in 1888. It stands in the north transept, and contains parts of the Renatus Harris case which was damaged by the fall of the tower in 1859. The illustration is Hill's original drawing (92). It is a double case and the choir case is functional. Although the pipe feet of the choir case increase proportionately, care has been taken to preserve their natural appearance. It will be seen that the pipe tops just fall short of the shades. The Peterborough case (94) was put up in 1904. Here, too, the front pipes look perfectly natural, and show

---

[1] The subscription lists include the following important names in British organ case history: J. L. Pearson, Norman Shaw, A. W. Blomfield, Somers Clarke, C. E. Kempe, Temple L. Moore, J. Norbury, J. Oldrid Scott, T. Garner.

96 *St. Andrew, Kirkandrews-on-Esk, 1893*

CASES BY TEMPLE MOORE

97 *St. Peter, Yaxley*

98 *Southwark Cathedral: case by Sir Arthur Blomfield, 1896*

99 *Winchester College Chapel: case by Caröe, 1908*

a proper decrease in scale and length. Many of the pipes in Hill's imposing double-fronted choir screen case at Beverley Minster are treated less successfully and this case, majestic though it is, cannot be included among his finest (95). It dates from 1916, and was probably Hill's last work. The greatest virtue is the splendidly contrived scale in relation to the building.

Examples of Dr. Hill's mastery on a smaller scale can be seen at St. Matthew's, Little London, Leeds (where there are two fronts, differently disposed), and at St. Mark's, New Milverton. The latter is especially attractive. It is a flat-fronted case with a tall central compartment, which faces from an elevated organ chamber into a small north transept. There is much delicately executed painting and carving, and the middle pipe of each compartment is embossed.

C. E. Kempe (1837–1907), who is known principally for his work in stained glass, also designed a few attractive organ cases in the Gothic revival style. Probably his most spectacular work in this field was at Epping Parish Church, but since this was substantially re-cast and re-decorated many years ago (by C. J. Hare) it cannot be regarded as typical of his work. An unaltered example of Kempe's work can be seen at St. Mary's, Petworth, Sussex.

The Gothic revival in its turn brought about a revival of the Renaissance style. One of its principal exponents, and certainly the most outstanding designer of Renaissance revival organ cases during the last quarter of the nineteenth century, was Sir Thomas Jackson. In many ways his organ cases are comparable to those of Bodley in the Gothic sphere. They have the same picturesqueness and romantic appeal; and quite often the same faults.

A very commendable case by Jackson at St. John-the-Evangelist, Northington (c. 1896), and his design for a west gallery double case at Radley College Chapel (1895), show that he could do well in the Gothic style when required. The Radley design was not improved by the substitution of very prominent side wings for the smaller ones originally proposed. This organ was taken down many years ago, but the chaire case survives in St. Andrew's Church, East Hagbourne.

Jackson carried out much restoration and other work at Oxford, where a few of his most characteristic cases are to be found. The double-fronted case on the screen at Brasenose College Chapel should get very high marks for originality and delicacy of treatment (86, 87). Each front is differently disposed, the western one being bolder in treatment. The overhanging sides, the low centre, the bold cornice with cresting, and the chubby but well-proportioned towers all contribute to its charm. Particularly delightful is the carving of the pipe shades with peacocks and foliage. The casework is light oak, and details are picked out in gold. The show pipes are also gilded. Unfortunately Jackson has fallen into the Bodleian error of making the line of the larger tower pipe mouths curve in the wrong direction. Other Jackson cases can be seen in the chapels of Wadham, Hertford and Corpus Christi Colleges. A design for Oriel College Chapel was never realised.

Jackson's case for the Willis organ at the Sheldonian Theatre, erected in 1877, has been much admired by Freeman and others (*89*). Although this case undoubtedly contains many beautiful features, in the authors' view it must be reckoned below the architect's best by reason of the incomplete effect of the two side 'pedal' towers, the lower parts of which are hidden by the gallery. Father Willis must take a just share of the blame for these unsatisfactory features. Jackson wrote in his *Recollections*, 'The new organ was to be a fine instrument, built by Henry Willis—Father Willis as he came to be called—the best of organ-builders but the most aggravating of men. His only idea of the building was that it contained an organ, and he wanted, in Wren's graceful gallery, to put an organ that overhung it by 4 ft. This I would not consent to, but the obstinate old fellow would not give way till the Vice-Chancellor, to whom I appealed, met us in the Theatre and said, "Mr. Willis, you must do as Mr. Jackson tells you". So I made him keep his organ within the front of the gallery, and in recompense let him fill with pipes the two gallery windows adjoining.'[1]

Except for some false-looking pipes in the two upper flats (a fault which is not apparent from the architect's drawing), Jackson's case at St. John's Parish Church, Hampstead, is an excellent pastiche of a seventeenth-century style (*91*). The kiosks above the towers are typical of many Continental Renaissance cases.

Three more instances may be cited of the use of the Renaissance style by other architects. The double case at St. Catherine's College Chapel, Cambridge (*88*), was designed by Bodley's partner, Thomas Garner, for the Norman & Beard organ of 1895. It is richly carved in light oak, and is a good instance of the effective use of carved wings. There are too many false-looking pipes in both cases, however, for this design to be regarded as completely successful.

Temple Moore designed several organ cases which show a proper

[1] In 1963 the organ was rebuilt, the case redecorated and the 'Pedal' Towers, happily, were removed.

100 *All Saints, Hove: case by F. L. Pearson, 1915*

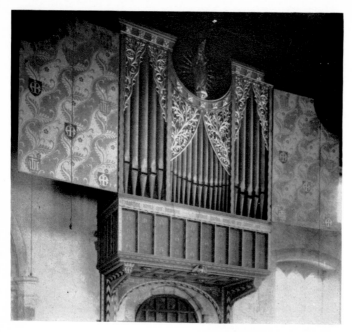

101 *St. Mary,*
Egmanton

CASES BY COMPER

102 *All Saints, Carshalton, double*
case, 1932

appreciation of the natural appearance of the instrument. For the church of St. Michael-and-All-Angels, Great Badminton, Gloucestershire, he designed an original case in mature British Renaissance style which is fully in keeping with the eighteenth-century classical church. The case was erected in 1908. It is a triple-tower design with corbelling. The centre tower, which is the tallest, interrupts the downward curve of the cornices above the intervening single-storey flats. The pipes of the latter are planted on steeply sloping toeboards. The only blemish is the proportionate feet lengths of the pipes in the towers, but this may not have been altogether the fault of the designer. The classical church of St. Andrew, Kirkandrews-on-Esk, Cumberland, was restored in 1893 by Temple Moore, when a new chancel screen and organ cases were provided. Here the Renaissance style has been used quite faultlessly. The organ is divided in identical cases on both sides of the chancel, and the south case is illustrated (96).

In his Gothic case at St. Peter's, Yaxley, Huntingdonshire, Temple Moore followed an early Italian precedent in giving the front pipes their true speaking lengths, and using pierced pipe shades well clear of the tops (97). He had adopted this practice earlier (1887–8) in another excellent case at St. Mary's, Old Malton, East Yorkshire.

The case of the famous T. C. Lewis organ of 1896 at Southwark Cathedral was designed by Sir Arthur Blomfield (98). Its style may be described as transitional Gothic to Renaissance in which Renaissance feeling predominates. The design owes much to the influence of early Italian models, principally in the disposition of the flats of pipes with horizontal mouths within an architectural framework. Looking at this case one can understand what Freeman meant when he referred to 'Blomfield's mantelpieces', an unfortunate resemblance which is emphasised by the belts around the two main towers. Nevertheless, this is a fine and, in many respects, an underrated case. Both tonally and visually this organ is worthy of a better position.

From about the beginning of the twentieth century, cases of real distinction become harder to find. The work of a few architects stands out from a mass of impoverished pipe fronts of unspeakable dreariness.

Some of the later work of J. O. Scott, Dr. A. G. Hill and Temple Moore, which belongs to this period, has been mentioned.

The spirit of Bodley continued in the work of his one time assistant, Sir Walter Tapper (1861–1924), whose beautiful Gothic case at the Church of the Annunciation, Marble Arch, dates from about 1913. There is also an excellent small Gothic case at Holy Trinity, Bramley,

Surrey, which dates from 1894. In the Lower Chapel of Eton College is a Renaissance case by Tapper, which is based on the design of the four-tower Father Smith case which formerly stood in the Upper Chapel (see p. 201).

An outstanding case of the Edwardian period is at Winchester College Chapel, designed by W. D. Caröe in 1908 (99). Freeman described this case as 'full of romance and adventure', but it is marred by two faults: the unattractive zinc colour of the front pipes (which does not show in the illustration), and the nonsensical treatment of some of them which are made to decrease in diameter as they increase in length. There are Caröe organ cases also at Southwell Minster, Malvern Priory, and St. Peter's, Cranley Gardens, London, among others. Several of his designs were never realised.

The double-fronted Gothic case by F. L. Pearson (son of J. L. Pearson) in his father's church of All Saints, Hove (100) must be included among the few outstanding designs of the early twentieth century. The church dates from 1890–1, and the organ (by Hill) from 1904, but the casework was not provided until 1915. Both fronts are finely carved in oak, and the pipes are of spotted metal. Although the conception is fine, it is not faultless. The chancel front is akin to J. L. Pearson's Westminster Abbey design (78), but less happy. There is a feeling that it has become compressed slightly in width to fit into the first bay of the chancel, there being no room for wings, the need for which is strongly felt. There are also a few obviously sham pipes in the smaller compartments, and some rather pointless Spanish trumpets. In the aisle front, width was clearly no problem, and the overall proportions are quite harmonious. The chancel organ case in Wakefield Cathedral was also designed by F. L. Pearson.

Another architect who designed several organ cases which were well above the general run of his day was Sir Charles Nicholson. His work is represented here by a design for a double case for St. Leonard's Church, Hythe, which is dated 1934 (93). While the design is not ideal, it is greatly superior to the one actually erected, as well as to Sir Charles's other important cases in the College Chapels of Harrow and Clifton.

Sir Giles Gilbert Scott's very effective, though not faultless, small case for the Lady Chapel of Liverpool Cathedral, erected in about 1910, led many critics to expect something really splendid for the main organ. Their hopes were not realised. Although the transept fronts embodying 32 ft. pipes are undeniably imposing, it is difficult not to agree with Freeman that the chancel designs are 'stodgy and commonplace'.[1] An

[1] *English Organ Cases*, p. 72.

unparalleled opportunity to produce a really outstanding British organ case of Continental scale was allowed to pass.

Sir Ninian Comper (1864–1960) was the designer of several very picturesque organ cases. The sumptuously decorated organ case and gallery at the west end of All Saints Church, Carshalton (1932), is a good example of Comper's doctrine of 'beauty by inclusion' (*102*). It also illustrates a basic error of scale to which some of his other cases are subject. Comper has tried to produce a design, comparable to large Continental cases in complexity, but compressed in scale to fit into an average British church. The result is not unlike a model of a case, with the smaller pipes reduced to the thickness of stair-rods, the whole being completely unrelated to the instrument it contains, or indeed to a real organ of any kind. The non-functional appearance is not improved by the lower flats all containing pipes of equal length. The chaire case is a non-functional screen.

An early case by Comper at St. Mary's, Egmanton, Nottinghamshire, erected in the 1890s, is without the faults which mar much of his later work (*101*). Here he has used real front pipes, and the scale of the case is properly related to the small one-manual instrument it contains. The twin flat towers, the concave cornice with its statuette, and the doors—all these reveal the influence of the case at Freiburg-im-Breisgau Cathedral which has been previously mentioned.

Stephen E. Dykes Bower is a leading church architect who is also an organist, and who deeply appreciates the importance of the outward appearance of the instrument. In an age when few organ cases of merit are being made, he has more beautiful designs to his credit than any other modern architect. His splendid restoration of the Pearson cases at Westminster Abbey has been mentioned.

Mr. Dykes Bower clearly favours the Renaissance style for organ cases. His most grandly conceived design is the double-fronted case which stands on the choir screen at Norwich Cathedral (*103, 104*). This was consecrated in 1950 and contains part of the instrument built by Messrs. Hill, Norman & Beard in 1946, after the previous organ and case (see p. 238) had been partially destroyed by fire. On the east front, the main case central tower is reminiscent of the famous Restoration period cases at Exeter and Gloucester. The choir case is after the manner of one or two small cases by Smith and Harris (Manchester Cathedral and Little Bardfield), and the arms of the See of Norwich (three gold mitres on a blue background) appear above it. The west front is the more original of the two, and contains features (such as the pointed compartments between the towers) which do not appear in any early British cases. Above the central tower is a golden crown on a crimson cushion, and the pipes of both fronts are gilded. The rather attenuated feet of the larger pipes would be more in keeping with a case of smaller scale, and they detract a little from the grandeur of the design.

The Rev. Andrew Freeman was vicar of the combined parishes of Standish and Hardwicke, Gloucestershire, from 1923 to 1947. The immense debt owed to Freeman by all students of organ history, particularly those who write books about it, has been acknowledged elsewhere. Mr. Dykes Bower designed the case of the instrument at St. Nicholas, Standish, which is known as the Andrew Freeman Memorial Organ (*105*). In accordance with Freeman's wishes the case was modelled on that of the parish church at Kitzbühel, in the Tyrol. The design was executed by Messrs. Boulton & Son, of Cheltenham, and the organ was built by Messrs. Percy Daniel & Co., of Clevedon. At Freeman's other church of St. Nicholas, Hardwicke, is a simple but most effective case by Mr. Dykes Bower, erected in 1938.

The restoration of war-damaged City of London churches during the 1950s has been accompanied in some instances by the construction of copies (or rather 'likenesses' since they are by no means exact copies) of the original cases. W. A. S. Lloyd's fine reproduction of the Smith case at St. Clement Danes (without the ugly Victorian extensions), and Cecil Brown's copy of the Harris case at St. Lawrence Jewry have already been mentioned. In the Commonwealth Chapel of St. Lawrence there is also a most effective and original small case in Renaissance style by Mr. Brown which contains the choir organ.

At All Hallows, Barking, is a reproduction of the original case, attributed to Renatus Harris, which has been mentioned on p. 218. This was designed by the architects of the church, Messrs. Seely & Paget. The case is painted cream (presumably because it was felt this would harmonise better with the new interior of the building) with some details picked out in gold. The front pipes are gold lacquered, not gilded. The old case had long since lost its overhanging sides, and these have been restored, but to a design which is too weak to be fully effective. The instrument is an example of the classical revival by Messrs. Harrison & Harrison. The number of pipes in the flats is less than originally owing to the different scale of the modern open diapason. It has been said that the copying of antique cases, or the designing of new ones in archaic styles, is out of place in the middle of the twentieth century, and that cases should be designed in a style expressive of the present day. The reproduction case

103, 104 (Above) *Norwich Cathedral: west front and east front*

CASES BY S. E. DYKES BOWER

105 (Left) *St. Nicholas, Standish* (*Andrew Freeman memorial organ*)

106 *Hyde Park Chapel, South Kensington: Wm. Hill & Son and Norman & Beard Ltd., 1961*

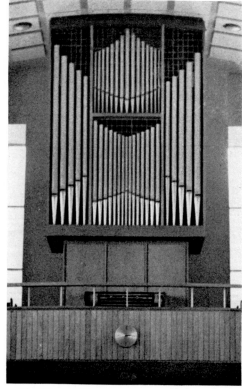

107 *St. Columba, Glenrothes: J. W. Walker & Sons Ltd., 1962*
108 *Christ the King, Glasgow: Wm. Hill & Son and Norman & Beard Ltd., 1961*

at All Hallows, at least, must surely be fully justified, because it enables us to see a very unusual design of the best period which would otherwise have been completely lost.

CONTEMPORARY STYLES

It cannot be said that many modern architects, or for that matter many organ-builders, are particularly interested in producing tasteful organ cases. It would be possible to produce an impressive list of instruments, new or rebuilt since the last war, whose appearance presents no improvement on the tasteless uncased fronts which have disfigured our buildings for the past hundred or so years. Some architects make no secret of their dislike of organs, and will hide them behind a screen, or in a chamber whenever possible. It is a pity, for instance, that in the recently restored Wren Church of St. Bride's, Fleet Street, the authorities saw fit to place the organ in a chamber at the west end of the church. A smaller, free-standing instrument would have served just as well; and the church could have been enriched by an organ case in a fine architectural setting.

There are some signs, however, of an improvement of taste, and these have come not from architects, but from organ-builders.

It has been shown in Chapter II that the tonal renaissance which originated on the Continent between the wars made little impression upon British organ-building until about 1950. This revival of classical tonal ideals, or *Orgelbewegung*, was accompanied by a revolution in the external appearance of the instrument. This, too, is only just being felt in our country.

The work-principle arrangement of Continental organs of the seventeenth and early eighteenth centuries was clearly expressed in the outward appearance of their cases. As previously explained, both the layout and the casework were essential to the characteristic musical effect. When the work-principle was gradually abandoned later in the eighteenth century, casework ceased to bear any particular relationship to the internal disposition of the instrument or the tonal result. Most Continental cases of the Rococo period and later are consequently little more than ornamental screens; and, as previously mentioned, the same applies to the majority of British nineteenth- and twentieth-century cases.

The Continental reaction against the romantic organ was accompanied by a reaction against 'romantic' casework. This manifested itself in two forms—the free standing unencased organ, and a return to the work-principle type of case, often in an undecorated and very austere form.

There was, of course, nothing new in the idea of an unencased organ;

275

it was simply a return to the earliest principles. The modern innovation was to bring the instrument out of its chamber, or from behind its screen, fully into the body of the auditorium, and to exploit the pleasing logarithmic curve of a natural sequence of pipes. Organs treated in this way are sometimes called 'functional' but this is not strictly accurate, because the pipes are usually arranged differently, and more attractively, than they would be on normal chests within a case. Unencased organs appeared first in Holland and Germany during the late 'twenties. At the same time they were pioneered in the U.S.A. by Walker Holtkamp, where they subsequently gained much acceptance.

Musically such arrangements can be two-edged. On the one hand the sounds can be clearly heard. But on the other hand the absence of casework can cause a lack of blend, and there is a tendency for the upperwork to sound rather 'spikey' when, as is usually necessary, the smaller ranks are displayed in the front.

Considered visually, these 'functional' displays are clearly a tremendous improvement upon the conventional uncased pipe fronts, and they can look very pleasing in a modern setting. But it is the authors' view that organ-builders of the fourteenth century, or thereabouts, showed good artistic judgment when they invented the organ case; and that unencased displays are best suited to modern architecture or very small organs.

Several British unencased organs have been made during the last decade by Messrs. Hill, Norman & Beard, and Messrs. J. W. Walker. The fine classical organ by the first-mentioned firm in the Hyde Park Chapel, South Kensington, is openly, though not completely, displayed (*106*). It is entirely appropriate in the modern architectural environment. The small positive organ which is bracketed out from the west wall of St. Columba's Church, Glenrothes, Fifeshire (*107*), by Messrs. Walker, shows how attractive such an arrangement can be for a small organ. The front contains pipes of the tapered (Spitzflöte) variety.

The Flentrop organ at Doetinchem (*109*), which has been previously cited, is a good example of a modern work-principle case. An impression of an undecorated work-principle case can be gained by imagining the Doetinchem one stripped of its pipe shades, tower cornices and ornaments. The result would be a series of boxes, one for each department, which is exactly how such cases are devised.

A completely uncompromising work-principle organ with each department separately encased has yet to be made in Britain. But at least two British organ-builders have adopted the principle of the box type of case in recent instruments. Messrs. N. P. Mander's Denham organ, a small

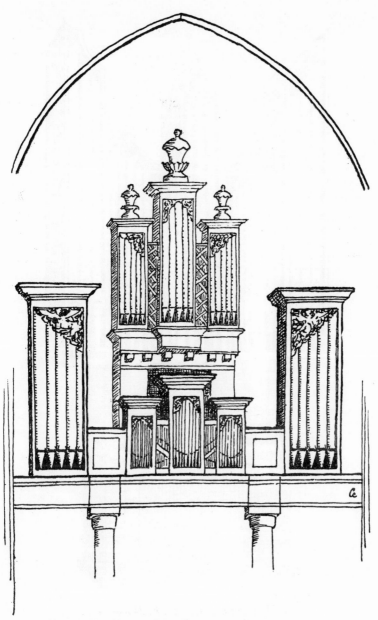

109 *Flentrop work-principle case at Doetinchem, Holland*
(Drawing by Cecil Clutton)

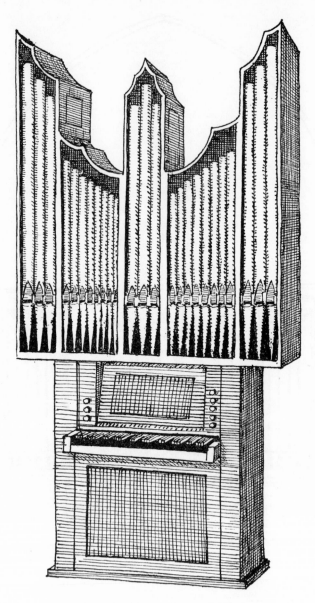

110 *Denham organ, by N. P. Mander Ltd.*
(Drawing by Cecil Clutton)

unenclosed utility instrument (*110*), was the first instance of the introduction of this type of case into the country. The winged form was
inspired by Flentrop's case at the Dutch Reformed Church at Groenlo,
in Holland. The organ at the Roman Catholic Church of Christ the King,
Glasgow (*108*), was built in 1961 by Messrs. Hill, Norman & Beard.
The case is extremely well devised, and is entirely worthy of the traditions
of a firm which, half a century earlier, were making the fine organ cases
of Dr. A. G. Hill.

Looking back on the survey of British organ cases which has just been
given it will be seen that they fall more or less naturally into three main
groups or periods, the second and third of which overlap slightly in time.

The first group consists of the few precious cases which are left to us
from the period *c.* 1500 to the Restoration of the Monarchy in 1660. With
one exception they are all in early Renaissance style. In the second group
are cases of Renaissance style made between 1660 and about 1800, during
which strength and dignity of design gradually gave way to weakness and
triviality, and the traditional form of the organ case was lost. The third
group contains a series of cases in revived Gothic, Grecian and Renaissance styles from 1760 to the present day, during which, largely as a
result of the purist Gothic revival of the 1840s, much of the lost form and
dignity was regained.

For about the past 200 years, designers of British organ cases have
been mainly content to draw upon past styles for their inspiration. It
remains to be seen whether they will continue to do so. A few modern
organs show the influence of contemporary Continental styles, but it is
too early as yet to see where this will lead.

GAZETTEER

This gazetteer does not, and cannot, aim to be exhaustive. Nor, since organs are frequently rebuilt, altered and sold, can it ever be completely up-to-date. Some limitation of scope is essential, and the following plan has been adopted.

(a) *Casework*. Organ cases of all periods have been mentioned. This includes many which are considered to be of interest, though not necessarily of outstanding merit.

(b) *Pipework*. This falls into two periods, dividing at about 1840, the approximate date when the Hill-Gauntlett influence began to be felt, and the British organ entered its modern phase. The aim has been to include so far as possible all pipework made before *c.* 1840 where this is known to exist in substantial quantity. After this date, only the work of the outstanding Victorian organ-builders has generally been mentioned (Gray & Davison, Hill, Lewis, Michell & Thynne, Schulze, Walker and Willis), although occasionally the work of a lesser builder has been mentioned by way of supplementary information. Occasionally it has been thought advisable to mention borderline examples rather than to omit them. No post-Victorian pipework has been mentioned. It should not be assumed that old pipework is in original condition unless specifically stated.

Dates given in brackets are inferred from secondary information, such as the date of erection or restoration of a building.

BEDFORDSHIRE

ARLESEY, *St. Peter:* Choir screen case by Geoffrey Lucas.
BEDFORD, *Holy Trinity:* Walker pipework, 1857.
    Moravian Church: Father Smith case, enlarged.
BOLNHURST, *St. Dunstan:* Probable F. H. Sutton design, case and pipework. Formerly in Keyhoe Church.
KEMPSTON, *All Saints:* Temple Moore case.
LEIGHTON BUZZARD, *All Saints:* Bodley case.
PERTENHALL, *St. Peter:* Hancock, 1783; case and pipes.
TURVEY, *All Saints:* Early Hill pipework.
WOBURN, *Parish Church:* Cases by Kempe.

BERKSHIRE

ABINGDON, *St. Helen:* Jordan case, 1725.
APPLEFORD, *St. Peter & St. Paul:* Green case and pipework, 1777.
BUCKLEBURY, *St. Mary:* Walker case and pipework, 1854.
CRANBOURNE, Church: Father Willis pipework.
EAST HAGBOURNE, *St. Andrew:* Choir case from Jackson's Radley College Chapel case.
LAMBOURN, *St. Michael-and-All-Angels:* Father Willis pipework, 1856.
READING, *St. Lawrence:* John Byfield senior case, 1741.
    St. Mary: Father Willis pipework.
    Town Hall: Father Willis pipework. Case by T. Lainson.
STOCKCROSS, *St. John:* Probably F. H. Sutton case. Hill pipework, 1860.
WELFORD, *St. Gregory-the-Great:* Bevington pipework, 1845.
WINDSOR, *St. George's Chapel:* Cases by Blore.

BRISTOL

The Cathedral: Harris screen case of 1685 divided and re-erected on the north side of the choir.
Christ Church, City: Renatus Harris case, 1707, altered. Some old pipework in rebuilt organ.
Christ Church, Clifton: Some Walker pipework, 1849 and 1884. Rebuilt.
St. George, Brandon Hill: John Smith (Bristol), 1854. Case and some pipework. Rebuilt.
St. James, Horsefair: Some Renatus and John Harris pipework, 1717–25. Rebuilt. Case gone.
Holy Trinity, Westbury-on-Trym: Hedgeland, 1860. Father Willis 1890 pipework. Rebuilt.
St. Thomas: Harris and Byfield case, 1728.
Charles Wesley's House, Broad Mead: Snetzler case and pipework, 1760. From Little Plumstead, Norfolk.
Clifton College
    Chapel: Nicholson case.
    Big School: Father Willis pipework.
Clifton Theological College: Bates of Ludgate pipework.

BUCKINGHAMSHIRE

CHALFONT ST. PETER, *All Saints:* Temple Moore case.
COLESHILL, *All Saints:* Hill case.

ETON COLLEGE, *Upper Chapel:* Hill pipework and J. L. Pearson cases.
Lower Chapel: Case by Tapper.
Memorial Hall: Dutch case from English Church, Rotterdam.
LACEY GREEN, *St. John-the-Evangelist:* Green case and pipework, 1792.
NEWPORT PAGNELL, *Parish Church:* Early Willis pipework.
STOKE POGES, *St. Giles:* Nicholson case.
STOWE School Chapel: Cases by Lorimer.
WEST WYCOMBE, *St. Lawrence:* An organ-less case.

CAMBRIDGESHIRE

CAMBRIDGE, *Christ's College Chapel:* Father Smith case, 1705. Slight modifications during present century.
Clare College Chapel: Old case enlarged by J. L. Simpson.
Emmanuel College Chapel: Father Smith double case, 1686. Front pipes, 1871.
Jesus College Chapel: Pugin case; Sir John Sutton tonal design; 1849. Bishop and Father Smith pipework. Harrison enlargements in 1927 left old work intact.
King's College Chapel: Thomas Dallam case on screen, 1605–6. Chaire case probably added by Pease, 1661.
Pembroke College Chapel: Father Smith double case, 1708.
Peterhouse College Chapel: Snetzler case and some pipework, 1765.
Queens' College Chapel: Bodley case.
St. Catherine's College Chapel: Double case by Garner, 1895.
St. John's College Chapel: Cases by J. O. Scott, 1889.
Trinity College Chapel: Father Smith double case, 1708. Main case enlarged by Blomfield, 1870. Chaire case probably 1694.
Holy Trinity: Gothic case, 1852. Walker pipework.
St. Andrew-the-Less: Almost certain Pugin-Sutton design; case and pipework.
St. Mary-the-Great, University Church: Father Smith case, 1697, and much pipework in original condition. Restored Hill, Norman & Beard, 1963.
St. Paul: Gothic case, 1842.
ELY, *the Cathedral:* Gilbert Scott case, 1851. (Important Harrison tonal scheme, 1908.)
HARLTON, *Our Lady of the Assumption:* Almost certain Sutton case and tonal design, 1869.

HORSEHEATH, *All Saints:* Churchwarden Gothic case.

LITTLEPORT Church: Eighteenth-century copy of Father Smith case at St. Mary-the-Great, Cambridge.

MELBOURN, *All Saints:* Caröe case.

CHESHIRE

ADLINGTON, nr. Macclesfield, *Adlington Hall:* Organ and case *c.* 1670 (including possibly earlier work) restored to original condition by Mander. Played by Handel in 1741 and 1751.

CHESTER, *The Cathedral:* Case by Gilbert Scott, 1876. Choir case by Hill.

DISLEY, *St. Mary:* Renn organ and case, 1836. Enlarged.

ECCLESTON, *St. Mary-the-Blessed-Virgin:* Bodley case (1899).

STOCKPORT, *St. George:* Case by Austin and Paley, re-cast.

St. Thomas: Samuel Renn pipework and case, 1834. Enlarged.

THURSTASTON, *St. Bartholomew:* Case by Norman Shaw.

CORNWALL

KILKHAMPTON Church: Shrider pipework (perhaps ex-Westminster Abbey). Restored in 1958 by Roger Yates.

LAUNCESTON, *St. Mary Magdalene:* Eighteenth-century case.

ST. COLUMB MAJOR, *St. Columba:* Bryceson Bros. & Ellis pipework. Rebuilt.

ST. MICHAEL'S MOUNT, *Chapel:* Avery *c.* 1786 case duplicated and enlarged. Some Avery pipework.

TRURO, *The Cathedral:* Main organ—Father Willis pipework, original. Lady Chapel—Harris and Byfield case.

CUMBERLAND

CROSBY-ON-EDEN, *St. John-the-Evangelist:* Hill pipework, *c.* 1850.

KIRKANDREWS-ON-ESK, *St. Andrews:* Temple Moore cases, 1893.

ST. BEES PRIORY Church: Father Willis pipework, 1899, original. Harrison additions.

DERBYSHIRE

DERBY, *St. John-the-Evangelist:* Father Willis pipework, 1872, rebuilt.

ELVASTON, *St. Bartholomew:* Bodley cases, chancel and west end.

DEVONSHIRE

DUNSFORD, *St. Mary:* Gothick case, *c.* 1840.

EXETER, *The Cathedral:* Loosemore case on choir screen, 1665.

COCKINGTON, nr. Torquay, *St. Matthew:* Nicholson case.

HOLSWORTHY, *St. Peter and St. Paul:* Harris case, 1671, formerly in Bideford Church.

PAIGNTON Church: Case by Mardon Mowbray (1889). Altered.

TAVISTOCK, *St. Eustace:* Curious case covered with statues. No pipes visible.

TEIGNGRACE, *St. Peter and St. Paul:* Eighteenth-century case and some pipework.

TIVERTON, *St. Peter:* Christian Smith case; Gibbons carving; 1696. Present instrument predominantly Father Willis, 1870.

TORQUAY, *St. Mary Magdalene, Upton:* Case attributed to Gilbert Scott, but probably redesigned by Temple Moore.

DORSET

BLANDFORD FORUM, *St. Peter and St. Paul:* G. P. England case and original pipework, 1794. Minor tonal alterations.

COLEHILL, nr. Wimborne, *St. Michael-and-All-Angels:* Caröe case.

SHERBORNE Abbey: R. C. Carpenter case, and Gray & Davison pipework, 1856, rebuilt.

WIMBORNE ST. GILES: Comper case.

COUNTY OF DURHAM

AUCKLAND Castle, *Bishop's Palace Chapel:* Father Smith case and pipework, 1688.

DARLINGTON, *Paradise Methodist Church:* Hill case.

DURHAM, *The Cathedral:* Main case of Father Smith organ of 1684–5 re-erected on south aisle wall.

 University College Chapel: Chaire case of Father Smith's Cathedral organ, 1684–5.

SEDGEFIELD, *St. Edmund:* Eighteenth-century case.

TYNE DOCK, *St. Mary:* Schulze pipework, 1864, largely original condition.

ESSEX

BARKING Church: Byfield and Green case, 1770.

COLCHESTER, *Moot Hall:* Case by J. Belcher.

EPPING, *St. John-the-Baptist:* Cases by Kempe, altered and redecorated by C. J. Hare.

FOXEARTH, *St. Peter and St. Paul:* Father Willis model organ, 1863–4. Rebuilt.

GREAT BARDFIELD, *St. Mary-the-Virgin:* Case Pugin-Sutton style, *c.* 1860. Pipework probably by Holdich.

GREAT MISTLEY Church: Chaire organ case from Worcester Cathedral.

GREAT WALTHAM, *St. Mary and St. Lawrence:* Nicholson case.

HARWICH, *St. Nicholas:* Flight and Robson case and pipework, 1822.

HIGH BEECH, *Holy Innocents:* Father Willis pipework, 1878.

LAMARSH, nr. Sudbury, *Holy Innocents:* Small G. P. England case and pipes.

LITTLE BARDFIELD, *St. Katherine:* Case and pipework, traditionally Renatus Harris, ex Jesus College, Cambridge. Almost untouched.

LITTLEBURY, *Holy Trinity:* Case by Gilbert Scott, 1852.

QUENDON, dedication unknown: Early nineteenth-century case re-cast by S. E. Dykes Bower.

RADWINTER, *St. Mary-the-Virgin:* E. Nesfield case.

SAFFRON WALDEN, *St. Mary-the-Virgin:* Early nineteenth-century Gothick case by Vincent; back parts by Bodley.

SOUTH BENFLEET Church: Nicholson case.

STANSTED MOUNTFITCHET Church: Caröe case.

THAXTED, *St. John, St. Mary-the-Virgin and St. Lawrence:* Two eighteenth-century cases, one formerly St. John's Chapel, Bedford Row. Some old pipework.

GLOUCESTERSHIRE

BARNSLEY, *St. Mary-the-Virgin:* Green case.

BROOKTHORPE, *St. Swithin:* Snetzler case.

CHELTENHAM, *All Saints:* Chancel case by H. A. Prothero. Aisle case by Hill. Hill pipework, 1887.

CIRENCESTER, *St. John-the-Baptist:* Father Willis pipework. Gilbert Scott case.

GLOUCESTER, *The Cathedral:* Main case Thomas Harris, 1666. Chaire case, 1579.

GLOUCESTER—*continued*

St. Mark: Hill case.

St. Nicholas: Case, c. 1790.

GREAT BADMINTON, St. Michael-and-All-Angels: Temple Moore, 1908.

HARDWICKE, St. Nicholas: Case by S. E. Dykes Bower.

KING'S STANLEY, St. George: Case by Bodley. Twin of St. Rose's R.C. Convent, Stroud.

NEWENT, St. Mary: Eighteenth-century case.

PARKEND, St. Paul: Case, possibly of Thomas Harris's Salisbury Cathedral chaire organ, with Gothick carving added.

PILNING, St. Peter: Case by Allen.

RODBOROUGH, St. Mary Magdalene: Case by John T. Lee.

STANDISH, St. Nicholas: Case of Freeman Memorial Organ by S. E. Dykes Bower.

STROUD, St. Rose's R.C. Convent: Bodley case. (See King's Stanley.)

TEWKESBURY Abbey: Milton organ—Formerly Magdalen College Chapel, Oxford. Case of John Chappington's organ of 1597, perhaps earlier. Much seventeenth-century pipework revoiced.

Grove organ—Michell & Thynne exhibition organ of 1885. Original pipework; no case.

WICKWAR, Holy Trinity: Case by Barnard & Partners.

WINCHCOMBE, St. Peter: Chippendale case c. 1730; hidden by modern screen.

WOTTON-UNDER-EDGE, St. Mary-the-Virgin: Shrider case formerly St Martin-in-the-Fields.

HAMPSHIRE

BASINGSTOKE, All Saints: Temple Moore case—no pipes visible.

COSHAM, St. Philip: Comper case, 1936.

EAST STRATTON, All Saints: Jackson case.

EASTNEY, St. Margaret: Hanging case by John T. Lee.

ECCHINSWELL, St. Lawrence: Bodley case.

ELLINGHAM, St. Mary: Jackson case.

GOSPORT, Holy Trinity: Jordan case, formerly Canons Park private Chapel.

MONK SHERBORNE, All Saints: Bodley case.

NORTHINGTON, St. John-the-Evangelist: Jackson case, c. 1896.

PORTSMOUTH, St. Mary, Portsea: Walker pipework original condition, 1891. Case.

ROMSEY Abbey: Walker pipework, 1848–88, original condition.

WESTBOURNE Church: Walker pipework, 1862-76-90.

WINCHESTER, *The Cathedral:* Case by Blore, 1819.

 Winchester College Chapel: West gallery case by Caröe, 1908. Choir organ case by S. E. Dykes Bower.

 St. Cross: Walker pipework, 1863.

HEREFORDSHIRE

BISHOPSTONE Church: Much altered remnant of Father Smith organ from Eton College.

BROMYARD, *St. Peter:* Churchwarden Gothic case, *c.* 1840.

BYFORD, *St. John-the-Baptist:* Pipework by Bates of Ludgate.

DINMORE MANOR Chapel: Green case and pipework, 1786.

EARDISLAND, *St. Mary-the-Virgin:* Case by H. B. Adderley, after Old Radnor.

HENTLAND, *St. Dubricius:* Walker pipework, 1869.

HEREFORD, *The Cathedral:* Father Willis pipework, 1892.

KINGTON, *St. Mary:* Walker pipework, 1883, rebuilt.

KINNERSLEY, *St. James:* Bodley case. (Bodley is buried here.)

LEOMINSTER Priory: Cases dated 1737 and 1924 respectively. Rebuilt instrument contains pipework by Avery, 1797, and Walker, 1842.

MOCCAS, *St. Michael-and-All-Angels:* Case of pleasing but inferior Bodley style.

MONKLAND, *All Saints:* Walker pipework, 1866.

WINFORTON, *St. Michael:* Old case.

YARPOLE, *St. Leonard:* Bishop and Star pipework.

HERTFORDSHIRE

CHESHUNT, *St. Mary-the-Virgin:* Bodley case.

HATFIELD House: Summer Drawing Room—Chamber organ, probably Flemish, 1609.

 Chapel—Lewis organ in case.

HOCKERILL, *All Saints:* Case by S. E. Dykes Bower.

ST. ALBANS, *The Cathedral:* J. O. Scott divided cases, 1908. Positive case by Cecil Brown, 1963.

 St. Peter: Parts of casework and pipes, formerly St. Martin-in-the-Fields, possibly Dallam.

HUNTINGDONSHIRE

ST. IVES, *All Saints:* Case attributed to Bodley, but in fact by Comper. Instrument taken out many years ago.

YAXLEY, *St. Peter:* Temple Moore case.

ISLE OF MAN

DOUGLAS, *St. Ninian:* Case by H. Wilson.

ISLE OF WIGHT

CARISBROOKE CASTLE: Chamber organ by E. Hoffheimer, 1602.

MOTTISTONE, *St. Peter and St. Paul:* George England case and some pipework, *c.* 1770.

RYDE, *All Saints:* Father Willis pipework, 1873, rebuilt.

KENT

BEXLEY, Danson Park: George England case and pipework, 1766, original condition. Restored by Mander.

BISHOPSBOURNE Church: Walker pipework, 1865–97.

CANTERBURY

    The Cathedral: Main organ—Father Willis pipework, 1888.
    Dean Bargrave's organ—case only (no pipes), 1629.

    St. Margaret: Gilbert Scott case.

CHATHAM, *St. Mary:* Green case and some pipework, 1795.

CHISLEHURST, *St. Nicholas:* Bodley case.

DEAL, *St. George:* Jackson case.

ELTHAM, *St. John-the-Baptist:* Father Willis pipework.

FOLKESTONE, *St. Peter:* J. F. Bentley case.

HATCHAM PARK, *All Saints:* see SURREY.

HYTHE, *St. Leonard:* Nicholson case.

ICKHAM, *St. John-the-Evangelist:* Walker 1897 pipework (partly earlier), and case.

LYDD Church: Father Willis model organ.

MAIDSTONE, *St. Paul:* J. L. Pearson case.

ROCHESTER, *The Cathedral:* Gilbert Scott cases divided on screen, 1875.

SHOREHAM, *St. Peter and St. Paul:* Chaire organ case from Westminster Abbey—Jordan.

LANCASHIRE

CHORLTON-ON-MEDLOCK, *St. Saviour:* Renn case and pipework, 1837.

HEATON PARK, nr. Manchester: Green pipework. Case probably by James Wyatt.

HEYSHAM, *St. James:* Snetzler case and pipework, formerly at Shaw House, Newbury.

HINDLEY, *St. Peter:* Schulze pipework, very little altered.

LEIGH, *St. Mary-the-Virgin:* Case by Austin and Paley. Green case of 1777 in vestry.

LIVERPOOL, *The Cathedral:* Cases by Giles Gilbert Scott. Main organ, 1924. Lady Chapel, 1910.

 St. George's Hall: Willis pipework, 1855. 'Casework' by C. R. Cockerell.

 St. Agnes, Sefton Park: J. L. Pearson case (1883).

 St. John the Baptist, Tue Brook: Bodley case.

MANCHESTER, *Town Hall:* Cavaillé-Coll pipework, rebuilt Lewis.

 St. George, Hulme: Renn case and pipework, 1829. Restored by Mander.

MIDDLETON, *St. Leonard:* Nicholson case.

PENDLEBURY, *St. Augustine:* Bodley case.

PRESTON, *St. Matthew:* Renn case and pipework, 1828–30.

 St. Oswald: Case by Tapper.

RAWTENSTALL, *St. Mary:* Case attributed to Hill, 1880.

RIPLEY, *Hospital Chapel:* Cases by Austin and Paley (two fronts).

ROCHDALE, *St. Mary:* Comper case (*c.* 1910).

SALFORD, *St. Philip:* Renn case and pipework, 1829. Slight additions. Restored by Mander.

WARRINGTON, *Parr Hall:* Cavaillé-Coll pipework and case.

WHALLEY, *St. Mary:* Gerard Smith case, 1729, originally in Lancaster Parish Church.

LEICESTERSHIRE

BOTTESFORD, *St. Mary-the-Virgin:* Case by J. Horsley.

GREAT BOWDEN, *St. Peter and St. Paul:* Case by Dallam, Thamar or Father Smith; probably pre-1670.

HOUGHTON-ON-THE-HILL, *St. Catherine:* Hill case.

LEICESTER, *All Souls:* Case by Hare.

 Bishop Street Methodist Church: Father Smith case, formerly at St. Margaret's Church.

 The Cathedral: Nicholson cases.

STAUNTON HAROLD, *Private Chapel:* Small mid-seventeenth-century organ, doubtfully attributed to Father Smith. Restored Mander.

SYSTON, *St. Peter and St. Paul:* Caröe case.

THEDDINGWORTH, *All Saints:* Case designed by F. H. Sutton, 1864–73. Some Snetzler pipework.

LINCOLNSHIRE

BOOTHBY PAGNELL, *St. Andrew:* J. L. Pearson case.

BRANT BROUGHTON, *St. Helen:* Case probably by Bodley, during incumbency of F. H. Sutton.

DENTON, *St. Andrew:* J. F. Bentley case. Poor imitation of Old Radnor.

EAST KIRKBY, *St. Nicholas:* Temple Moore case.

GRANTHAM, *St. Wulfram:* Tapper case.

LAUGHTON, *All Saints:* Bodley case.

LINCOLN, *The Cathedral:* Case by E. J. Willson, 1826. Father Willis pipework, 1898.

St. Andrew: Bodley case.

Bishop's Hostel Chapel: Case by Temple Moore.

MORTON-BY-GAINSBOROUGH, *St. Paul:* Case by Micklethwaite and Somers Clarke.

SKIRBECK, *St. Nicholas:* Temple Moore case.

LONDON

BERMONDSEY, *St. James:* Case by Savage. Early Bishop pipework.

St. Mary, Rotherhithe: Largely original Byfield pipework, 1764, and case.

BETHNAL GREEN, *St. Augustine, Haggerston:* Father Willis pipework.

St. Peter's Organ Works: Chamber organ—Christianus Smith, 1643. Chamber organ—Father Smith, formerly in the possession of Sir John Sutton, formerly New College, Oxford.

CAMBERWELL, *Dulwich College Chapel:* George England case, 1760, and some pipework.

Emmanuel Church, West Dulwich: Hill pipework, 1877.

St. Giles, Camberwell: Bishop pipework, 1844, restored by original builders.

CHELSEA, *Christ Church:* England and Russell case and some pipework, 1799. From St. Michael, Queenhithe, in 1876.

Holy Trinity, Sloane Street: Walker pipework of 1891, somewhat modified.

Royal Hospital Chapel: Case may be by Renatus Harris.

St. Luke: Churchwarden Gothic case, early nineteenth century, extended.

CITY OF LONDON, *All Hallows, London Wall:* Hill pipework in effective Italian style case, *c.* 1870. Formerly in Highbury Barn, Islington.

All Hallows-by-the-Tower: Copy of war-destroyed case (Harris-Gerard Smith) by Seely and Paget.

St. Andrew Undershaft: Harris case, 1696. Organ rebuilt and moved.

St. Andrew-by-the-Wardrobe: Snetzler case and pipework, original condition; formerly at Teddesley Hall.

St. Botolph, Aldgate: Renatus Harris case, 1707.

St. Botolph, Bishopsgate: J. Byfield junior case divided and spoilt.

St. Catherine Cree: Father Smith case, 1686. Front pipes not original.

St. Clement, Eastcheap: Renatus Harris case, 1695.

St. Dunstan-in-the-West, Fleet Street: Gothick case by James Shaw, 1839.

St. Edmund-the-King, Lombard Street: Case attributed to Renatus Harris in west gallery. Modern facsimile on north wall.

St. Ethelburga, Bishopsgate: Comper case.

St. Helen, Bishopsgate: Case, T. Griffin, 1742 (Jordan-Byfield-Bridge).

St. James, Garlickhithe: Father Smith case, 1697, altered by J. Knopple, 1718. Much Smith pipework.

St. Lawrence Jewry: Reproduction of war-destroyed Harris main case by Cecil Brown. New choir organ case in Commonwealth Chapel.

St. Magnus-the-Martyr, London Bridge: Jordan case, 1712.

St. Margaret, Lothbury: G. P. England case of 1808, enlarged 1862 and 1881 with cases from St. Mildred, Poultry.

St. Margaret Pattens: Case and some pipework, T. Griffin, 1749 (Jordan-Byfield-Bridge).

St. Martin, Ludgate: Bates pipework, *c.* 1845, and early nineteenth-century case.

St. Mary-at-Hill, Billingsgate: Hill pipework mostly 1848, original condition. Contemporary case.

St. Mary Woolnoth: Case probably by Robert Dallam.

St. Paul's Cathedral: Wren-Gibbons cases of 1695–96 Father Smith organ divided north and south of the choir. Predominantly Father Willis pipework of 1872 and later.

Father Willis model organ 'on wheels' in north transept, 1881.

CITY OF LONDON—*continued*

St. *Peter, Cornhill:* Father Smith case enlarged by Hill and Gauntlett in 1840. Hill-Gauntlett console in vestry.

St. *Sepulchre, Holborn Viaduct:* Harris case 1670 thrice altered and spoilt.

St. *Stephen, Walbrook:* George England case, 1765.

St. *Vedast, Foster Lane:* Harris-Byfield case and pipework, 1731, originally in St. Bartholomew-by-the-Exchange. Restored and rebuilt by Mander, 1961.

DEPTFORD, St. *Paul:* Bridge case, 1730.

FINSBURY, St. *James, Clerkenwell:* Case and some pipework, G. P. England, 1792.

GREENWICH, St. *John, Blackheath:* Good modern case.

Royal *Naval Hospital Chapel:* Green pipework, 1789, and contemporary case in Grecian idiom.

HACKNEY, St. *James, Clapton:* Caröe case.

HAMMERSMITH, St. *John:* J. F. Bentley case.

HAMPSTEAD, St. *John-the-Evangelist:* Jackson case. Father Willis pipework.

St. *Luke:* Case by Basil Champneys (1898.)

St. *Stephen:* Father Willis pipework.

Fenton *House:* Bible Regal, c. 1700.

HOLBORN, St. *Andrew:* Case from the Foundling Hospital Chapel.

St. *Anselm and St. Cecilia, Kingsway (R.C.):* G. P. England case and pipework, 1802—formerly in Sardinian Embassy Chapel, Lincoln's Inn Fields.

St. *Ethelreda, Ely Place (R.C.):* Divided cases by J. F. Bentley.

St. *George, Bloomsbury Way:* Gray & Davison pipework and case, c. 1850—formerly in Emmanuel Church, St. John's Wood.

St. *Giles-in-the-Fields:* Case attributed to Father Smith, 1671, but possibly by Christian Smith, 1699.

ISLINGTON, St. *Augustine, Highbury:* Father Willis pipework, 1889.

St. *Mary Magdalene, Holloway Road:* G. P. England pipework and case, 1819. Father Willis was organist here for nearly 30 years.

Union *Chapel, Compton Terrace:* Father Willis pipework, 1873.

KENSINGTON, St. *Barnabas, Addison Road:* Case, c. 1850.

Holy *Trinity, Brompton:* Case by Hare.

Holy *Trinity, Kensington Gore:* Case by Hare.

St. *Peter, Cranley Gardens:* Case by Caröe.

Victoria and Albert Museum: Remains of organ-harpsichord by Lodowicus Theewes, 1579, formerly in the chapel of Ightham Mote House.

German table organ, 1627.

German Chamber organ, *c.* 1540.

Positive organ, formerly in the Church of Santa Cruz, Madeira, *c.* 1540.

Case of chamber organ, Chippendale design.

LAMBETH, *St. John, Waterloo Road:* Grecian style double case, 1824. Restored after war damage by Mander.

PADDINGTON, *St. John, Southwick Crescent:* Hill pipework, 1865.

St. Mary Magdalene, Crypt Chapel: Small case by Comper.

ST. MARYLEBONE, *All Souls, Langham Place:* Case in Grecian style.

Church of the Annunciation, Marble Arch: Case by Tapper. *c.* 1913

St. Katherine, Regent's Park: Green case, 1778.

ST. PANCRAS, *St. Pancras New Parish Church:* Case by S. S. Teulon (slightly modified).

St. Dominic's Priory, Haverstock Hill (R.C.): Father Willis pipework, unaltered.

SHOREDITCH, *St. John, Hoxton:* Old case.

St. Leonard: Case of Bridge organ, 1754.

SOUTHWARK, *The Cathedral:* T. C. Lewis pipework, 1896. Case by Sir Arthur Blomfield.

St. Dunstan, Bellingham: Case formerly in Chapel Royal, St. James's Palace. Hill pipework, 1866.

Holy Trinity: Case and some pipework by Timothy Russell, 1824.

STEPNEY, *St. Anne, Limehouse:* Gray & Davison pipework; 1851 Exhibition organ.

Christ Church, Spitalfields: Bridge case and pipework, 1731.

WANDSWORTH, *Holy Trinity, Clapham:* Case by Beresford-Pite (1902.)

St. Peter, Streatham: A. G. Hill case.

All Saints, Tooting Graveney: Tapper case.

WESTMINSTER, *The Abbey:* Cases by J. L. Pearson, 1899; re-erected and decorated by S. E. Dykes Bower, 1960.

St. Barnabas, Pimlico: Bodley cases.

St. Clement Danes, Strand: Reproduction of war-destroyed Father Smith case, *c.* 1690, by W. A. S. Lloyd.

St. Gabriel, Warwick Square, Pimlico: Case by Blomfield.

St. George, Hanover Square: Gerard Smith case enlarged by Blomfield. (Hope Jones pipework.)

WESTMINSTER—*continued*

Grosvenor Chapel: Case, *c.* 1732, extended.

St. James, Piccadilly: Renatus Harris case, 1686–8; formerly in 'Popish' Chapel, Whitehall; erected in church, 1691. Chaire case added 1852.

King's College Chapel, Strand: Father Willis pipework.

Marlborough House Chapel: Snetzler case and some pipework, 1760.

St. Margaret: Walker pipework, 1897.

St. Mark, North Audley Street: Cases by Blomfield.

St. Martin-in-the-Fields: Double case by Allom, 1854.

Our Lady of the Assumption, Warwick Street: Case by John Byfield, *c.* 1790; tastefully extended by Mander.

St. Paul, Covent Garden: Case of Elliot organ, *c.* 1800; Bevington pipework, 1860.

Third Church of Christ, Scientist, Curzon Street: Case by W. Dunne and R. Watson.

MIDDLESEX

BRONDESBURY, *St. Anne:* Case and Lewis pipework from Hanover Square Concert Rooms.

CHISWICK, *Parish Church:* Cases by J. L. Pearson; Bryceson pipework.

EALING, *Christ-the-Saviour, formerly Christ Church:* Bodley case.

ENFIELD, *St. Andrew:* Bridge case, 1753.

HARROW, *St. George, Headstone:* Case by F. Rothwell, Senior.

Harrow School Chapel: Nicholson case.

HORNSEY, *Alexandra Palace:* Father Willis pipework, 1875.

KINGSBURY, *St. Andrew:* Father Willis pipework, ex-St. Andrew, Wells Street, London.

SOUTHALL, *St. George:* Jordan case formerly at St. George, Botolph Lane, London.

TWICKENHAM, *All Hallows:* Renatus Harris case, 1703. Pipework by Harris and Gray & Davison. Formerly at All Hallows, Lombard Street.

NORFOLK

BLICKLING, *St. Andrew:* Snetzler case, 1764; pipework altered.

CAWSTON, *St. Agnes:* G. P. England Gothick case and pipework, 1813. Formerly St. Stephen, Norwich.

EAST BRADENHAM, *St. Mary:* Green case and pipework, 1786.

HILLINGTON, *St. Mary-the-Virgin:* Snetzler case and pipework, 1756.

KING'S LYNN, *St. Margaret:* Snetzler case and some pipework, 1754. Dr. Burney was organist here from 1751 to 1760.

MUNDFORD, *St. Leonard:* Comper case.

NORWICH, *The Cathedral:* Double-fronted screen case by S. E. Dykes Bower. Snetzler case and pipework, *c.* 1745, in St. Saviour's Chapel.

St. Andrew: Case by H. F. Green.

St. George, Colegate: G. P. England case and pipework, 1802; altered.

King Edward VI Grammar School: Choir case from old Norwich Cathedral organ.

PULHAM, *St. Mary-the-Virgin:* Bodley case (1885).

REDENHALL, *Assumption of the Blessed Virgin Mary:* Holdich case and pipework, 1843.

SANDRINGHAM Church: Blomfield case.

SCULTHORPE, *St. Mary and All Saints:* Snetzler case and pipework, 1756.

SOUTH PICKENHAM, *All Saints:* Pugin case, *c.* 1850, ex-St. Mary, West Tofts.

THORNAGE, *All Saints:* Thomas Elliot case and pipework, 1812, original.

UPPER SHERINGHAM, *All Saints:* Hill case.

WYMONDHAM Abbey: Gothick case in west gallery. Organ built by James Davis for Longman & Broderip, 1793. Restored by Hill, Norman & Beard, 1954.

NORTHAMPTONSHIRE

ASHLEY, *St. Mary-the-Virgin:* Gilbert Scott case.

BARBY, nr. Rugby, *St. Mary:* Case and pipework by Flight and/or Robson, *c.* 1810. Gauntlett associations.

CASTLE ASHBY, *St. Mary Magdalene:* Case by F. H. Sutton; Nicholson pipework; 1872.

DAVENTRY, *Holy Cross:* Father Willis rebuild of Holdich, *c.* 1865. Double-fronted case.

EASTON NESTON, *St. Mary-the-Virgin:* Early Father Willis pipework.

EASTON-ON-THE-HILL Church: Holdich case and pipework, 1845.

EDGECOTE, *St. Peter and St. Paul:* Holdich pipework, *c.* 1850. Barrel attachment.

FARTHINGSTONE, *St. Mary-the-Virgin:* Allen Gothic case and pipework.

FINEDON, *St. Mary-the-Virgin:* Shrider case and pipework, 1717; Holdich; restored by Mander.

HIGHAM FERRERS, *St. Mary:* Temple Moore case.

ISLIP, *St. Nicholas:* Temple Moore case.

KETTERING Church: Blomfield case.

NORTHBOROUGH, *St. Andrew:* Green case and pipework.

NORTHAMPTON, *All Saints:* Schwarbrick case.

    St. Peter: J. O. Scott case.

OLD Church: Holdich; case and pipework, 1853.

PETERBOROUGH, *The Cathedral:* Hill case, 1904.

PIDDINGTON Church: Holdich. Similar to Old Church, but barrel removed.

SOUTHWICK Hall: Holdich pipework, *c.* 1840, in churchwarden Gothic case.

STANFORD-ON-AVON, *St. Nicholas:* Unrestored organ case in west gallery, *c.* 1580 (later dummy chaire case). Probably from Chapel Royal, Whitehall.

THRAPSTON, *St. James:* Jackson case.

TOWCESTER, *St. Lawrence:* Case from Fonthill Abbey.

WELLINGBOROUGH, *St. Mary:* Comper case.

NORTHUMBERLAND

HEXHAM Abbey: Avery case from Carlisle Cathedral, much altered.

NEWCASTLE-UPON-TYNE, *The Cathedral:* Harris case 1676 enlarged by R. J. Johnson, 1891; in north transept. 'Back-front' of 1710 faces east into St. George's Chapel. Choir organ case in chancel by Johnson.

    St. Dominic's Priory (R.C.): Father Willis pipework, *c.* 1880.

    St. George, Jesmond: Lewis pipework rebuilt, 1886.

    St. John-the-Baptist: Nicholson case.

TYNEMOUTH, *Christ Church:* Old case in west gallery.

NOTTINGHAMSHIRE

CLUMBER, *St. Mary-the-Virgin:* Gray & Davison pipework, *c.* 1890; Bodley case.

EGMANTON, *St. Mary:* Early Comper case (*c.* 1895).

NOTTINGHAM, *St. Catherine:* Case, *c.* 1780, formerly in Tockington Hall.

    St. Mary: Gilbert Scott case, 1872, recast by Temple Moore in 1916. Also separate case by Temple Moore.

    St. Peter: Snetzler case rearranged by S. E. Dykes Bower.

NEWARK, *St. Mary Magdalene:* Gilbert Scott case; Father Willis pipework, 1865; rebuilt.

PLUMTREE Church: Bodley case, 1873-4. Sutton influence.

SNEINTON, *St. Stephen:* Case by Hare.

SOUTHWELL Minster: Case by Caröe.

WEST RETFORD, *St. Michael-and-All-Angels:* Father Willis pipework, *c.* 1875.

WILFORD Church: Father Willis pipework, *c.* 1880.

WOLLATON, *St. Leonard:* Father Willis pipework, 1865.

OXFORDSHIRE

BAMPTON Church: Pipework by Gray; Gothick case; *c.* 1840.

CHURCHILL, *All Saints:* Late eighteenth-century case and pipework.

DEDDINGTON, *St. Peter and St. Paul:* Case by Hare.

HORLEY, *Parish Church:* Unusual eighteenth-century case with original pipework.

OXFORD, *Brasenose College Chapel:* Jackson case, 1892.

Christ Church Cathedral: Father Smith case, 1680; enlarged by Gilbert Scott in 1870 and later.

Corpus Christi College Chapel: Case rearranged by Jackson.

New College Chapel: Gilbert Scott case.

Oriel College Chapel: Old case recast by Jackson.

Pembroke College Chapel: Old case from Sheldonian Theatre, recast by Kempe.

Sheldonian Theatre: Case by Jackson, 1877.

University College Chapel: Case by Sir Albert Richardson.

Wadham College Chapel: Jackson case; Father Willis pipework.

St. James, Cowley: Gothick case, *c.* 1840, ex-Carfax, Oxford.

St. John the Evangelist (Cowley Fathers' Church): Bodley case; Michell & Thynne pipework, rebuilt.

St. Mary the Virgin, University Church: Father Smith case, 1675-6; west front gothicised by Plowman, 1827.

WOODSTOCK, *Blenheim Palace:* Father Willis organ, 1891, in Long Library. Untouched.

RUTLAND

BELTON, *St. Peter:* Nicholson case.

EDITH WESTON, *St. Mary:* Green case and pipework, 1787.

STOKE DRY, *St. Andrew:* Lincoln case and pipework, 1813.

SHROPSHIRE

ATTINGHAM House: Green chamber organ.

ELLESMERE, *College Chapel:* Nicholson case.

KINLET, *St. John-the-Baptist:* Early nineteenth-century Bishop pipework and case.

LUDLOW, *St. Laurence:* Snetzler case, 1764, and some pipework. Case spoiled by the addition of 'Spanish tubas'.

RICHARD'S CASTLE, *All Saints:* Case by Norman Shaw (1891–2).

SHIFNAL, *St. Andrew:* G. P. England, 1811; case and some pipework.

SHREWSBURY, *St. Mary:* Case by Byfield and Harris, 1729.

WHITCHURCH, *St. Alkmund:* Shrider case and some pipework.

SOMERSET

BATH, Abbey: Jackson case.

MOORLYNCH, *St. Mary-the-Virgin:* James Davis, eighteenth or early nineteenth century. Case and pipework.

MUCHELNEY, *St. Peter and St. Paul:* Gray & Davison barrel organ, 1835–40.

NETTLECOMBE COURT: House organ by John Loosemore, *c.* 1665. Case. Rebuilt in eighteenth century.

SHEPTON MALLET Church: Old case altered.

PORTISHEAD, *Congregational Church:* Case and pipework possibly John Smith, *c.* 1830.

TAUNTON, *Holy Trinity:* Hill pipework, 1845. Gothick case.

St. John-the-Evangelist: Father Willis pipework, 1864. Rebuilt, Yates, 1963.

STAFFORDSHIRE

BARTON-UNDER-NEEDWOOD, *St. James:* Case by Basil Champneys.

BURTON-ON-TRENT, *St. Chad:* Bodley case.

St. Paul: Bodley case.

St. Modwen: Snetzler case, 1771.

ECCLESHALL, *Holy Trinity:* Caröe case.

HOAR CROSS, *Church of the Holy Angels:* Bodley case.

LICHFIELD, *The Cathedral:* Main organ—cases by J. O. Scott, 1907, Hill pipework.

Parish Church: Case probably by J. O. Scott.

LONGSDON, *St. Chad:* Case by G. Horsley.

RUGELEY, *Dominican Church*: Father Smith case, *c.* 1700, ex-Eton College.

STAFFORD, *St. Mary*: Case by John Geib, 1790.

STRETTON, *St. Mary*: Case by Micklethwaite & Somers Clarke (1897).

WEST BROMWICH, *St. Andrew*: Snetzler case, 1777.

WOLVERHAMPTON, *St. John*: Renatus Harris case and some pipework from Christ Church Cathedral, Dublin, 1697. Some pipework from rejected Temple Church instrument.

SUFFOLK

EDWARDSTONE, *St. Mary*: Case in Bodley style.

ELVEDEN, *St. Mary and St. Patrick*: Caröe case.

FALKENHAM, *St. Ethelbert*: Green case and pipework; restored by Bishop, 1957.

FRAMLINGHAM, *St. Michael*: Case, *c.* 1580, and some pipework by Thamar, 1674. Formerly Pembroke College, Cambridge.

GROTON Church: Father Willis model organ.

HADLEIGH, *St. Mary*: Father Smith case, *c.* 1687; formerly in Donyland Hall.

HENSTEAD, *St. Mary*: Caröe case.

HITCHAM, *All Saints*: Some Flight and Robson pipework.

HOO, *St. Andrew*: Old pipework, *c.* 1830.

LOUND, *St. John the Baptist*: Comper case.

LYNDSEY Church: Hugh Russell case and pipework, 1801.

NAUGHTON Church: Gray chamber organ, 1777. Case. Restored Bishop, 1955.

NAYLAND, *St. James*: Some Green pipework, *c.* 1786. Case discarded 1914.

PAKENHAM, *Blessed Virgin Mary*: Bates pipework, *c.* 1850.

SHADINGFIELD, *St. John-the-Baptist*: Case and pipework by Parsons of Bloomsbury, *c.* 1820.

SHELLAND, *King Charles-the-Martyr*: Bryceson barrel organ, *c.* 1820.

SOUTHWOLD, *St. Edmund*: Walker pipework.

SWEFFLING, *St. Mary-the-Virgin*: Parsons chamber organ, *c.* 1850.

TANNINGTON, *St. Ethelbert*: Pipework may be by Bryceson, *c.* 1840. Rebuilt.

THELNETHAM, *St. Nicholas*: Bates pipework, 1855.

WINSTON Church: Pipework possibly by Russell, *c.* 1840.

WISTON, *St. Mary*: Gray barrel organ.

YOXFORD, *St. Peter*: G. P. England case, 1790, from Moravian Chapel, Fetter Lane, London.

SURREY

BEDDINGTON, *St. Mary-the-Virgin:* Lewis pipework, 1869, original; William Morris organ screen.

BRAMLEY, *Holy Trinity:* Tapper case; Lewis pipework, 1894.

CARSHALTON, *All Saints:* Double case by Comper, 1932.

COLDHARBOUR, *Christ Church:* Caröe case.

CROYDON, *St. John-the-Baptist:* Case by J. O. Scott, 1893; Hill pipework.

 St. Matthew: Lewis pipework, 1882.

 St. Michael-and-All-Angels: Bodley case and Father Willis pipework. Rebuilt Mander.

DORKING, *St. Paul:* Late Hill pipework.

EPSOM, *St. Martin of Tours:* Nicholson cases.

FETCHAM, *St. Mary:* Early Father Willis pipework.

GODALMING, *St. Peter and St. Paul:* Hill case.

HAM COMMON, *St. Andrew:* Bodley case.

HAMPTON COURT, *Chapel Royal:* Case by Shrider, 1712.

HATCHAM PARK, *All Saints:* Lewis pipework, 1871.

REDHILL, *St. John:* Father Willis pipework.

RICHMOND, *Parish Church:* Old case.

 St. Matthias: Blomfield case; Lewis pipework.

ROEHAMPTON, *Holy Trinity:* Case by Fellowes-Prynne.

WALTON-ON-THAMES, *St. Mary:* Case may be Father Smith, ex King's Private Chapel, Windsor, 1673.

WEYBRIDGE, *St. James:* J. L. Pearson case (*c.* 1865).

WHITELEY VILLAGE, *St. Mark:* Tapper case.

SUSSEX

BRIGHTON, *St. John-the-Evangelist, Carlton Hill:* Bates pipework, possibly from Chapel Royal, Brighton, or Royal Pavilion.

 St. Martin: Case by Somers Clarke. Hill pipework.

 St. Peter: Father Willis pipework, 1889; rebuilt.

CHICHESTER, *The Cathedral:* Case by Hill, 1888. Much old pipework.

 St. John: England case, 1812, enlarged and spoilt.

DANEHILL, *All Saints:* Bodley case (1890).

HASTINGS, *All Saints:* Willis pipework, 1878.

HORSHAM, *Christ's Hospital, Big School:* Case by James Shaw, *c.* 1832.

HOVE, *All Saints:* Double fronted case by F. L. Pearson, 1915.

ICKLESHAM Church: Late eighteenth- or early nineteenth-century case.

MID-LAVANT, *St. Nicholas:* Blomfield case.

NEWHAVEN, *St. Michael:* Bates case and pipework, *c.* 1854.
PETWORTH, *St. Mary and St. Thomas:* Case by Kempe.
PIDDINGHOE, *St. John:* Barrel organ, *c.* 1800.
RYE, *St. Mary:* Jackson case.
SOUTHEASE, dedication unknown: Allen chamber organ. Case.
TICEHURST, *St. Mary:* Walker pipework, 1866.
WILLINGDON, *St. Mary:* Hill case.
WINCHELSEA, *St. Thomas-the-Apostle:* Case by Mervyn Macartney.

WARWICKSHIRE

BIRMINGHAM, *The Cathedral:* Schwarbrick case, 1715.
   Church of the Messiah: Hill pipework, 1882.
   Town Hall: Case of Hill organ, 1834.
BROWNSOVER, nr. Rugby, *St. Michael-and-All-Angels:* Chaire organ
   case from St. John's College Chapel, Cambridge, post 1660.
   (See St. Mark, Old Bilton.)
COMPTON WYNYATES: Father Smith chamber organ; case and pipework,
   original.
GREAT PACKINGTON, *St. James:* Bridge case and pipework, formerly at
   Gopsall Hall. Original condition. Designed by Handel.
NEW MILVERTON, *St. Mark:* Hill pipework and case, *c.* 1880.
OLD BILTON, *St. Mark:* Dallam main organ case from St. John's College
   Chapel, Cambridge, 1635–6. F. H. Sutton restoration. Nicholson
   pipework, *c.* 1870.
RUGBY, *Holy Trinity:* Bodley case.
STRATFORD-ON-AVON, *Guild Chapel of St. James:* Case by S. E. Dykes
   Bower.
   Holy Trinity: Bodley case.
TEMPLE BALSALL, *St. Mary:* Gilbert Scott case.
WARWICK, *St. Mary:* Schwarbrick casework.

WESTMORLAND

APPLEBY, *St. Lawrence:* Case and some old pipework, probably from
   Carlisle Cathedral, pre-1571. Case shortened and spoilt.

WILTSHIRE

ASHTON KEYNES, *Holy Cross:* Bishop pipework, 1840.
CHIPPENHAM, *St. Andrew:* Gray & Davison pipework, 1879; and
   case.

CRICKLADE, *St. Sampson:* Nicholson of Worcester pipework, 1820, an original case.

DEVIZES, *St. John:* Snetzler case.

MARLBOROUGH, *College Chapel:* Bodley case.

SALISBURY, *The Cathedral:* Father Willis pipework, 1876–77.

St. Thomas: Green pipework, 1792, ex-Cathedral.

STANTON FITZWARREN, *St. Leonard:* Gray & Davison barrel organ rebuilt, 1865.

SWINDON, *Christ Church:* Gray & Davison pipework, 1851, rebuilt.

St. Mark: Temple Moore case.

WARMINSTER Church: G. P. England case and some pipework.

WORCESTERSHIRE

GREAT WITLEY, *St. Michael:* Eighteenth-century case in style of Baroque church. Nicholson of Worcester pipework.

MALVERN, Priory Church: Caröe case.

OMBERSLEY, *St. Andrew:* Gray Gothick case and pipework, 1829.

POWICK, *St. Peter:* Eighteenth-century case.

STOURBRIDGE, *St. Thomas:* G. P. England case and some pipework, 1809–11.

TENBURY, *St. Michael's College:* Father Willis pipework, 1874.

UPTON-ON-SEVERN, *St. Peter and St. Paul:* Eighteenth-century case.

WORCESTER, *The Cathedral:* Transept and choir cases by Gilbert Scott.

St. Swithin: Eighteenth-century case.

YORKSHIRE

BARNSLEY Church: Eighteenth-century case.

BARTON-LE-STREET, *St. Michael-and-All-Angels:* Temple Moore case.

BEVERLEY, *Minster:* Hill case 1916. Much Snetzler and Hill pipework.

BRADFORD, *The Cathedral:* Case by Sir Edward Maufe.

CAWTHORNE, *All Saints:* Bodley case.

DONCASTER, *Christ Church:* Schulze pipework.

St. George: Schulze pipework, 1862.

GIGGLESWICK School Chapel: Jackson case.

HALIFAX, *Parish Church:* Snetzler case retained as north aisle front. Chancel case by J. O. Scott, 1879.

Victoria Hall: Hill case.

HULL, *City Hall:* Case by Philip Selfe of Forster & Andrews.

ILKLEY, *All Saints:* Lewis pipework, 1882, rebuilt. Cases by J. Stuart Syme.

LANGTOFT, *St. Peter:* Hill case.

LEEDS, *All Souls (Hook Memorial Church):* Case by A. Crawford Hick.
St. *Aidan:* Twin cases by A. Crawford Hick.
St. *Bartholomew, Armley:* Schulze pipework; case by Walker & Athron, 1879.
St. *Matthew, Chapel Allerton:* Bodley case.
St. *Matthew, Little London:* Hill cases.
St. *Peter (Parish Church):* Case of 1841. No pipes visible.
Brunswick Chapel: Case and some pipework; J. Booth, 1828.

LYTHE, St. *Oswald:* Tapper case on screen; no pipes visible (1910–11).

MIDDLESBROUGH, St. *Columba:* Temple Moore case.

NEWBY HALL: Case probably by Robert Adam, *c.* 1775.

OLD MALTON, *Priory Church,* St. *Mary:* Temple Moore case, 1887–8.

RIPON, *The Cathedral:* Gilbert Scott case, 1878, on choir screen; slightly modified.

ROTHERHAM, *All Saints:* Snetzler case and some pipework, 1777.

ROWLEY, St. *Peter:* Hill case.

SCARBOROUGH, St. *Martin:* Bodley case.

SELBY Abbey: Divided organ with J. O. Scott cases, 1909.

SHEFFIELD, St. *Paul:* Snetzler case.
St. *Marie, Norfolk Row (R.C.):* J. F. Bentley case, 1875.

WAKEFIELD, *The Cathedral:* Case of 1720, altered. Chancel case by F. L. Pearson.

WHITBY, St. *Hilda:* Case by R. J. Johnson.

YORK Minster: Case of Elliot & Hill organ, 1829, on choir screen, slightly modified. Also Lincoln chamber organ.

WALES

BANGOR, Caerns, *The Cathedral:* Cases by Gilbert Scott, 1873.

CARDIFF, Glam., St. *German, Roath:* Bodley case (1882).
St. *Saviour, Roath:* Bodley case (1888).

CARMARTHEN, St. *Peter:* G. P. England case, 1796.

DINGESTOW Court, Mon.: Father Smith pipework, provided with new case and soundboards by Robert Gray, 1773. Restored Mander.

HAVERFORDWEST, St. *Mary:* Harris-Byfield case, 1737.

MOLD, Flints., St. *Mary:* Jackson case.

OLD RADNOR, Radnorshire, St. *Stephen:* Casework, *c.* 1500, restored by F. H. Sutton, 1872. Front pipes and new instrument by Walker, 1872.

USK, Mon., St. *Mary:* Gray & Davison pipework, 1861, ex-Llandaff Cathedral, 1898.

ST. ASAPH, Flints., *The Cathedral:* Hill pipework, 1898; rebuilt 1932.

ST. DAVID'S, Pembs., *The Cathedral:* Father Willis pipework, rebuilt.

SCOTLAND

BLAIR ATHOLL Castle, Perthshire: Positive-regal by Loosemore, 1650. Part casework missing.

DUNBLANE, Perthshire, *The Cathedral:* Case by Lorimer.

EDINBURGH, *St. Mary's Cathedral:* Case by Sir Gilbert Scott.

McEwan Hall: Case by R. Anderson.

Palmerston Place United Free Church: Case by Washington Browne.

GLASGOW, *Art Gallery:* Case by J. W. Simpson.

Christ-the-King (R.C.): Case by Hill, Norman & Beard, 1960.

Westbourne United Free Church: Case by Whystock & Reid.

PAISLEY, Renfrews., *The Abbey:* Lorimer case.

STIRLING, *Church of the Holy Rude:* Case by James Miller.

NORTHERN IRELAND

BELFAST, *Ulster Hall:* Hill pipework, 1861, minor rebuild in 1904.

DOWNPATRICK, *Down Cathedral:* Green pipework in Gothick case, erected *c.* 1800. Rebuilt 1914.

SELECTIVE BIBLIOGRAPHY

BLANTON, J. E., *The Organ in Church Design* (Albany, Texas, 1958).

BONAVIA-HUNT, N. A., *Modern Organ Stops* (London, 1923).

CLUTTON, C. and DIXON, G., *The Organ: Its Tonal Structure and Registration* (London, 1950).

FREEMAN, A., *English Organ Cases* (London, 1921); *Father Smith* (London, 1932); *Church Organs and Organ Cases* (London, 1946).

HILL, A. G., *The Organ and Organ Cases of the Middle Ages and Renaissance* (London, 1883 and 1891).

HOPKINS, E. J. and RIMBAULT, E. F., *The Organ: Its History and Construction* (London, 1855; 3rd ed. 1877).

NORBURY, J., *The Box of Whistles* (London, 1887).

PEARCE, C. W., *Notes on English Organs of the Period 1800–1810 ... Taken Chiefly from the MS of Henry Leffler* (London, 1911); *Notes on Old City Churches, Their Organs, Organists, and Musical Associations* (London, 1911).

SUTTON, F. H., *Church Organs* (London 1872; 2nd ed. 1883).

SUTTON, Sir JOHN, *A Short Account of Organs Built in England from the Reign of King Charles the Second to the Present Time* (London, 1847).

SUMNER, W. L., *The Organ: Its Evolution, Principles of Construction and Use* (London, 1952; 3rd ed. 1962).

THE ORGANS ADVISORY COMMITTEE OF THE COUNCIL FOR THE CARE OF CHURCHES *Organs and Organ Cases for Parish Churches* (London, 1962).

Current Periodical Publications

Musical Opinion.

Musical Times.

The Organ—published quarterly since 1921; an indispensable source of pictorial and written information about all aspects of the British organ.

INDEX

The numbers in **heavy type** refer to the *Figure Numbers* of the illustrations

Abingdon, St. Helen, 226, 281
Adam of Darlington, 46, 47
Adam, Robert, 303
Adams, Thomas, 94
Adlington Hall, organ at, 64–6, 165, 169, 208, 220, 283; **23**
Aeolian Skinner Co., 44, 117
Alkmaar, St. Laurance, Schnitger organ at, 35, 149
Allen, 286, 295, 301
Allom, T., 241, 294; **75**
American organ building, 27, 44, 107, 117, 157
uncased organs, 276
Amiens Cathedral, 162, 165
Amorbach, Fürstlichen Hofkirche, Stumm organ, 35
Anderson, R., 304
Antegnati organ school, 40, 51
'Antheme' stop, 63
Appleby, St. Lawrence, 175, 178
Appleford, St. Peter and St. Paul, 281
Armley, St. Bartholomew, 98, 99, 109, 255; **69**
Ashley, St. Mary-the-Virgin, 295
Ashmole, Elias, *Order of the Garter*, 188
Ashton Keynes, Holy Cross Church, 301
Atkinson, Robert, 218
Attingham House, Salop, 298
Auckland Castle, Bishop's Palace, Chapel, 223, 284
Austin, 283, 289
Austrian school of organ-building, 25
Avery, 84, 183, 283, 287, 296

Bach, J. S., 28, 30–3, 44, 45, 91, 94, 120, 137, 157
registration, 32–4
use of reeds, 30
Bampton, 297
Bancroft, Bishop, 50
Bangor Cathedral, 256, 303
Barbier, N., organ at Gisors, 36
Barby, Northants, St Mary, 295
Bargrave, Dr. Isaac, 187
Barker, Charles Spackman, his lever action, 42, 99
Barking, All Hallows, 48, 272, 291
Barnard & Partners, 286
Barnsley, Glos., St. Mary-the-Virgin, 285
Barnsley, Yorks., 302
Baroque organs, 25, 29, 30, 32, 42, 157
terraced dynamics, 32
Barrel Organs, 299, 301
Barton-le-Street, 302

Barton-under-Needwood, 298
Basingstoke, All Saints, 286
Basse de Cromorne, 38
de trompette, 38
Bassoon, 43, 82, 87, 103
Bates (of Ludgate), 237, 281, 287, 291, 299, 300, 301; **56**
Bath Abbey, 298
Beddington, St. Mary-the-Virgin, 300
Bedford, Holy Trinity, 280
Bédos, Dom, 129
Belcher, J., 284
Belfast, Hill Organ at Ulster Hall, 94, 304
Bellows, 10th century, 21–2
diagonal, 22
Belton, Rutland, 297
Bennett, 126
Bentley, J. F., 161, 288, 290, 292, 303
Richard, 75
Beresford-Pite, 293
Best, W. T., 43, 94, 102–4
on mixtures (qu.), 24
orchestral arrangements, 43
on Thomas Adam, 93
Beverley Minster, Snetzler organ, 87, 166, 265, 302; **95**
diapered pipes at, 170
Bevington, 241, 281, 294
Bexley, Kent, Danson Park, 288
Birmingham Cathedral, 161, 166, 228, 301; **27**
Town Hall, 92, 243, 301
Bishop, J. C., 95, 145, 241, 282, 285, 290, 299, 300, 301 [301
Bishopstone Church, 287
Bishopsbourne Church, 288
Blair Atholl Castle organ, 52, 304
Blandford Forum, 230, 284
Blanton, J. E., *The Organ in Church Design*, 177, 178, 182
Blenheim Palace, 169, 297
Blewitt, Jonas, 126–9, *Complete Treatise on the Organ*, 126, 127
Blickling, St. Andrew, 294
Blockwerk, 23–5, 32, 49
South German, 32
Blomfield, Sir Arthur, 202, 262, 269, 293, 294, 300; **98**
Blore, 238, 281, 287
Blow, John, 70, 75, 122, 125, 126
Bodley, G. F., 161, 252, 257, 258, 261, 262, 269, 280, 282, 285–90, 293–303; **79–81**, **83**, **84**
Bolnhurst, Beds., St. Dunstan, 252, 280
Bologna, S. Petronio, organ, 23, 40, 51, 258
Bolton Town Hall, organ specification, 103, 104
Bombarde, 39, 43

307

Booth, J. (of Wakefield), 90, 302, 303
Boothby Pagnell Church, 258, 290
Bosanquet family, 74
Bottesford, Leics., St. Mary, 289
Boulton and Son (Cheltenham), 272
Bourdon, 36–8, 43, 63, 92, 96, 101, 103, 104
Bower, S. E. Dykes, 159, 228, 258, 271, 285–7, 293, 295, 296, 301; 103–5
Bradford Cathedral, 302
Brahms, Johannes, 19
Bramley, Holy Trinity, 269, 300
Brant Broughton, 290
Brescia, 40, 51
Bridge, Richard, 83, 84, 217, 226, 228, 234, 291–4; 25
Bridgetown, Barbados, St. Michael, 198
Brighton, 300
Bristol Cathedral, 59, 214, 281; 35
    Charles Wesley's House, 281
    Christ Church, 281
    Clifton College, 270, 281
    Clifton Theological College, 281
    Holy Trinity, 281
    St. George, St. James and St. Thomas, 231, 281
    St. Mary Redcliffe, 82, 131; 66
British organs, 21, 39
    Middle Ages to 1650, 45–61
    Restoration Period, 62–81
    Eighteenth century, 81–9
    Hill–Gauntlett Revolution, 89–97
    Willis, Schulze and Hope-Jones, 97–115
    Post-war revival, 115ff.
    musical adaptability and use of, 120–46
    registration for French and German music, 137–45
Broderick, Cuthbert, 244
Bromyard, St. Peter, 287
Brondesbury, St. Anne, 294
Brookthorpe, Glos., St. Swithin, 285
Brown, Cecil, 214, 272, 291
Browne, Washington, 304
Brownsover Church, 184, 301
Brustwerk, 26
Bryceson Brothers and Ellis, Messrs., 238, 283, 294, 299
    Barrel organ, 299; 55
Bucklebury, St. Mary, 281
Bull, John, 61
    Randolph, 48
    William, 59, 121
Burgess, William, 255
Burney, Dr., 68, 69, 72, 82, 148, 295
Burton-on-Trent, 298
Burward, John, 54
Buxtehude, 45
Byfield, John, senr., 76, 81, 129, 161, 217, 228, 233, 281, 283, 291, 294, 298, 303; 43, 66
    John (the 2nd), 76, 83, 84, 227, 291
    John (the 3rd), 76, 81
Byford, St. John, 287
Byrd, 59, 121

Cambridge, All Saints, 172
    Christ's College, 172, 204, 282
    Clare College, 282
    Emmanuel College, 204, 206, 223, 282; 49
    Holy Trinity, 282
    Jesus College, 60, 61, 78, 159, 161, 162, 169, 170, 172, 223, 247, 282; 61
    King's College, 53, 54, 60, 159, 162, 172, 175, 183, 192, 282; 6, 7
    Pembroke College, 68, 178, 197, 204, 282, 298; 29
    Peterhouse, 226, 282
    Queens' College, 261, 282
    St. Andrew-the-Less, 248, 282
    St. Catherine's College, 162, 169, 266, 282; 88
    St. John's College, 184, 257, 282, 301
    St. Mary-the-Great Church, Father Smith organ in, 119, 166, 198, 223, 282; 46
    St. Paul's Church, 282
    Trinity College, 53, 54, 75, 166, 202, 225, 233, 282; 48
Camden Society, 237, 244
Camidge, Dr. John, 90
Canterbury Cathedral, 47, 64, 66, 102, 257
    Dean Bargrave's organ, 175, 187, 288
    Lancelot Pease's organ, 191; 37
Canterbury, St. Andrew, 49
    St. Margaret, 288
Cantus Firmus, 39
Capel, Jutland, organ specification, 27, 35
Cardiff, St. German and St. Saviour, 303
Carisbrooke Castle, I.O.W., 172
Carmarthen, 303
Carlisle Cathedral, 59, 178, 301
Caröe organ cases, 283–5, 287, 292, 297–301; 99
Carpenter, R. C., 165, 255, 284; 70
Carshalton, All Saints, 231, 300; 102
'Cart' stop, 77
Caseless organs, 233ff., 275–6
Cases, double, 165
Casework, 156ff.
    decoration and appendages, 166ff.
Casson, Thomas, his influence on Dixon, 111
Castle Ashby, St. Mary Magdalene, 295
Cathedrals, organ position in, 147ff.
Cavaillé-Coll, Aristide, 40–2, 97, 98, 145, 146, 289
    stop-control system, 41, 145
Cave, Sir Thomas, 181
Cawston, St. Agnes, 294
Cawthorne, All Saints, 302
Central Council for the Care of Churches, 119
Chaire organ, 54, 56, 59, 63, 64, 73, 82, 122, 125, 165; 11
Chalfont St. Peter, All Saints, 281
Chamberlayne, John, 47
Chamber organs, 87, 172, 187, 293; 33, 34, 44, 45, 56
Champneys, Basil, 292, 298
Chapman and Hartop, 183

Chappington, John, 56, 182, 286
Charles I, 50
Charles II, 181
Chartres, 178
Chatham, St. Mary, 288
Cheltenham, All Saints, 285
Cheshunt parish church, 161, 261, 287; 80
Chester Cathedral, 206, 256, 283
Chichester Cathedral, 76, 165, 300; 92
Chippendale, 234, 286, 293
Chippenham, Wilts., 95, 301
Chippenham, St. Andrew, 301
Chirk Castle, organ at, 54, 55, 58
Chislehurst, St. Nicholas, 288
Chiswick parish church, 258, 294
Choir organ, 65, 77, 78, 87, 96, 101, 104, 109, 128, 130
Chorlton on Medlock, 289
Chorus, 31, 34, 37, 72, 74, 75, 79, 83, 99, 106, 108, 115, 125, 130, 142, 145
Chorus, French Diapason, 37
  German Diapason, 31
  Rückpositiv, 31
Christchurch Priory, 184
Christian worship, introduction of the organ into, 20, 21
Churches, Parish, organ position in, 155ff.
Churchill, Oxon., 297
Churchwarden Gothic, 283, 287, 291
Cirencester, St. John the Baptist, 285
Clarabella, 93, 96, 103, 104, 107
Clarinet, 30, 43, 96, 103, 131, 142
Clarion, 36, 37, 43, 63, 82, 85, 87, 93, 96, 103, 104, 106, 128
Clarion mixture, 106
Clarke, Somers, 262, 290, 299, 300
Classical organ, 35, 40, 118, 119, 157
Claviorganum, 89
Clermont-Ferrand, Rabiny organ at Notre Dame du Port, 36
Clicquot, 37, 39
Clumber, Notts., St. Mary, 296
Clutton, Cecil, 66, 112, 115
Cockerell, C. R., 243, 289; 76
Cockington, Devon, 284
Colchester Moot Hall, 284
Coldharbour, 300
Colehill, Dorset, 284
Coleshill, All Saints, 281
Commonwealth, organs during the, 50, 57, 187
Communication, 77
Compenius, 51, 52, 66
Compass, 'C', Gauntlett's, 90
  'GG', 132-8
Comper, Sir Ninian, 171, 271, 284, 286-9, 291, 293, 295, 296, 299, 300; 101
Composition pedals, 145
Compton, John, 112
Compton Wynyates, Smith organ at, 74, 211, 301; 33
Console, 26, 32
Contra fagotto, 103

Cor Anglais, 103
Cornet, 27, 36-8, 71-4, 82, 85, 87, 93, 127, 129
  Dulciana, 84
  Introduction into England, 71
Corno di Bassetto, 104, 130
Corno flute, 93, 128
Cornopean, 93, 96, 101
Cosham, St. Philip, 286
Cotsgrave, Dandle, Dictionary of the French and English Tongues (qu.), 60
Couplers, 42, 142
Coventry, Holy Trinity, 49
  St. Michael, Schwarbrook organ at, 83
Cranbourne Church, Berks., 281
Crang and Hancock, 198
Cremona, 38, 73, 93, 127, 131
Cricklade, St. Sampson, 302
Cromorne, 36, 37, 82
  Basse de, 38
Cromwell, Oliver, 55
Crosby-on-Eden, St. John, 283
Croydon, St. John, St. Matthew, 300
  St. Michael and All Angels, 155, 258, 261, 300; 84
Croyland Abbey, 150
Cymbal, 29, 36, 37, 52, 63, 74, 128
Cymbelstern, 27, 195

Dallam, George, 76
  Ralph, 188, 189
  Robert, 55, 57, 62, 63, 66, 67, 69, 76, 172, 291; 8
  Thomas, 53, 54, 60, 76, 86, 122, 282, 287
  genealogy, 76
  organ for the Sultan, 48
Danehill, All Saints, 261, 300; 81
Daniel, Percy, and Son, Messrs. (Clevedon), 272
Darlington, Paradise Methodist Church, 284
Daventry, Holy Cross, 295
Davis, James, 237, 295, 298
Davison, Frederick, 94
Deal, Kent, St. George, 288
Delft, Nieuwekerk, 24
Denham organ, 159, 276; 110
Denton, St. Andrew, 290
Derby, St. John, 283
Devizes, St. John, 302
Devonshire, Duke of, 88
Diapason, 27, 44, 57, 72-5, 79, 82, 83-7, 92, 93, 96, 99, 101, 109, 125-31
Diapason chorus, French, 37
  German, 31
Diapason phonon, Hope-Jones's, 106
Diapason, Smith's, 74
Dictionary of English Furniture, 234
Dingestow Court, Mon., Smith's chamber organ, 74, 231, 303; 44, 45
Dinmore Manor Chapel, 287
Disley, Ches., St. Mary, 283
Dixon, Lt. Col. George, 108, 127
  Casson's influence on, 111
  selective registration, 127

Doetichem, Flentrop organ at, 26, 276; **109**
Doggerell, Mr. (gilder), 188, 189
Doncaster parish church, 98, 302
Doors, 169
Dorking, St. Paul, 300
Double cases, 165, 282; **14, 16, 29, 92, 93**
Doubled stops, 58, 59
Double organ compositions, 122–6
Double organ Voluntary, 66, 67, 68
Douglas, I.O.M., St. Ninian, 288
Downes, Ralph, 116, 119
Downpatrick, Down Cathedral, 237, 304; **53**
Dryden, Sir Henry, 175
Dublin, Christ Church Cathedral, 217, 299
  St. Mary, 78, 217; **19**
Duddyngton, Anthony, and his Contract, 48, 60
Dugdale, *History of St. Paul's Cathedral*, 172
  Monasticon Anglicanum, 165
Dulcet, 96
Dulciana, 85, 88, 92, 93, 96, 127
  cornet, 84
Dulcimer, 83
Dulzian, 27, 28
Dunblane, 304
Dunne, W., 294
Dunsford, Devon, 284
Durham Cathedral, 70, 72, 150, 152, 196, 201, 204, 284; **47**
  Rites of, 50
  University College Chapel, 202, 284
Dutch Reformed Church, 32
Dutch School: *See* Netherlands

Ealing, Christ the Saviour, 294
Eardisland, St. Mary-the-Virgin, 287
East Bradenham, St. Mary, 295
East Hagbourne, St. Andrew, 265, 281
Eastney, St. Margaret, 286
East Kirkby, 290
Easton Neston, 295
Easton-on-the-Hill, 295
East Stratton, All Saints, 286
Ecchinswell, St. Lawrence, 286
Eccleshall, Church of Holy Trinity, 298
Eccleston, St. Mary, 261, 283
Echo, 39, 93, 103, 126, 128
  compass, 39
  organ, first English, 73, 77, 78
  18th cent. use of, 129
Edgecote, St. Peter and St. Paul, 295
Edinburgh, 256, 304
Edwards, F. G., 102
Edwardstone, Suffolk, 299
Egmanton, Notts., St. Mary, 271, 296; **101**
Electric action, 115, 118
Elgar, organ sonata, 107
Elizabeth, Queen, her organ for the Sultan, 48
Ellesmere, Salop, 298
Ellingham, St. Mary, 286
Elliot, Thomas, 89, 152, 238, 294, 295, 303; **57**
Eltham, St. John, 288
Elvaston, Derbyshire, 283

Elveden, 299
Ely Cathedral, 108, 152, 255, 256, 282; **71**
  organ specification, 109
Ely, Marquis of, 83
Enfield, St. Andrew, 229, 294
England, George, 84, 229, 234, 288, 290, 292, 299; **51, 65**
England, George Pike, 84, 89, 284, 285, 291, 292, 294, 295, 298, 302, 303
  tonal characteristics, 84
England, John, 84
Epping, St. John the Baptist, 265, 285
Epsom, St. Martin, 300
Eton College organ, 50, 53, 60, 201, 270, 282
  Snetzler organ, 88
Evelyn, John (qu.), 55, 57, 75
Exeter Cathedral organ, 59, 67, 122, 150, 152, 170, 191, 213, 271, 284; **14**
  Song school, organ specification, 67
'Expressive' organ, 42
'Extension' organ, 112

Falkenham, St. Ethelbert, 299
Farquhar, Dr. Theodore, 151
Farthingstone, St. Mary-the-Virgin, 295
Fellowes-Prynne, 300
Fetcham, 300
Finedon, Church, Northants., Shrider organ at, 81, 166, 170, 225, 296; **39**
Flentrop, 276, 279; **109**
Flight and Robson, Messrs., 217, 285, 295, 299
Flue, 33; **17**
Flue-controlled voicing, 34
Flutes, 34–9, 48, 63, 73, 77, 82, 83, 85, 87, 93, 96, 98, 103, 104, 126, 127, 141, 142
Folkestone, St. Peter, 288
Foothole-controlled voicing, 34
Forkel, 33
Forster and Andrews, Messrs., 30
Foundling Hospital, 131
Foxearth, Essex, St. Peter and St. Paul, 285
Framlingham Church, 68, 159, 162, 175, 178, 299; **4**
Franck, César, 19, 42, 146
Fredericksborg Castle, 51, 66
Freeman, Rev. Andrew, 56, 150, 177, 178, 181, 189, 191, 217, 229, 234, 256, 262, 266, 272
Freiburg-im-Breisgau, 'swallow's nest' case at, 261, 276
French composers, 43, 138, 142, 146
  diapason chorus, 37
  music, 17th and 18th cent., 39
  organ building, 25, 35–9, 100, 106, 117
  organ pipes, 170
  pedal organ, 39
Frescobaldi, 40, 61
Furniture, 36, 37, 63, 77, 87, 128

Galpin Collection, 52
Gamba, 43, 96, 103
Gambette, 96
Garner, T., 162, 261, 262, 266, 282; **88**

Gauntlett, Dr. Henry John, 103, 132, 214, 280, 292, 295
  his 'C' compass, 90
Gauntlett Revolution, the, 89–97
Gedackt, 27, 72, 73, 101
Geib, John, 233, 299; 52
Gemshorn, 27, 96, 101
George III, 84, 218
  VI, Coronation of, 111
German chamber organs, 172, 293
  compass, 132, 135
  composers, 137, 142, 145, 146, 149
  diapason chorus, 31
  flute, Snetzler's, 89
  mixtures, 31
  organ-building, 23, 25–35, 38, 44, 59, 97, 98, 100, 106, 117, 118, 120, 196
  organ cases, 162
  romantic organ, 42, 43
  table organ, 293; 18
  uncased organs, 276
  17th and 18th century music performed on British organs, 137–42
'GG' compass, substitute for on a 'C' organ, 132–7
Ghent altarpiece by Van Eyck, 22
Gibbons, Christopher, 55
  Grinling, 115, 195, 207, 214, 284, 291
Giggleswick School Chapel, 302
Gilding, 169, 183
Gisors, St. Gervais, Barbier organ specification, 36
Glasgow, 279, 304; 108
Glenrothes, Fife, St. Columba, 276; 107
Gloucester Cathedral, 99, 152, 175, 178, 181, 213, 271, 285; 3
Glynn and Parker, Messrs., 65
Godalming, St. Peter and St. Paul, 300
Godwin, *London Churches*, 206, 214, 228
Gonnesse, 170
Gopsall Hall, 83
Gosport, Holy Trinity, 286
Gothick organ cases, 162–6, 175, 177, 234, 282–6, 297, 302, 304
Grand Jeu, 129
Grand Ophicleide stop, 92
Grand Orgue, 36, 37, 42
  Compass, 39
  20th century, 44
Grand Plein Jeu, 37
Grantham, St. Wulfram, 290
Gray & Davison, Messrs., 94, 95, 103, 130, 137, 165, 244, 286, 292–6, 298, 301–3
Gray, John, 95
Gray, Robert, 74, 231, 299, 302
Great Badminton, St. Michael-and-All-Angels, 269, 286
Great Bardfield, 159, 160, 169, 252, 285; 68
Great Bowden, 289
Great Exhibition (1851), 97, 99
Great Mistley, 285
Great Organ, 23, 25, 56–9, 64, 72, 77, 82, 87, 96, 103, 104, 122; 12

Great Packington, Bridge organ at, 83, 301
Great Waltham, 285
Great Witley, 302
Great Yarmouth parish church, 218, 228
Green, H. F., 295
Green, Samuel, 81, 83, 89, 126, 191, 218, 225, 233ff., 281, 282, 285–8, 292, 293, 295, 297–9, 302, 304; 53
Griffin, T., 229, 291
Groenlo, Holland, 279
Groton, 299
Grove, Mr., 105
Guilmant, 41

Haarlem, St. Bavo, Muller organ, 24, 25, 35, 148, 149
  tracker action at, 26, 27
Hadleigh, Suffolk, 295
Halberstadt Cathedral, 23
Halifax parish church, Snetzler organ, 88, 302
Hamburg, Johanneskirche, Schnitger organ, 27, 35
Ham Common, 300
Hampton Court, 55, 300
Hancock, 280
Handel, 65, 83, 126
  on pedals, 82
Hardwicke, Glos., St. Nicholas, 272, 286
Hare, C. J., 265, 292, 297
Harlton, Cambs., 169, 251, 282; 67
Harmonics—Arthur Harrison, 108
Harmonium, 53
Harp, 83
Harpsichord, 121, 293
Harris, John, 76, 81, 228, 281
  and Byfield partnership, 81, 82, 281, 283, 298, 303; 66
Harris, Renatus, 55, 57, 65, 68, 76–81, 83, 97, 148, 170, 183, 196, 211ff., 220ff., 238, 271, 272, 281, 284, 285, 291, 294, 299; 16, 19, 22, 30, 35, 54, 58
  behaviour and character, 79
  genealogy, 76–81
  tone and diapason chorus, 76
Harris, Thomas, 56, 68, 76, 170, 178, 196, 286
Harrison and Harrison, Messrs., 108, 116, 142, 202, 237, 247, 258, 272, 282, 283
Harrison, Arthur, 107, 108, 137
  his solo organ, 109, 110
Harrison, Cuthbert, 116
Harrison, Donald, his work in America, 44, 117
Harrow, St. George, Headstone, 294
Harrow School Chapel, 270, 294
Harvey, S. W., 191
Harwich, St. Nicholas, 285
Hastings, 301
Hatfield House, 172, 287
Hatcham Park, Surrey, All Saints, 300
Hauptwerk, 26–8, 32, 33
Hautbois, 37, 43, 82, 85, 87, 93, 104, 126, 127, 131
Haverfordwest, St. Mary, 303
Hawkins, 69

Hawksmoor, 229
Heaton Park, Lancs., 289
Hedgeland, 281
Henry VII, 177
    VIII, 39, 51, 52, 177
Henstead Church, Suffolk, 299
Hentland, St. Dubricius, 287
Herschel and Snetzler, 88
s'Hertogenbosch Cathedral, 148
Hexham Abbey, 296
Heysham, St. James, 289
Hick, A. Crawford, 303
Higham Ferrers, 296
High Beech, Essex, Holy Innocents, 285
Hill, Dr. A. G., 87, 152, 165, 166, 170, 177,
    213, 238, 252, 279, 291–3, 300–4; 57, 92,
    94, 95
    Organs and Organ Cases of the Middle Ages,
    262
Hill, Arthur, 102
Hill, Thomas, 102
Hill, William, and Son, Norman and Beard,
    Messrs., 59, 116, 118, 119, 130, 137, 183,
    204, 237, 257, 266, 271, 276, 279, 288,
    290, 293, 295, 298, 300, 304
Hillington Church, 88, 295
Holdich, G. M., 94, 252, 295, 296
Holyrood House, Triptych at, 22, 156; 1
Hoo, Suffolk, 299
Hope Jones, 102, 106, 111, 119, 293
    tonal characteristics, 106
Hope, W. St. John, History of Windsor
    Castle, 188
Hopkins and Rimbault, 73, 85, 148
    The Organ: its history and Construction,
    100, 188, 189
Horley, Oxon., 297
Horseheath, Cambs., All Saints, 283
Horsham, Christ's Hospital, 79, 300
Horsley, G., 298
Houghton-on-the-Hill, 289
Hove, All Saints, 270, 300; 100
Howe, John ('Father'), 50, 53
Howe, John (the Younger), 47, 49, 53
Howe, Thomas, 50, 53
Hull, 115, 302
Huntingdon, St. Mary, Snetzler organ, 89
Hydraulus (Roman organ), 20
Hythe, St. Leonard, 270, 288; 93

Ickham, St. John the Evangelist, 288
Icklesham Church, 300
Ightham Mote House, 293
Ilkley, All Saints, 302
Innsbruck, Silbernenkapelle, 40, 51
Inventions Exhibition (1885), 101, 105
Isaac, 24
Islington Chapel of Ease, 84
Islip, St. Nicholas, 296
Italian concerto, 32
    influence, 51
    mutation, 30
    organs, 23, 25, 29, 39, 45, 100, 162

Jackson, Dr. Francis, 118
Jackson, Sir Thos., 161, 166, 169, 252, 265,
    281, 286, 297, 298, 301, 302; 86, 87, 89, 91
Jeans, Susi, 122
Jeux de Combinaisons, 41
Jeux de fonds, 41
Jebb, Dr. John, 244
    Three Lectures on the Cathedral Service of
    the Church of England, 152
'Jebbism', 191
Johnson, R. J., 211, 303
Jones, 89
Jones, W. C., reed voicer, 112
Jordan, Abraham, senior and junior, 79, 86,
    226–31, 281, 286, 288, 291; 28
    introduction of swell organ from Spain, 86

Kempe, C. E., 262, 265, 280, 285, 301
Keraulophon, 96
Kettering, 296
Keyboard, balanced, 22
    changes of, 140
    Halberstadt, 23
    second, 165
    slider-type, 21
    Snetzler's, 89
Keyhoe Church, 280
Kiedrich, Germany, St. Valentine, 248
Kilkhampton, Cornwall, 283
Kingsbury, Middlesex, 294
Kingsgate, Davidson and Co., Messrs., 115
King's Lynn, St. Margaret, 165, 218, 226,
    295; 24
King's Stanley, Glos., 286
Kington, St. Mary, 287
Kinlet, 298
Kinnersley, St. James, 287
Kirkandrews-on-Esk, 269, 283; 96
Kitzbühl, Tyrol, 272
Klosterneuberg, Abbey Church organ, 23, 33,
    35
Knopple, John, 201, 291
Krummhorn, 30, 73

Lacey Green, St. John, 282
Lainson, T., 281
Lamarsh, Essex, 285
Lambourn, Berks., 281
Landini (organist of St. Peter's, Rome), 23
Langley, Batty, Gothic Architecture Improved,
    234
Langtoft, St. Peter, 302
Languid, the, 33, 34; 17
Larigot, 36, 38
Laud, Archbishop, 50
Laughton, All Saints, 290
Launceston, St. Mary Magdalene, 283
Leckingfield Proverbs, 49
Lee, John T., 286
Leeds, All Souls, 303
    Brunswick Chapel, 90, 303
    Parish Church, 151, 303
    St. Aidan, 303

St. Bartholomew, 303
St. Matthew, Chapel Allerton, 261, 303
St. Matthew, Little London, 265, 303
Town Hall, 244
Legh Family, 64, 65, 220
Leicester, 198, 201, 289
Leigh, St. Mary-the-Virgin, 289
Leominster Priory, 287
Lewis, T. C., 99, 105, 107, 269, 289, 293, 294, 300
Lichfield Cathedral, 93, 94, 150, 257, 298
Parish Church, 298
Lieblich gedackt, 101
Lille Cathedral, 255
Lilley, H. T., 191, 201, 206, 211; 37, 46, 75
Lincoln (organ builder), 297
Lincoln Cathedral, 59, 165, 172, 238, 290; 10
Bishop's Hostel Chapel, 290
St. Andrew, 290
Lip shapes, Pipe, 170, 197; 26
Liszt, Franz, 19, 44
Little Bardfield, St. Katherine, 78, 223, 271, 285; 30
Littlebury, Holy Trinity, 256, 285
Little Plumstead, Norfolk, 281
Littleport, Cambs., 283
Liverpool Cathedral, 112, 270, 289
Exhibition (1886), 105
George St. Chapel, 92, 107
St. Agnes, 289
St. George's Hall, 99, 100, 102, 105, 289; 76
St. John the Baptist, 289
St. Peter, 217
Llanano, 48
Lloyd, W. A. S., 202, 272, 293
Locke, John, 75, 122, 125
Lockyar, Daniel, 49
London
Albert Hall, 100, 244
Alexander Palace, 100, 244, 294
All Hallows-by-the-Tower, 218, 291; 21
All Hallows, Lombard Street, 79, 115, 218; 22
All Hallows, London Wall, 291
All Hallows, Twickenham, 79, 115, 169, 218, 294; 22
All Saints, Tooting Graveney, 293
All Souls, Langham Place, 241, 293
Christ Church, Chelsea, 290
Christ Church, Newgate St., 91, 211, 214
Christ Church, Spitalfields, 228, 293
Church of the Annunciation, Marble Arch, 269, 293
Dulwich College Chapel, 234, 290; 51
Emmanuel Church, St. John's Wood, 292
Emmanuel Church, West Dulwich, 290
Foundling Hospital Chapel, 132, 292
Grosvenor Chapel, 294
Highbury Barn, Islington, 291
Holy Trinity, Brompton, 292
Clapham, 293
Kensington Gore, 292
Sloane Street, 106, 290

Southwark, 293
Hyde Park Chapel, South Kensington, 276; 106
Italian Church, Hatton Garden, 116
Jesuit Church, Farm Street, 112
King's College Chapel, Strand, 294
Marlborough House Chapel, 294
Our Lady of the Assumption, Warwick Street, 233, 294; 43
Panopticon of Science and Art, 105
Queen's Chapel, Whitehall, 214
Royal Festival Hall, 115, 119, 120
Royal Hospital, Chelsea, 290
Royal Naval Hospital, Greenwich, 238, 292; 59
St. Alban, Fulham, 228
St. Andrew, Holborn, 217, 292
St. Andrew-by-the-Wardrobe, 88, 291
St. Andrew Undershaft, 197, 214, 291
St. Andrew, Wells Street, 294
St. Anne, Limehouse, 293
St. Anselm and St. Cecilia, Kingsway, 292
St. Augustine, Haggerston, 290
St. Augustine, Highbury, 292
St. Augustine, Kilburn, 257
St. Barnabas, Addison Road, 292
St. Barnabas, Pimlico, 293
St. Bartholomew, Cripplegate, 228
St. Bartholomew-by-the-Exchange, 228, 292
St. Botolph, Aldgate, 217, 225, 291
St. Botolph, Bishopsgate, 291
St. Bride, Fleet Street, 77, 211, 217, 275
St. Catherine Cree, 214, 223, 291; 63
St. Clement, Eastcheap, 79, 220, 291
St. Clement Danes, 202, 272, 293
St. Dionis Backchurch, 218
St. Dominic's Priory, Haverstock Hill, 293
St. Dunstan, Bellingham, 293
St. Dunstan-in-the-West, 46, 291
St. Edmund-the-King, 220, 291
St. Ethelburga, Bishopsgate, 291
St. Ethelreda, Holborn, 292
St. Gabriel, Pimlico, 293
St. George, Bloomsbury Way, 292
St. George, Botolph Lane, 229, 293
St. Giles, Camberwell (Bishop organ), 95, 241, 290
St. Giles, Cripplegate, 228
St. Giles-in-the-Fields, 217, 228, 292
St. Helen, Bishopsgate, 228, 291
St. James, Bermondsey, 95, 290
St. James, Clerkenwell, 292
St. James, Garlickhithe, 201, 291
St. James, Piccadilly, 162, 166, 197, 214, 223, 233, 294; 36
St. James's Palace, Chapel Royal, 293
St. John, Blackheath, 292
Hoxton, 293
Hammersmith, 161, 292
Lambeth, 241, 293; 60
Paddington, 293
Red Lion Square, 257, 258

London (*contd.*)
St. John-the-Evangelist, Hampstead, 166, 266, 292; 91
St. Katherine, Regent's Park, 293
St. Lawrence, Commonwealth Chapel of, 272
St. Lawrence Jewry, 213, 218, 220, 272, 291; 16
St. Leonard, Shoreditch, 226; 25
St. Luke, Chelsea, 291
Hampstead, 292
Old Street, 228
St. Magnus-the-Martyr, London Bridge, Jordan organ, 86, 231, 291; 28
St. Margaret, Lothbury, 230, 291
St. Margaret Pattens, 229, 291
St. Margaret, Westminster, Walker organ, 106, 148, 294
St. Mark, East Walworth, 218
St. Mark, North Audley Street, 294
St. Martin, Ludgate, 291
St. Martin-in-the-Fields, 52, 189, 218, 241, 287, 294; 75
St. Mary-at-Hill, Billingsgate, 291
St. Mary, Lambeth, 217
Rotherhithe, 83, 84, 129, 166, 229, 290; 41
Southwark, 293
St. Mary Woolnoth, 291
St. Mary Magdalene, Islington, 84, 231, 292; 42
St. Mary Magdalene, Milk Street, 150
St. Mary Magdalene, Paddington, 293
St. Mildred, Poultry, 85, 291
St. Michael, Queenhithe, 290
St. Nicholas, Deptford, 206
St. Olave, Tooley Street, 90
St. Pancras, 293
St. Paul, Covent Garden, 294
Deptford, 228, 292
St. Paul's Cathedral, 47, 72, 73, 79, 80, 97, 101, 146, 148, 165, 172, 195, 197, 207, 291; 32
proposed Harris organ, 79–81
Visitation (1598), 50
St. Peter, Cornhill, 91
Cranley Gardens, 270, 292
Streatham, 293
St. Peter-ad-Vincula, The Tower, 198
St. Peter's Organ Works, Bethnal Green, 175, 187, 290; 34
St. Sepulchre, Holborn, 166, 196, 211, 218, 220, 292; 54
St. Stephen, Hampstead, 292
St. Stephen, Walbrook, 85, 229, 292; 65
St. Vedast, Foster Lane, 118, 161, 166, 228, 292; 40
Southwark Cathedral, 99, 269, 293: 98
Temple Church organ, 71, 72, 79, 197, 202, 206, 217; 50
Third Church of Christ, Scientist, Curzon Street, 294
Union Chapel, Islington, 292
Victoria and Albert Museum, 252, 293

Westminster Abbey, 46, 93, 111, 233, 258, 271, 293; 78
Roman Catholic Cathedral, 112
Whitehall, Royal Chapel, 68, 70, 181, 198
Longman and Broderip, 237, 295
Longsdon, St. Chad, 298
Lorimer, 282, 286, 304
Loosemore, John, 52, 67, 172, 191, 192, 284, 298, 304; 13, 14
Loppersum, 71
Lound Church, Suffolk, 299
Lucas, Geoffrey, 280
Ludlow, 298
Lugge, John, 61, 122
Lüneburg, St. John, 162
Lure, 83
Lydd Church, 288
Lyndsey, Suffolk, 299
Lythe, Yorks., 303

Macartney, Mervyn, 301
Mace, Thomas, *Musick's Monument*, 59
Macrory, *Notes on the Temple Organ*, 206
Madeira, Church of Santa Cruz, 72, 293
Maidstone, St. Paul, 288
Malvern Priory, 270, 302
Manchester Cathedral, 223, 256, 271
St. George, 289
Town Hall, 289
Mander, Messrs. N. P. Ltd., 115, 207, 228, 233, 241, 262, 276; 110
Mander, Noel, 58, 65, 66, 74, 75, 83, 88, 118, 159, 175, 187, 208, 220, 226, 233, 289, 294, 300
Marlborough College Chapel, 302
Marsh, John, 126–9
Maufe, Sir Edward, 302
Medemblik, 71
Melbourn, Cambs., All Saints, 283
Mendelssohn, 19, 44, 91, 214
Mersenne, 129
Harmonie Universelle (on reed-voicing), 101
Michell and Thynne, 102, 280, 286, 297
development of the romantic organ, 105, 106
Micklethwaite, 290, 299
Middlesbrough, 303
Middleton, St. Leonard, 289
Mid-Lavant, St. Nicholas, 300
Miller, James, 304
Milton, John, 55
Mixtures, 27, 28, 44, 63, 72, 74, 85, 93, 98, 101, 106, 108, 112, 122
Bernard Smith's, 74
chorus, 20, 31
early history, 24
German, 31
Renatus Harris's, 78
Moccas, Herefs., St. Michael-and-all-Angels, 287
Mold, Flints, St. Mary, 303
Monkland, All Saints, 287
Monk Sherborne, All Saints, 286

Montre, 37, 43
Moore, Temple, 161, 256, 262, 266, 269, 280, 281, 283, 286, 288, 290, 296, 302, 303; 96, 97
Moorlynch, St. Mary-the-Virgin, 298
Morris, William, 300
Morton-by-Gainsborough, 290
Mottistone, St. Peter and St. Paul, 288
Muchelney, 298
Muller, Christian, 35
Mundford, St. Leonard, 295
Musical Times, correspondence re pedals, 61
on Father Willis, 102
on Stanford-on-Avon, 181
Mutations, 29, 34, 36, 39
Cavaillé-Coll, 41
Mutation stops, 142
French, 38
Italian, 39
Myddleton, Sir Thomas, 54

Nachthorn, 27, 28
Nasat, 27, 74
Nason, 77, 83, 85
Naughton Church, Suffolk, 299
Nayland, St. James, 299
Nazard, 29, 36-8, 104, 142
Neo-Baroque voicing, 34
Nesfield, E., 285
Netherlands, 25-7, 44, 71, 117, 196, 276
organs without pedals, 71
Nettlecombe Court, 67, 192, 298; 13
Newark, 297
Newbury, Shaw House, 289
Newby Hall, 303
Newcastle-upon-Tyne, 78
Cathedral (St. Nicholas), 196, 211, 217, 296; 20
Newent, St. Mary, 286
Newhaven, St. Michael, 301
New Milverton, St. Mark, 265, 301
Newton, Isaac, 75
William, 238
Nicholson of Worcester, 95, 302
Nicholson, Sir Charles, 270, 281, 284-5, 288, 294, 297, 298, 300, 301
Nightingale, 48
Norbury, John, *The Box of Whistles*, 207, 211, 213, 262
Nordlingen, St. George, 166
Northborough, St. Andrew, 265, 296
North, Hon. Roger (qu.), 67
Northampton, Marquis of, chamber organ, 74, 75, 208
Northampton, All Saints and St. Peter, 296
Town Hall, 98
Northington, St. John, 265, 286
Norwich Cathedral, 112, 238, 271, 295; 103, 104
Norwich, Military Company of, 59
St. Andrew, St. George and King Edward VI Grammar School, 295
St. Peter Mancroft, 78, 218, 228

Nottingham, St. Catherine, 296
St. Mary, 256, 257, 296; 72
St. Peter, 296
Nutt, John, partner with Ohrman, 89

Oberwerk, 26, 138
Obrecht, 24
Octava, 27, 72
Octave coupler, 96
Octavin, 43
Ohrman, Jonathan, foreman to Snetzler, partner with Elliott and Nutt, 89
Old Bilton, Warwicks., St. Mark, 175, 184, 301; 8
Old Church, Northants., 296
Old Malton, Yorks., 269, 303
Old Radnor, 48, 49, 157, 159, 165, 303; 2, 31
Old stops, 49
Ombersley, 302
Open-foot voicing, 34, 40, 87
Ophicleide, 92
Orchestral arrangements, 43
Orchestrion, 90
Ordnance of the Lords and Commons for the Demolition of all organs (1644), 151, 172
Organ and clockmaking, mechanical, 47
Organ, Blockwerk, 23, 24, 25, 32
portative, 22
positive, 22, 24, 25, 28, 32, 33, 36, 39, 94, 172, 293, 303; 1
Organ cases, 148, 159ff; 8, 13, 14, 16, 22, 24, 25, 27, 29, 32, 35, 38, 43, 46, 48, 49, 51-4, 57, 58, 61-6, 70-5, 77-81, 83-9, 91-101, 103, 104
Orgelbewegung, 275
Orgelmakers, Guild of, 47
Ottobeuren, Riepp organ at, 35
Ouseley, Rev. Sir Frederick Gore, 101, 110, 191
Oxford, Brasenose College Chapel, 159, 265, 297; 86, 87
Christ Church Cathedral, 71, 198, 297
Corpus Christi College, 266, 297
Examination Schools, Portrait of Bernard Smith, 76
Hertford College, 266
Magdalen College, 47, 54, 55, 57, 286
New College, proposed organ, 62, 63, 67, 76, 290, 297
Oriel College, 161, 266, 297
Pembroke College, 297
St. James, Cowley, 297
St. John the Evangelist, 261, 297; 83
St. John's College, 54
St. Mary the Virgin, 206, 238, 297; 15
Sheldonian Theatre, 71, 101, 266, 297; 89
Wadham College, 266, 297

Paignton Church, Devon, 284
'Pair' of organs, 46
Paisley Abbey, 304
Pakenham, Suffolk, 299
Paley, 283, 289

Palma Cathedral, Majorca, 166, 237
Paris, Sainte Clothilde, 42, 43
    Saint Denis, organ, 41
Parkend, Glos., St. Paul, 286
Parratt, Walter, 102
Parsons, 299
Parton, *History of Parish of St. Giles*, 228
Pearson, F. L., 270, 300, 303; **100**
Pearson, J. L., 155, 252, 257, 262, 282, 288, 289, 293, 300; **77**
Pease, Lancelot, 64, 183; **37**
Pedal organ, 24, 25, 95
    French, 39
    Independent, 32
    Opposition to, 93
Pedal pipes, 93, 97, 101
Pedals, 24, 28, 32, 36, 39, 60, 61, 82, 92, 116, 122, 135
    early existence in England, 60, 61, 82
    composition, 145
    development by Camidge and Gauntlett, 90
Pendlebury, St. Augustine, 289
Pertenhall, St. Peter, 280
Peterborough Cathedral, 262, 296; **94**
Petit Plein Jeu, 37
Petworth, St. Mary, 265, 301
    St. Thomas, 301
Phillips, Gordon, 126
Piccolo, 103, 107
Piddinghoe, St. John, 301
Piddington Church, Northants., 296
Pilning, Glos., St. Peter, 286
Pipe arrangements, 159; **18**
    embellishments, 169ff., 182, 183, 272
    embossed, 169, 183, 192
    false lengths, 229
    lip shapes, 170, 197; **26**
    shades, 161; **18**
Pipes, 33, 158ff.; **17**
    copper, 21, 169
    lead, 51, 169
    pedal, 93, 97, 101
    tin, 49, 57, 68, 169
    wood, 51, 57, 67, 69, 74, 93
    zinc, 169
Pistons, 99, 100, 145
Plainsong, 22, 24, 61
Plein Jeu, 36, 43
    use of, 38
Plowman, Thomas, 206, 238, 297
Plumtree Church, Notts., 297
Pneumatic action, 115
    organ, origin of, 20
Poitiers Cathedral, Clicquot organ, 39
Portative, the, 22
Portishead, Somerset, 298
Portsea, St. Mary, Walker organ at, 106, 286
Portuguese organs, 38, 40, 86
Posaune, 93, 96
Positif (Positive), 22, 24, 25, 28, 32, 33, 36, 39, 44, 94, 172, 293, 303; **1**
    compass, 39
    20th century, 44

Post-war revival and Continental Neo-Baroque, 115–19
Powick, St. Peter, 302
Praetorius, *Syntagma Musicum*, **23**
Prestant, 37, 38, 43, 72
Preston (composer), 61
Preston, St. Matthew and St. Oswald, 289
Primitive organ, the, 20
Principal, 71, 74, 77
Prothero, H. A., 285
Pugin, A. W. N., 197, 244, 247, 252, 261, 282, 285, 295; **61, 90**
Pulham, St. Mary-the-Virgin, 258, 295; **79**
Purcell, 75, 125, 126

Quarte de Nazard, 38, 77
Quendon, Essex, 285
Quimper Cathedral, 183
Quint, 93, 96, 103, 109
Quintade, 27, 28, 72
Quintadena, 27, 28
Quinteflûte, 36

Rabiny organ at Clermont-Ferrand, 36
Radley College, 265, 281
Radwinter, St. Mary-the-Virgin, 285
Rauschpfeife, 27, 28
Rawnce, Nicholas, 47
Rawtenstall, St. Mary, 289
Reading, St. Lawrence, 49, 281
    St. Mary, and Town Hall, 281
Récit, 39, 44
Récit-compass, 39
Récit Expressif, 39, 44
Redenhall, Assumption of the Blessed Virgin, 295
Redford, 61
Redhill, St. John, 300
Reeds, 52, 63, 85, 99, 105, 108, 112, 118, 122, 129, 142
    Cavaillé-Coll, 41
    Spanish and Portuguese, 40
    stops, 25, 38, 82
    use of, by Bach, 30
    weighting of tongues, 101
Rees *cyclopaedia* (1819), 91
Regal, the, 26, 30, 31, 39, 52, 172, 303
Regal stops, 26, 52, 53
    in France, 39
Reger, Max, 44, 145
Registration, Bach, 32–4
    Basse de Cromorne, 38
    Basse de trompette, 38
    Cavaillé-Coll, 42
    Double organ voluntary, 66
    Grand and Plein Jeu, 38
    Late 17th cent., 126
    18th century, 127–9
    Rollschweller, 43
    Schnitger, 32, 33
Renaissance organs, 25, 35
    organ cases, 162, 165, 166, 182, 189, 231, 279
    pipe embellishment, 169
    Revival, 265

Renn, Samuel, 283, 289
Repton School Chapel, Harrison organ, 110, 120, 140
Restoration organ before Father Smith, 62–8
organ cases, 189ff., 226, 279; 37
Richard's Castle, Salop, 298
Richardson, Sir Albert E., 214
Richmond, Surrey, 300
Riepp, Karl, organ at Ottobeuren, 35
Ripley Hospital Chapel, 289
Ripon Cathedral, 150, 256, 303
Robertsbridge MSS, 22
Robinson, John, 86
Robson, 295
Rochdale, St. Mary, 289
Rochesson, Louis Eugène, 116
Rochester Cathedral, 152, 256, 257, 288
Rococo organ, 25, 35, 157, 229, 275
Rodborough, St. Mary Magdalene, 286
Roehampton, Holy Trinity, 300
Rollschweller, 43, 145
Romantic composers, 43, 114
organ, 30, 41
Rome, St. Peter, 23
Romsey Abbey, Walker organ at, 95, 287
Rood lofts, 150
Rotherham, All Saints, 303
Rothwell, F., 294
Rotterdam, English Church at, 282
Rowley, St. Peter, 303
Rückpositiv, 26, 28, 31, 137, 165
chorus, 31
Rugby, Holy Trinity, 301
Rugely, Dominican Church, 299
Russell, Hugh, 84, 290, 299
Timothy, 293
William, *Fugue from Voluntary XII*, 136, 138–9
Ryde, I.O.W., All Saints, 288
Rye, St. Mary, 301

Sackbut, 61, 63
Sadt, 73
Saffron Walden, St. Mary, 285
St. Albans Cathedral, 257, 287; 74
St. Peter-in-the-East, 189, 218, 287
St. Asaph's Cathedral, 304
St. Bees Priory Church, 111, 283
St. Columb Major, Cornwall, 283
St. David's Cathedral, 304
St. Ives, Hunts., 288
St. Michael's Mount, 283
Saint Pol-de-Léon, 184, 189
Saint-Saëns, 41
Salamanca Cathedral, 157, 258
Salford, St. Philip, 289
Salicet, 104
Salicional, 43
Salisbury Cathedral, 47, 54, 57, 77, 217, 286, 302; 58
organ specification, 78
St. Thomas, 302
Sandringham Church, 295

Saqueboute, 36
Savage, 290
Scandinavia, 26, 27, 44, 51, 66, 100, 117
Scarborough, St. Martin, 303
Scherer family, 27, 45
Schmidt, Bernard and Christianus, *see* Smith
Schnarrwerk, 31
Schnitger, Arp, 27, 32, 35, 36, 45
registration, 32
Schreider, *see* Shrider
Schudi, Burkhardt, 89
Schulze, Edmund, 97, 105, 119, 255, 280, 284, 289, 302, 303; 69
Great Exhibition organ, 98, 99
Schulze and Lewis, 105
Schwarbrick, Thomas, 56, 83, 161, 217, 228, 301; 27
Scott, Sir George Gilbert, 95, 152, 170, 184, 213, 252, 255, 270, 282, 284–8, 295–7, 301, 302; 71, 72
Recollections, 152
Scott, John Oldrid, 252, 257, 262, 282, 287, 298, 300, 303; 73, 74
Screens, removal of stone, 152
Sedgefield, St. Edmund, 284
Sculthorpe Church, 226, 295; 64
Seely and Paget, Messrs., 272, 291
Selby Abbey, 257, 303; 73
Selfe, Philip, 302
Sesquialtera, 27–31, 38, 71, 74, 77, 82, 83, 85, 87, 93, 115, 126, 127
Shadingfield, 299
Shallots, 30
Shaw, James, 291, 300
Norman, 262, 283, 298
Watkins, 126
Sheffield, 303
Shelland, Suffolk, 299
Shepton Mallet, 298
Sherborne Abbey, 165, 169, 255, 284; 70
Sheringham, All Saints, 295
Shifnal, 298
Shoreham, St. Peter and St. Paul, 288
Shrewsbury, St. Mary, 298
Shrider, Christopher, 73, 75, 81, 87, 202, 225, 283, 286, 298, 300; 39
pedals at St. Paul's, 82
Sifflet, 27, 36, 63
Silbermann, 34, 45
Silvering (of pipes), 169
Simpson, J. L., 282
Simpson, J. W., 304
Simpson, Dr. Sparrow, 208
Sion, Notre Dame de Valère, 35, 157, 251
Skinners Company, 50
Skirbeck, St. Nicholas, 290
Slider-chest, 23
Small Principal, 57
Smart, Henry, 244
Smith, Bernard ('Father'), 50, 51, 62, 66, 68–75, 83, 89, 148, 181
organ cases, 195, 197, 198, 208, 220ff., 270, 271, 280–4, 289–92; 29, 46–50, 63

Smith, Bernard ('Father') (*contd.*)
  his nationality, 68–70
  letter, re Durham, 70
  chamber organs, 74; 33, 34, 44, 45
Smith, Christian, 75, 224, 284, 292; 38
Smith, Christianus, 58, 69, 175, 187, 189, 290
Smith, Christopher, 79
Smith, Gerard, 68, 75, 218, 289, 291, 293
Smith, John (of Bristol), 281, 298
Sneinton, Notts., 297
Snetzler, Johann, 69, 81, 84, 86, 87, 224
  cases, 225ff., 281, 282, 285, 288, 289, 291,
    294, 296–9, 302–3; 24, 64
  claviorgan, 89
  bureau organs, 88
Solo, 104
Southall, St. George, 229, 294
South Benfleet Church, 285
Southease, Sussex, 301
South Pickenham, Norfolk, 247, 295
Southwark Cathedral, 99, 107, 293
Southwell Minster, 270, 297
Southwick Hall, Northants, 296
Southwold, 299
Spanish organ building, 38, 40
  cases, 158, 162
  swell organs, 86
Specifications of organs:
  Adlington Hall, 65
  Beverley Minster, 87
  Bolton Town Hall, 103, 104
  Canterbury Cathedral, 64
  Capel, 27
  Chirk Castle, 55
  Christianus Smith's chamber organ, 58
  Clermont-Ferrand, 37
  Dallam's organ for the Sultan, 48
  Ely Cathedral (great and solo only), 109
  Eton College, 53
  Exeter Cathedral Song School, 67
  Gisors, 36
  Innsbruck, Silbernenkapelle, 40, 51
  Italian Church, Hatton Garden, 117
  Liverpool, George Street Chapel, 92
  New College, Oxford, Dallam's proposed
    organ, 63
  Oxford, Christ Church Cathedral, 71
  Paris, Sainte-Clotilde, 43
  Repton School Chapel, 110
  Rotherhithe, St. Mary, 83
  St. Bride, Fleet Street, 77
  St. Mary Redcliffe, Bristol, 82
  St. Paul's Cathedral, 74
    organ on wheels, 101
  St. Stephen, Walbrook, 85
  Salisbury Cathedral, 78
  Temple Church, 72–3
  Tewkesbury Abbey, 'Grove' organ, 105
  Wallasey Parish Church, 103
  Winchester Cathedral, 67–8
  Worcester Cathedral, 57
    Shire Hall, 96
  York Minster, 57

Spectator (qu.), 86
'Spit', 34
Spitzfloit, 27, 276
Spofforth, Samuel, 94
Springlade system, 23
Stafford, St. Mary, 233, 299; 52
Standish, Freeman Memorial organ at, 159,
  272, 286; 105
Stanford-on-Avon, 166, 169, 175, 178, 181,
  296; 5
Stanley, 126
Stansted Mountfitchet Church, 285
Stanton Fitzwarren, St. Leonard, 302
Staunton Harold, Leics., 290
Steele, John, 122
Steinkirchen, Schnitger organ at, 26, 35
Stirling, Church of Holy Rude, 304
Stockcross, St. John, 160, 161, 281; 85
Stocklist, organbuilder's (1515), 51, 52
Stockport, Ches., St. George, 283
Stoke Poges, St. Giles, 282
Stop-control, Cavaillé-Coll system, 41, 145
  mechanism, invention of, 23
Stops, 27ff., 49, 83, 85, 87, 101, 103, 106, 108,
  128, 145
  'Antheme', 63
  Baroque, 30
  Bombarde, 39
  Borrowing by communication, 65
  'Cart', 77
  Clarinet type, 30
  Cornet, 38, 71
  Cromorne, 38
  Cymbel, 29
  Doubled, 58, 59
  Dulciana, 84, 88, 89
  Early introduction of, at Old Radnor, 49
  Fifteenth, 29
  Flute, 39
  French mutation, 38
  Grand ophicleide, 92
  Grosse Nazard, 38
  Harmonics, 108
  'Harp, lute and dulcimer', 83
  Hautbois, 39
  Italian, 39
  Krummhorn, 30
  Larigot, 38
  Mutation, 29, 30, 38
  Nazard, 29, 38
  Nineteenth, 29
  Pedal, 39
  Principall, Small, 58
  Quarte de Nazard, 38
  Reed, types of, 30
  Regal, use of, 26, 30, 31, 39, 52, 53
  Sesqualtera, 29, 31
  Seventeenth, 29
  Shaking, 48
  Spanish and Portuguese reed, 40
  Smith's Diapason, 74
  Terz-cymbel, 29
  Terzian, 29, 31

Tierce, 38
Trumpet, 30
Twelfth, small, 58
Twenty-second, 29, 59
Violin (Cremona), 73
Vox Humana, Voix humaine, Voce Humana, 31, 39
Stowe School Chapel, 282
Strasbourg, 256
Stratford-on-Avon, 301
Strawberry Hill, 234
Street, G. E., 213, 252
Stretton, St. Mary, 299
String tone, 118
Stubington, H., *The Dallams in Brittany*, 183
Stuart, 'Athenian', 238
Stumm brothers, organ at Amorbach, 35
Suabe flute, 93, 96
Sumner, W. L., *The Organ: its History, etc.*, 188
   The Organs of St. Margaret's, Leicester, 201
   The Organs of St. Paul's Cathedral, 207
Superoctave, 96
Sutton, Rev. A., 248
Sutton, Rev. F. H., 175, 178, 187, 238, 244, 252, 255, 280, 282, 285, 290, 301, 303; 62, 85
   The Organ at St. Stephen's, Old Radnor, 175
   Church organs: their positions and construction, 175
Sutton, Sir J., *Short Account of Organs built in England* (qu.), 75, 84, 86, 87, 96, 155, 195, 196, 207, 225, 233, 244, 247, 282, 290
Sweffling, Suffolk, 299
Swell box, 35, 79, 94, 122, 128
   Cavaillé-Coll, 41
   in Germany, 35
Swell organ, 82–7, 96, 101, 103, 104, 142
   18th century use of, 128, 129
Swindon, 302
Sydney Town Hall, 107
Syme, J. S., 302
Syston, Leics., 290

Table organ, 293; 18
Tannington, Suffolk, 299
Tapper, Sir Walter, 269, 282, 289, 290, 293, 300
Taunton, Holy Trinity, 298
   St. John-the-Evangelist, 298
Taunton, Robert, 66
Tavistock, St. Eustace, 284
Taylor, Prof. Edward, 58
Teddesley Hall, 88, 291
Teigngrace, Devon, 284
Temple Balsall, 301
Tenbury, St. Michael's College, 302
Tenoroon, 92
Terraced dynamics, 32
Terz-cymbel stops, 29
Terzian, 29, 31, 38

Teulon, S. S., 293
Tewkesbury Abbey, 56
   Grove organ, 56, 105, 286
   Milton organ, 161, 166, 169, 175, 182, 286; 9
Thamar, Thomas, 67, 68, 181, 183, 184, 299
Thaxted, Essex, 285
Theddingworth organ case, 160, 252, 290; 62
Theewes, Lodowicus, 172, 293
Thelnetham, 299
Theodosius, organ on Obelisk of, 20, 22
Theophilus, *De Variis Artibus*, 21
Thornage, All Saints, 295
Thorne, E. H., 135
Thrapston, St. James, 296
Thumb pistons, 99
Thurstaston, Ches., St. Bartholomew, 283
Thynne, 102, 106, 119, 280
'Tibia clausa' and 'tibia plena', 107
Ticehurst, St. Mary, 301
Tierce, 37, 38, 77, 82, 83, 87, 96, 105, 116
Timber, Philip, 62
Tirlemont, Belgium, organ case at, 251
Tiverton, St. Peter's, Willis organ, 130, 224, 284; 38
Toeboards, curved and sloping, 162
Tompkins, Thomas, 121
Tongues, 30
Torquay, St. Mary Magdalene, 284
Towcester, St. Lawrence, 296
Towers, 161, 183, 211
Tracker-action, 26, 115, 118, 119
Tractarian Movement, 151, 155, 241
Travers, 126
Tremulant, 27, 53, 63, 96, 104
Trevelyan, Sir George, 67
Tromba, 108, 145
Trombone, 93, 96, 103, 104
Trompette, basse de, 38
Trumpets, 27, 30, 36–8, 41–4, 66, 72–4, 77, 82–7, 93, 96, 103, 104, 108, 126, 127, 141
   French, 146
Truro Cathedral, 257, 258, 283
Tuba, 101, 142, 298
Tuba mirabilis, 92, 93, 103
Tudor school of organ music, 121, 122
Turkey, Sultan of, 48
Turvey, All Saints, 280
Two-manual organs, 53, 54
Tyne Dock, St. Mary, 98
Tynemouth, 296

Upton-on-Severn, 302
Ushaw College Chapel, 252; 90
Usk, Mon., Gray & Davison organ, 95, 303
Utrecht, St. Nicolai, 24

Valetta, St. Paul's Cathedral, 206
Van der Goes, Hugo, Triptych, 22, 156; 1
Van Eyck, Ghent altarpiece by, 22
Ventil, 23
   stop control, 41, 42
Victoria and Albert Museum, 252

Victorian organs, 46, 243; **75, 76**
Vincent, 285
Viola, 103
Viol de gambe, 43, 96
Violin stop, 96, 103, 104
Virginal, 51
Vogler, Abbot, his orchestrion, 90, 91
Voicing, 40, 87, 99
  flue-controlled, 34
  foothole-controlled, 34
  open-foot, 34, 98
  Neo Baroque, 34
Vox Humana, 31, 36–40, 43, 66, 74, 82, 83, 85, 87, 103, 104, 126, 127, 131

Wainwright, 88
Wakefield Cathedral, 270, 303
Walcha, Helmut, 27
Wald flute, 93, 96
Walker and Athron, Messrs, 255, 303
Walker, Joseph, 86, 94, 95
Walker, J. W. and Sons, Messrs., 57, 86, 101, 106, 112, 116, 119, 130, 137, 175, 276, 280, 281, 282, 286–8, 290, 294, 301–3
Wallasey Parish Church, 102–104
Walond, 126
Walpole, Horace, 234
Walter, l'Orgoner, 47
Walton-on-Thames, 300
Warman, John W., 191
Warminster, 230, 302
Warrington, Parr Hall, 289
Warwick, St. Mary, 150, 301
Watson, R., 294
Weingarten, 149
Weitz, Guy, 112
Welford, St. Gregory, 281
Wellingborough, 296
Wells Cathedral, 66
Werkprinzip, *see* Work Principle.
Wesley, S. S., 95, 100, 122, 132, 135
  his music, 132, 135, 141
  pedal board, 100
Wesley, Samuel, 126, 132
Westbourne Church, Hants., 287
West Bromwich, St. Andrew, 299
Westminster Abbey, *see* London.
West Retford, Notts., 297
West Tofts, St. Mary, 159, 160, 169, 247, 248, 252; **82**
West Walton, Norfolk, 207
West Wycombe, St. Lawrence, 282
Weybridge, 160, 161, 258, 300; **77**
Whalley, St. Mary, 289
Whitby, St. Hilda, 303
Whitchurch, St. Alkmund, 298
Whitehaven, St. Nicholas, Harrison organ at, 108, 111
Whitely Village, St. Martin, 300
Whystock & Reid, Messrs., 304
Wickwar, Glos., Holy Trinity, 286

Widor, 42
Wilford, Notts., 297
Williams, C. F. Abdy, 148
Willingdon, St. Mary, 301
Willis, George, reed-voicing, 101
Willis, Henry ('Father'), 50, 57, 84, 95, 99–102, 108, 119, 130, 137, 142, 192, 201, 208, 213, 224, 258, 266, 280–2, 285, 287–304
Willis, Henry 'III', 112
Willson, E. J., 238, 290
Wilson, H., 288
Wimborne St. Giles, 284
Winchcombe, St. Peter, 286
Winchelsea, 301
Winchester Cathedral, 21, 45, 99, 238, 286
  organ specification, 67, 68
Winchester College Chapel, 270, 287; **99**
Wind-chest, 21, 41, 65, 98
  slider, 23
  springlade, 23
Wind pressure, 33, 35, 40, 41, 65, 92, 98, 99, 100, 101, 106, 112, 146
  Cavaillé-Coll, 41
  French, 37
Windsor, St. George's Chapel, 183, 184, 188, 233, 281; **11, 12**
Winforton, St. Michael, 287
Winston Church, 299
Wiston, St. Mary, 299
Wollaton, Notts., 297
Wolverhampton, St. John, 72, 299
Wood, Anthony (qu.), 71
Woodman, Dr., 62
Woodroffe, George, 191
Worcester Cathedral, 54, 57, 59, 64, 66, 68, 107, 122, 183, 184, 223, 256, 285, 302
  Dallam's double organ, 122
  Shire Hall, 95
  Nicholson organ specification, 96
Work-principle organs, 275, 276; **109**
Worthington, Dr., 92
Wotton-under-Edge, St. Mary, 286
Wren, Sir Christopher, 73, 75, 80, 195, 207, 208, 291
Wulstan; his organ at Winchester, 21
Wyatt, James, 289
Wymondham Abbey, Norfolk, 237, 295

Yarpole, Hereford., 287
Yates, Roger, 192, 298
Yaxley, St. Peter, 161, 162, 269, 288; **97**
York, John, 54
York, St. Helen, 118
  Minster, 46, 50, 54, 57, 59, 90, 118, 150, 152, 172, 238, 303; **57**
  organ specification, 57
Yoxford, St. Peter, 299

Zaragoza Cathedral, 162, 237, 261
Zimbel, 27, 28